THE MAKING OF MIAMI BEACH: 1933–1942

The Architecture of Lawrence Murray Dixon

Jean-François Lejeune and Allan T. Shulman

Foreword by
Paul Goldberger

Edited by
Sonia R. Chao

BASS MUSEUM OF ART
MIAMI BEACH FLORIDA 2000

First published in the United States of America in 2000 by
Rizzoli International Publications, Inc. 300 Park Avenue South,
New York, NY 10010.

This catalogue was supported by grants from the National Endowment
for the Arts, the Florida Department of State Division of Historical
Resources, the Henry Luce Foundation, Inc. and the Graham Foundation
for Advanced Studies in the Fine Arts.

The Bass Museum of Art is recognized for artistic excellence by
the State of Florida and receives funding through the Florida
Department of State, the Florida Arts Council and the Division of
Cultural Affairs. Major support is provided for the Museum by the
City of Miami Beach and Friends of the Bass Museum. The Museum
also receives funding from the Metropolitan Dade County Cultural
Affairs Council, the Miami Beach Cultural Arts Council, the Institute of
Museum and Library Services and the National Endowment for the Arts.
American Airlines is the official airline for the Bass Museum of Art.

GRAHAM FOUNDATION FOR
ADVANCED STUDIES IN THE FINE ARTS

Bass Museum of Art
2121 Park Avenue
Miami Beach, Florida 33139
305 673 7530

e-mail:
info@bassmuseum.org

World Wide Web:
www.bassmuseum.org

Individual text copyright: Jean-François Lejeune and Allan T. Shulman

Photographs of works from the Collection of the Bass Museum of Art
by Peter Harholdt, West Palm Beach, Florida, unless otherwise noted.

Book Design: Frank Begrowicz, FBGD, Inc., Coral Gables, Florida

front cover inset:
View of the lobby of the Tides looking toward Ocean Drive, Miami Beach. Photograph by
Samuel H. Gottscho. © Doris Schleisner. Collection of the Bass Museum of Art. Gift of
Lawrence M. Dixon Jr.

front cover background:
Night view of the façade of the Tides taken from Ocean Drive. Photograph by Samuel H.
Gottscho. Collection of the Bass Museum of Art. Gift of Lawrence M. Dixon Jr. © Doris
Schleisner.

back cover:
Miami Beach Library and Art Center (John Collins Memorial Library, now the Bass Museum
of Art), Collins Avenue and 22nd Street, Miami Beach. Russell Pancoast, 1930. Collection of
the Bass Museum of Art.

previous page:
Project for an hotel, Collins Avenue, Miami Beach. Perspective, pencil on tracing paper,
18 x 30". Lawrence Murray Dixon, c. 1935-36. Collection of the Bass Museum of Art.
Gift of Richard B. Dixon.

THE MAKING OF MIAMI BEACH: 1933–1942

The Architecture of Lawrence Murray Dixon

CONTENTS

ACKNOWLEDGMENTS

Ruth Grim

This book was made possible through the generosity of several grant agencies. An initial grant from the National Endowment for the Arts started the project by funding the research of the collection and this was followed by another for the book's publication. We owe David Bancroft at the NEA a great deal of thanks for helping with our grant application. Many thanks also to the Henry Luce Foundation and Ellen Holtzman; the Florida Department of State Division of Historical Resources and Vicki Cole; and The Graham Foundation for Advanced Studies in the Fine Arts and Richard Solomon. All were instrumental in seeing this project through to publication and it is a great source of pride to us that such important local, state and national institutions saw as much value in the project as we did. Thanks also to Jean-Louis Cohen and Richard Guy Wilson for their support letters.

But, by far, we owe the greatest thanks to Lawrence Dixon Jr. and Richard B. Dixon, the sons of Lawrence Murray Dixon, for the generous donation of the works upon which this book is based. As this collection represents virtually all that is left of the records of their father's prolific career, their generosity was more than magnanimous. It also proved to be the impetus for a great deal of very valuable research into the architecture of this area and we hope this book is merely the first and will inspire more to follow. I must also thank Larry Dixon Jr. for his help during research by filling in details of his father's life and career as well as for his patience in seeing this project completed. We hope both Dixons feel we have done well by their father and are pleased with this publication.

Many other individuals deserve thanks for contributing their time and talents to making this book a reality. I would like to thank Diane Camber for her encouragement throughout and for trusting me to manage this project. Jean-François Lejeune and Allan Shulman deserve considerable thanks for their hard work and dedication to the project from its inception, involving everything from assisting with grant applications to researching Dixon's career and his place within the history of Miami Beach from top to bottom. Paul Goldberger, noted architecture critic and writer for the *New Yorker*, has honored us with a foreword to the book and for this we are deeply grateful. We also owe a great deal of thanks to David Morton, Editor at Rizzoli International Publishing, for his support in bringing this book to completion. It is indeed an honor for all involved that the book is to be published with the prestigious Rizzoli "R" on the cover.

Frank Begrowicz of FBGD, Inc. contributed his considerable talents as graphic designer of the book. It is indeed a beautiful volume and we owe a great deal of that to him. Sonia Chao proved invaluable in her role as guest editor. The quality of this publication is due, in large part, to her. Peter Harholdt provided his excellent eye as the photographer and we owe him many thanks for his beautiful work as well as his patience and perseverance.

Rachel Garick, Bass Museum Registrar, worked diligently over long hours coordinating image captions, credit lines and reproduction permission, among other crucial tasks on this project. As always, we are very indebted to her. Wanda K. Texon, Bass Museum Curator of Education, is also to be thanked for her help and insight in reviewing some of the text. Additional thanks to E. Bann Williams, former Bass Museum Registrar, for his help and encouragement with this project and Amanda Perez, Curatorial Assistant, for assisting in collection cataloguing and other tasks during the organization of the material for this book.

In addition, we owe thanks to the Raleigh Hotel and Mr. Dean Peters, Head of Marketing and Sales; the Museum Walk Apartments and Ruth Reedy, Manager; the Plymouth Hotel and Nellie Rivera, Manager; the Miami Beach Ocean Resort and Mr. Klaus Voss, General Manager and his assistant, Nicole Paquette; and the Lincoln Road Association and Sally Baumgartner, Director, for agreeing to let us photograph works related to Dixon's architecture in their buildings.

The contribution of the University of Miami School of Architecture also needs to be recognized. Four graduate assistants were instrumental in gathering the research for this publication. Fern Primov initiated the research at Miami Beach City Hall and in several archives; Christopher Keidaish and Peter Berenz spent considerable time in front of microfilm machines to gather the hundreds of pages of the *Miami Herald* and the *Miami News* documenting the construction of Miami Beach; and Amber Ortiz helped compile the bibliography and the index. Finally, special thanks to Silvia Ros, designer, for her indispensable help in browsing through hundreds of architectural journals and discovering critical missing data on Miami Beach architecture within the *Avery Index of Periodicals*. The authors also thank Professor Aristides Millas for sharing his knowledge of Miami Beach. His enthusiasm for the architecture and urbanism of the city, coupled with his deep belief in historic preservation, helped spur their own interest and motivation.

For archival help, the authors also owe thanks to Dawn Hugh and Becky Smith at the Historical Museum of Southern Florida; Sam Broderick and George Faust at the Florida Collection of the Miami-Dade Public Library; and Francis X. Luca at The Wolfsonian–FIU Library. Special thanks also to The Wolfsonian–FIU for allowing access to and reproduction from the Schultze & Weaver Archives, particularly Cathy Leff, Director; Wendy Kaplan, Associate Director of Exhibitions and Curatorial Affairs; Marianne Lamonaca, Curator; Neil Harvey, Collections Manager; and David Burnhauser, Registrar.

Jean-François Lejeune wishes to thank Roselyne Pirson for her support and infinite patience. Allan Shulman thanks Lisa B. Palley for her advice and encouragement and Hector Burga, Matt Ligas and Ligia Labrada for keeping the office on an even keel during the writing of this book.

Ruth Grim
Curator, Bass Museum of Art

PREFACE

Diane Camber

Years ago all of Greater Miami's radio stations were located in the island city of Miami Beach. The call letters for one of those established in the 1930s — WIOD — stood for Wonderful Isle of Dreams. Out of dreams and coconuts came the start of this city's short but vivid history. About one hundred years ago the dream of cultivating a substantial coconut industry brought seven adventurous New Jersey men to southeast Florida to buy land. They bought a large tract which ran from Jupiter, north of Palm Beach, to Cape Florida (the tip of Key Biscayne) for thirty-five cents an acre and in 1882 planted 216,000 seed coconuts, thousands of which were on what is now Miami Beach. Rabbits quickly ate the sprouting palms and the Northerners retreated back to civilized New Jersey, leaving their dream behind. After the railroad pushed south, one of the original investors, a determined Quaker farmer named John Collins, returned to attempt once again to develop some of this property. He planted an avocado orchard on the island in 1907. A few years later he was joined by his daughter and son-in-law, Thomas Pancoast. But Thomas Pancoast had a different dream — to develop the island as a resort. Whether farming or recreation would prevail remained to be seen but father and son-in-law agreed that a bridge was needed to the mainland. Four months into the project and halfway across the bay, the money ran out for what had come to be called "Collins Folly." Financial rescue came from yet another dreamer, Prest-o-Lite Battery magnate and builder of the Indianapolis Speedway, Carl Fisher. The bridge was finished in 1914. Fisher was never one to do things by halves and, in accord with Pancoast, he envisioned Miami Beach as an American Riviera for the well-to-do, with elegant hotels and residences on the waterfront (ocean and bay). Although impetuous, he had the money and clout to realize his dream. In return for financing the bridge, Fisher was given a tract of property. He quickly drained and filled swampy land, sold plots for homes and built nightclubs, swimming casinos, polo fields, golf courses, hotels and other attractions to lure winter residents and visitors. Out of Fisher's elitist dream of an American Riviera came the grand hotels and private estates of the 1920s, built in the Mediterranean eclectic style. Today few of the grand hotels and oceanfront estates of this period remain. While Pancoast and Fisher created a winter playground to cater to the rich and famous, others carved out a middle-class enclave between the ocean and the bay, mostly inland and south of 23rd Street in what is now known as South Beach.

In 1916 there was only one hotel on Miami Beach, Fisher's Lincoln, with sixteen rooms. By 1925 there were at least 234 hotels and apartment houses, 8,000 permanent residents, 300 shops and offices, eight bathing casinos, three schools, four polo fields, three theaters and two churches. High society traveled south by train and ship to keep up the frantic pace of the Jazz Age. But in September 1926 the hurricane of the century struck, taking a toll on human life and sweeping boating piers into the sea. But the big hotels, built soundly on concrete piles, remained intact.

The damage to Miami Beach's reputation was greater than the damage to its structures. Investors stayed away and the great land boom went bust. The stock market crash further impeded financial recovery. The attitudes of elitist dreamers such as Fisher no longer dominated. In spite of it all, a recovery was made but it took another form.

By the mid-1930s a different dream prevailed. Tourism for the middle class rather than land development for the rich became the major focus. Instead of the ornate Mediterranean revival style, developers built less costly Deco streamlined two- and three-story hotels and apartments designed for the new arrivals who began to dominate South Beach from 1st Street to Lincoln Road. It was a future-oriented style that associated itself with industrial design and the machine as symbols of progress. It contained the streamlined vocabulary of the great ocean liners with mast-like marquees, shiny glass and metal surfaces. Exterior trim lines were painted in bright, sun-drenched colors. Greens, blues, oranges and pinks were set off against neutral backgrounds of beige and white.

By 1940 Miami Beach was jam-packed. The fortune seekers occupied the new Deco hotels of South Beach while the older, more imposing Mediterranean-style Roney, Nautilus and Floridian hotels were once again filled with celebrities and high society. Development and dreams however, came to a temporary halt with Pearl Harbor. By 1942 there was a blackout and German submarines were off the coast. Air Force personnel displaced tourists in hotels large and small. Fisher's stately Nautilus Hotel was converted to an army hospital. Undaunted, Miami Beach came back after the war and experienced another boom. Investors came with bigger dreams and more money than ever to construct huge hotels — such as the Fontainebleau and Eden Roc — to the north. They turned their backs on the fanciful but small buildings of South Beach. New residential architecture of a larger scale became the focus of developers throughout the 1950s, 1960s and the 1970s.

In 1972 the architect, Denise Scott Brown, who had visited Morris Lapidus's famous Fontainebleau Hotel in the 1960s, returned to Miami Beach with her husband, architect Robert Venturi. It was on this trip that they discovered South Beach. In a letter to the president of the Miami Chapter of the American Institute of Architects they observed that its buildings were "a priceless heritage of the early 1930s." Later, in a 1975 planning proposal to the City of Miami Beach, they wrote that South Beach was "one of America's great treasure chests of architecture in the art deco style." They noted that most of the buildings had been designed by a handful of architects, among them Lawrence Murray Dixon, the focus of this book. At the time I was living and working elsewhere but on a visit home I came across what must have been an excerpt from the AIA letter published in *Florida Architecture* describing the Miami Beach art deco phenomenon. I was fascinated. After my mother's death in 1976, I moved to Miami Beach to renovate my family home, built in 1937. I became aware of the existence of a fledgling preservation group, the

"Greetings from Miami Beach." c. 1940. Postcard. Collection Allan T. Shulman.

Miami Design Preservation League, and met Barbara Capitman, its visionary leader. As an art and architectural historian I was recruited to organize the first Art Deco tours and to write articles alongside Barbara Capitman to propagandize the newest Miami Beach dream. This dream was of a restored South Beach.

In 1978 we succeeded in placing a square mile of South Beach on the National Register of Historic Places, to become America's largest twentieth-century historic district. For the first time the past began to be seen as part of the city's future, as a result of the efforts of our small band of intrepid preservationists. During my work for the League I met Larry Dixon Jr., L. Murray Dixon's son, also a practicing architect. When I left the League to join the Bass Museum of Art and resume my previous museum career, I maintained my contact with Larry. I knew that the Dixons had saved vintage photographs, drawings and other material of their father's and I hoped to persuade them that it be cared for and exhibited at the Bass Museum of Art.

In the early 1980s I began to organize a series of architectural exhibitions at the Museum and actively cultivated donation and purchase of material for a design collection that now numbers over one thousand works. This growing collection of architectural material captured the attention of the national art press, which recognized it as an innovative collecting strategy. Some of the exhibitions toured the country. Although the Bass Museum of Art's collection includes postwar international

works, it has considerable strength in works from Miami Beach's Art Deco period as well as mid-century design, including works by Morris Lapidus. Larry Dixon Jr. and his brother, Richard, eventually entrusted their father's archives to the Bass, which we celebrate with this publication.

I should like to express my appreciation to the authors Allan Shulman and Jean-François Lejeune, whose research and interpretation has illuminated the amazingly extensive Florida career of an architect whose life was tragically cut short. I am particularly grateful to Curator Ruth Grim for her enthusiasm for the material and her oversight of the research and publication.

Special note must be made of the ongoing contribution of the Friends of the Bass Museum. This organization, more than any other, has enabled the design collection's growth, publication and exhibition. They have continued their generosity with the publication of this book. I also want to express my personal appreciation to the Graham Foundation, the Luce Foundation, the National Endowment for the Arts and the Florida Department of State Division of Historical Resources for their significant support and endorsement of *The Making of Miami Beach: 1933–1942, The Architecture of Lawrence Murray Dixon.*

Diane Camber
Executive Director, Bass Museum of Art

FOREWORD

Paul Goldberger

Lawrence Murray Dixon embodied Miami Beach in its formative years — and Miami Beach in its formative years embodied one of the most pleasing architectural episodes in the history of the United States. It is no longer necessary to talk about the Art Deco hotels, apartment buildings, motels and public buildings that were built in Miami Beach in the years between the world wars in the defensive tone that one had to assume a generation ago, when only a handful of quirky aficionados thought these buildings worthy of praise. In the 1970s the architectural and political establishments shared the view that the Art Deco architecture of Miami Beach (or Art Moderne, as this work is often called to distinguish it from European Art Deco architecture) had been no better than superficial and trivial when new and, worse, that it had become seedy and all but worthless when old. It was with some pride that the City of Miami Beach talked about redeveloping South Beach in the early 1970s. Anyone could see that the Art Moderne hotels were small, tired and economically unproductive. Why not tear them down and put something worthy in their place?

How that did not happen — how a band of zealots convinced politicians and cultural authorities alike to rethink South Beach — is a story that has been well documented, in this book and elsewhere. Suffice it to say here that the shift that saved South Beach is one of the triumphant moments in the saga of twentieth-century American architecture, for it demonstrated not only the change in attitude toward older urban neighborhoods that was happening in many cities — an increasing willingness to respect what was there, and to build on the existing fabric rather than try to replace it wholesale — it also represented a recognition that this architecture that lined Ocean Drive and Washington Avenue and the surrounding streets was a remarkable and uniquely American achievement. The art moderne buildings of Miami Beach are not like anything that had come before. They make a language of their own, a language as accessible, and as fully American, as that of jazz or the American musical theater. It is no accident that these buildings began to earn the serious respect of architectural scholars at more or less the same time that jazz was becoming more an object of serious musical inquiry. And yet the rising interest in art moderne architecture, like that of jazz, was not only scholarly, but also popular. More and more people found in this architecture a tremendous sense of joy.

Several of Dixon's buildings are worth studying in detail — the Royal Arms and Ester apartments, which take tentative steps, from a safe Mediterranean style toward art moderne; the Atlantis, a fully realized miniature skyscraper of a hotel whose demolition in 1973, just as the movement to save these buildings was coming into its own, was a tragic loss; his other hotels in the form of beautifully composed little skyscrapers, the Tides, the Raleigh and the Ritz; and the jaunty low buildings like the Flamingo, the Drexel, the Marlin, the Miljean and the Clyde. In each case Dixon created gracefully composed façades with

powerful, jazzy rhythms. His architecture was shaped by a sense of fantasy controlled by an overriding geometric discipline. Fantasy tempered by geometry is as good a definition as any of what makes all of Miami Beach's art moderne architecture work, Dixon's and that of his peers. The fantasy is of a new world, of faith in a machine age that would be lyrical, spirited and light, not somber, harsh and dark.

Together the Art Moderne buildings of Dixon and his colleagues made a place. That is their most important contribution, of course — they accentuate the most important urban idea, the one from which all urban design flows, which is that the whole is greater than the sum of its parts. Every one of these buildings is good, but the urban whole that they make as they join together is truly great. Ocean Drive, parts of Collins Avenue, Washington Avenue and some of the side streets of Miami Beach constitute an urban architectural ensemble as important as any in America — and unlike almost every other first-rate urban ensemble, these streets were created entirely in the twentieth century.

Where did the Art Moderne of Dixon and his contemporaries come from? We can think of it as being born of one part International Style puritanism, one part Art Deco indulgence. It yearned to look modern, to feel new, yet it rejected both the ascetic, stern order of the high modernism of the International Style and the astonishing lushness of Parisian Art Deco. Out of these two strains Dixon and the other architects working in Miami Beach made a hybrid that managed to feel as modern as the International Style and as sensual as Art Deco, while being not quite like either of its parents. Miami Beach Moderne possesses modernity without austerity, sensuousness without ornateness. These buildings are crisp in the way International Style buildings of glass and steel are crisp, and yet they are also lyrical and easy, something the tight, rigid International Style could never allow itself to be.

I first became acquainted with South Beach the old-fashioned way, so to speak — I went to visit my grandmother, who lived for many years in the Netherlands Hotel on Ocean Drive and 13th Street, and before that in the Beacon at 7th Street. It was the early 1970s, and she thought that if anything had historical value, it was herself and her neighbors, not the buildings they lived in. She did not live to see the new South Beach, or to discover that her address is now a set of fancy condominiums, and I do not know that she would have understood what all the fuss was about. To her, these buildings were easy and relaxed; they let in the breezes and offered views and public spaces that were both dignified and energetic, and private spaces that were nurturing. They made their occupants feel like they were part of a street, part of a neighborhood, part of a community — part of something larger than themselves. But that, of course is precisely what the art moderne buildings of Lawrence Murray Dixon still do today, more than half a century after they were first built. Now, for a very different world, this architecture makes a larger and a later Miami Beach a civilized and exuberant urban place.

BUILDING AND REBUILDING:
THE MAKING OF MIAMI BEACH

Allan T. Shulman

There comes a time in the life of every real estate development when it takes on a life of its own independent of the men (or corporations) who started it.[1]

On the eve of the United States' entry into World War II, Miami Beach was the booming metropolitan center of a unique resort culture: it was America's Winter Playground. However, as late as 1912, Miami Beach was described as a wilderness. It was a subtropical barrier island comprising three interrelated ecosystems: a beach along the Atlantic oceanfront that merged with dunes and the remnants of earlier coconut tree plantings; a low scrub forest in the interior; and a belt of mangroves facing Biscayne Bay on its west side. Over a span of the next thirty years, entrepreneurs, land speculators, engineers and architects successively transformed this landscape for a variety of uses, from Anglo-American suburb to urban seaside resort.

The land development potential of South Florida, and specifically Miami Beach, was ignited by the extension of the Florida East Coast Railway to Miami in 1896. The parallel rise of sun and sea bathing at the end of the nineteenth century made Miami Beach's destiny seem fated — its offshore location, surrounding warm waters, consistent sun and mild weather made it an ideal winter sanctuary for the rich and newly mobile middle-class tourists. Like "thermal bathing" before it, sun and sea bathing were largely an excuse for taking a vacation, and for the creation of a resort.

The foundations of Miami Beach as a resort were established by three development companies in an innovative and prescient land speculation scheme, one that would be repeated many times along both Florida coasts. The clearing and lifting of its native terrain was the key first step of its elaboration. A vast and specialized mechanical armada was used in the first industrial-scale creation of fresh land in Florida.[2] First, the existing palmetto and mangrove roots were cut using a unique sixteen-ton traction engine tractor, its wheels fitted with knives. Next, the inland water edges were neatly contoured with concrete seawalls, which gave shape to the city. Lastly, suction dredges, installed on barges in Biscayne Bay, vacuumed up bay bottom and redeposited it within the new perimeter. Miami Beach was transformed into a table of bleached sand, neatly fringed and crisscrossed by canals, lakes and lagoons.

A critical figure in this land transformation plan was Carl Fisher, a publicity man and auto industry tycoon. He accelerated and financed the preparation of the landscape for the new city, stimulating an active real estate market among the newly arrived developers and residents of the city. Fisher was also absorbed in the challenge of town-making, and took charge of the many facets associated with the city's evolution. He was described as a man "with a philosophy for a new design for living, who considered play as soul-saving as work or religion."[3] This tireless developer directed a massive publicity campaign that established the image of Miami Beach as a playground, an effort critical to its ultimate success as a development venture.

The first planning act occurred in 1912, when two Miami bankers, John N. Lummus and James E. Lummus, formed the Ocean Beach Realty Company and platted a small ocean-facing portion of their land at the southern tip of Miami Beach. Here, a gridiron of streets and avenues, aligned with the Atlantic Ocean, was laid out near the old ferry terminal that was the gateway to the island. The blocks were generally four hundred feet by three hundred feet, bisected by alleys and parceled into fifty-foot-wide lots. Henceforth this common American block, with its characteristic division into narrow lots, was adopted in large areas of Miami Beach. Wide avenues flowed north and south while the narrower streets and interstitial spaces between buildings flowed east to the beach, where a boardwalk and bathing casinos were built. The pattern was extended north along the shore by John Collins, an agriculturally-minded pioneer, who formed the Miami Beach Improvement Company in 1913 and built the first automobile link between Miami and Miami Beach: a two-and-one-half-mile wooden bridge that was the longest in the world when completed. Both the Lummuses and Collins were influenced by an earlier American seaside resort, Atlantic City, New Jersey. In *The Miracle of Miami Beach*, J. N. Lummus emphasized the role of this archetypal resort in the layout of Miami Beach, especially in regard to the relationship of the city to the sea.[4]

opposite:

View of Miami Beach looking north. Photograph by Richard B. Hoit, 1915. Courtesy of the Historical Museum of Southern Florida. Notation verso, "Taken from the 'Jenny Plane' — Earl Rader, pilot, from 7,000 feet. There were only 12 structures of any sort at this time on all this area and the white patch in lower left center was the Curtiss Air Field, which was the only landing spot in the greater Miami area."

1   Polly Redford, *Billion Dollar Sandbar* (New York: E.P. Dutton, 1970), 204.

2   John Rothchild, *Up for Grabs* (New York: Viking Books, 1985), 39. John Rothchild refers to Miami Beach as "the founding example of what happened along both Florida coasts. Once the dredges corrected the basic defect, developers were left with a tabula rasa of dried silt, as empty and devoid of precedent as an atoll after a nuclear strike."

3   Jane Fisher, *Fabulous Hoosier* (New York: Robert M. McBride, 1947), 125.

4   John Newton Lummus, *The Miracle of Miami Beach* (Miami: The Teacher Publishing Co., 1940).

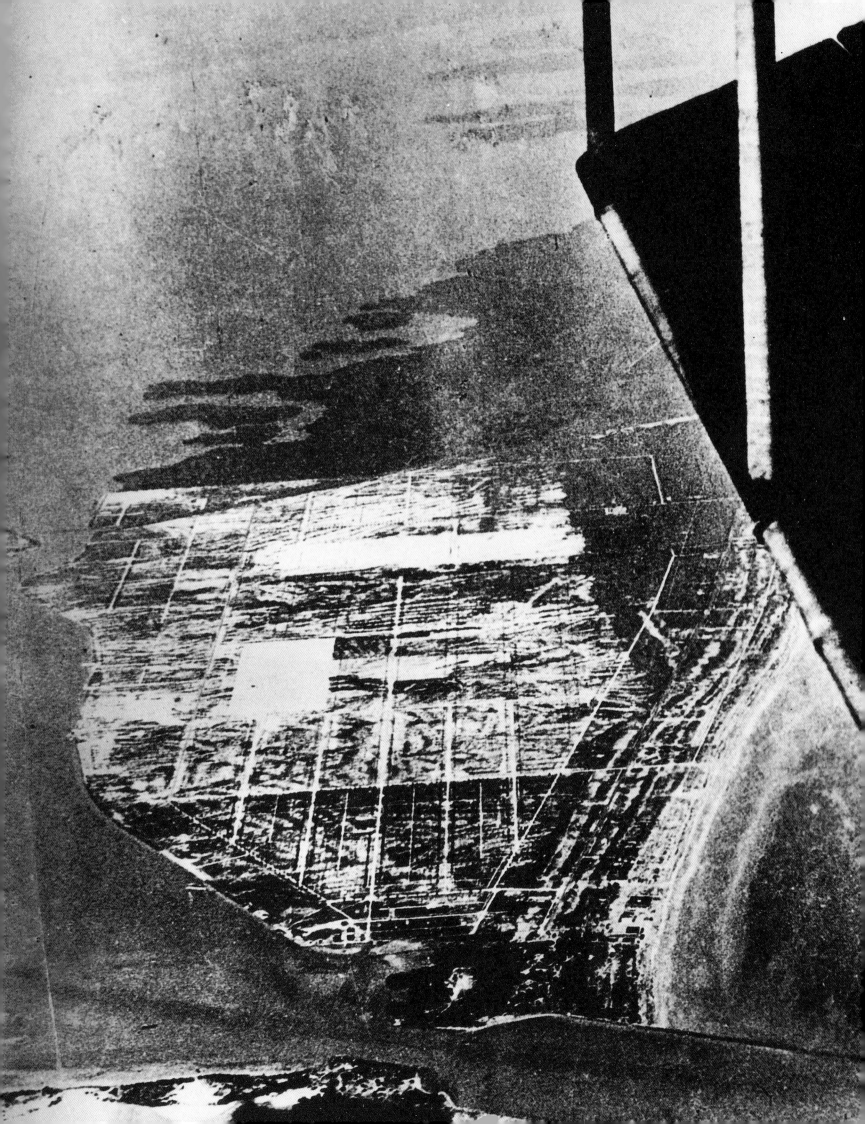

Meanwhile Carl Fisher, who founded the Alton Beach Realty Company in 1913, extended the gridiron on his lands as well. As the centerpiece of his domain, he planned Lincoln Road, a grand commercial boulevard connecting Biscayne Bay on the west and the Atlantic Ocean on the east. Here, formal planning features reminiscent of the City Beautiful movement were initiated. Designed according to the instructions of Fisher on the model of *rue de la Paix* in Paris, it was one hundred feet wide with corner lots that swept around, coordinated rows of coconut trees, a gate on its west end and a monumental olive tree on its east end. This shade tree was planted near Fisher's own home at the foot of Lincoln Road, in the Caribbean tradition of urban foundation. It was dedicated by the Indiana poet James Whitcomb Riley to mark the inaugural moment of the new city.

The remainder of Miami Beach was planned according to a pattern of successive subdivisions which were designed and realized by independent developers including Collins, the Lummuses, Carl Fisher and the various syndicates they formed. In the district south of Collins Canal, known as South Beach, most subdivisions followed the previously established gridiron pattern, producing incongruities and irregularities reflecting their piecemeal planning. The most notable discontinuity was a shift in the street grid between the earlier ocean-facing parcels and the purely north-south gridiron behind the oceanfront.

In addition to the area around Lincoln Road, Fisher came to control almost the entire west side of South Beach as well as the area north of the canal. Along the western flank, in 1920 and 1922, he constructed grand hotels like the Flamingo and Nautilus, while to the north he established picturesque residential neighborhoods organized around a spine of recreational amenities like golf courses and polo fields. More grand

hotels, like the King Cole (1925) and the Boulevard (1925), were built facing these amenities.

As early as 1914, Miami Beach was the suburban setting for modest homes and palatial mansions. A promotional brochure and map produced by Ocean Beach Realty Corporation illustrated the early development of the city, where many homes were built according to Florida vernacular wood traditions; other houses were faced in masonry and stucco. Within the suburban interval of the fifty-foot lots, the scale and character of these homes helped establish the pattern of an Anglo-American suburb. Functional zoning maintained the residential integrity and character of most of the city, while uniform setbacks and the general regularity of height reinforced the suburban scale. Northward and along the waterfront, guidelines established by Carl Fisher required larger and more expensive homes. Here, Fisher gathered men of his ilk, primarily Midwestern industrialists like Harvey Firestone (Firestone Tire Company) and Frank Sieberling (Goodyear Tire Company).

Miami Beach was incorporated as a city in 1915. Well-embroidered myths of the resort as an ideal city, formulated largely by Fisher, propelled its subsequent development. "Miami Beach is calling you" was the rhetorical appeal of a publicity campaign intended to spur growth. Tourists and developers responded positively; in the 1920s Miami Beach, along with the rest of Florida, experienced an unprecedented boom in land sales, construction and tourism. Newspapers paraded the developers' claim that the resort was the fastest growing city in the country.

The Great Florida Land Boom coincided with, and perhaps influenced, the ascendancy of the Mediterranean revival in Florida architecture. As it reformed the vernacular and eclectic traditions of early Miami Beach architecture, the Mediterranean revival introduced a more urban vision,

as well as a more finely developed architecture of illusion and association. It became the canonical style of Miami Beach during the 1920s, and was soon assimilated into almost every type of project, including the small hotels and apartment buildings that arose in areas originally planned for small homes. The scale of buildings became grander, with tall, urban, palace-like façades facing the street. Their stucco-faced walls were adorned with elaborate door surrounds, arches, decorative grillwork and parapets. Scenographically, the Mediterranean Revival was used to particular effect in the realization of unified streetscapes, such as the Artist's Village built on Española Way in 1922.

The boom and the Mediterranean Revival ended definitively with the Great Depression of 1929. Yet Miami Beach began growing again in the early 1930s, setting the stage for another giant construction boom. As early as 1935 Miami Beach was once again the fastest growing city in the country with a per capita building rate twenty times higher than next highest city, Washington D.C. "A hotel for every group of 75 permanent residents is the unusual offering of Miami Beach," declared the *Miami News*.[5] Between 1935 and 1942, the year when the city was virtually converted into a military training center, this phenomenal growth produced hundreds of new and modern resort structures.

It was in the post-Depression 1930s that Miami Beach achieved the definitive form and iconic imagery for which it is noted. Its architects became agents of an urban and architectural transformation that accommodated new building types, novel styling and changing patronage. Lawrence Murray Dixon (1901–1949), along with Henry Hohauser (1895–1963), Roy France (1888–1972), Anton Skislewicz (1895–1967), Albert Anis (1889-1964) and others, were responsible for a large number of buildings, each becoming an imaginator of the new city.

Panorama of Miami Beach. From left to right, the gridded district of South Beach, with Ocean Drive and Lummus Park; the Collins Canal; the picturesque mid-Beach district with its golf courses and polo fields (in the foreground, Collins Avenue). Date and artist unknown. Courtesy of the Historical Museum of Southern Florida.

The Layers of Miami Beach

Oh what a tangled web we weave, when first we practice to deceive.[6]

Cyclical rhythms of development characteristic of twentieth-century America calibrated the development of Miami Beach. Successive periods of expansion — the city's foundation, the Great Florida Land Boom (1920–1926) and the post-Depression boom (1935–1942) — were interrupted by hurricanes, economic decline and both world wars. Each boom and its related production of buildings were tied to important moments of social change, depositing a new set of priorities and meanings. These details are buried in a web of history and myth that are the patrimony of Miami Beach.

Seven urban and architectural strata were most influential in the development of Miami Beach up to 1942. Although they are connected with issues of style they are in fact independent of them. First, the transformation of the terrain from a coastal strand into an ideal landscape laid the foundation for town planning. Second, the city was conceived as a leisure suburb extension of greater Miami, as well as a playground for wealthy Northern industrialists. American land use traditions established the structural pattern for a winter resort, while vernacular housing traditions provided models for residential development. Third, Mediterranean

5 "Hotels Number: One for Each 75 Beach Residents," *Miami News*, 23 January 1938.

6 Sir Walter Scott, *Marmion*, canto V, st. 12 [*Lochinvar*, st. 17], 1808.

and Caribbean traditions supplanted this vernacular tradition during the 1920s with a new imposing scale and urbanism. Emerging housing types, including towers and low-rise apartment blocks, accommodated a growing population. Fourth, the modern movement, with its emphasis on innovation and efficiency, became dominant starting in the 1930s. New standards of light, air and open space transformed the ground plane of the city. The urban implications of the Mediterranean Revival were nevertheless preserved and advanced, regardless of the theoretical anti-urban impulses often associated with the modern movement. Fifth, a distinctly metropolitan identity and scale of development became apparent in the late 1930s, particularly in the previously undeveloped areas closest to the oceanfront. Sixth, beginning in the 1920s, the southern part of Miami Beach became the promised land of the working middle class, bringing perhaps for the first time an ethnic and immigrant culture to a Florida resort. Finally, the city evolved to reflect a multiplicity of historical intentions and meanings.

Miami Beach is a layering of consecutive urban visions, built one on top of the other and compacted in time and space. Each vision left an architectural and urban imprimatur on its structure, influencing the development of an eclectic local vocabulary of buildings and spaces.[7] Most interesting, though, is the intermingling between layers, producing a high degree of urban and stylistic continuity, as well as an urban assemblage between diverse fragments.

At work landscaping Miami Beach. Date unknown. Courtesy of the Historical Museum of Southern Florida.

Layer One: From Wilderness to Landscape

John Levi, a courageous engineer
Knew how to make swamplands disappear.
Three million cubic yards of sand it took
To fill the swamp and give it that new look,
As from the bottom of blue Biscayne Bay
Land rose — at fifty thousand dollars a day.[8]

Romantic Miami Beach is Utopia, endeavoring to be the most beautiful place in the world.[9]

Where has there been a more convenient opportunity to remodel the surroundings than Florida in the modern age?…The favorable Florida climate and new methods of horticulture made it possible to impose an eclectic landscape, gathered and installed outdoors.[10]

Miami Beach was not a likely place for the establishment of a city; its mucky swamps and dense brush had to be tamed in order to fulfill its destiny of enticing tourists and selling homesites. Yet, its domestication created a physical utopia of green lawns, neat rows of feathery trees, flowering plants, and a clean beach raked daily of seaweed. The transformation of Miami Beach reveals a critical ingredient in the city's creation: the ways and means to completely reinvent the environment as the context for a new type of resort city. This reinvention was part of a development plan that began, Denise Scott Brown noted, "by elaborating the values of nature and then adding the architecture."[11]

Like other new cities of the Progressive Era in America, Miami Beach responded to the dream of escape from the industrial city and the search for an ideal climate and landscape. The health-giving power of sun, the paradisiacal winter climate and the exoticism of the tropics were consequently mobilized toward the notion of an enchanted "land of romance." Miami Beach was projected as a convincing image of a perfect existence, a utopian environment reflective of the leisure that the tropics could offer. In fact, the natural setting of South Florida was transformed to reflect what a generation of Americans thought the tropics should look like, rather than a naturally evolved landscape.

7   Established local traditions of building are evidence of a coherent building typology. For more information on the development of typology in Miami Beach, see Allan T. Shulman, "Miami Beach as Urban Assemblage: A Unique Culture of Housing," *The New City* 3 (1996): 25-49.

8   Irving Zieman, *Miami Beach in Rhyme* (Boston: Meador Publishing Company, 1954), 31.

9   Brochure, *Paradise Under the Sun*, Archives and Special Collections, Otto G. Richter Library, University of Miami.

10 Rothchild, 38-42.

11 Denise Scott Brown, *City of Miami Beach (Florida) Washington Avenue Revitalization Plan, City of Miami Beach* (Miami Beach, Florida: City of Miami Beach, 1979).

Nature was objectified and idealized as the infrastructure and exterior furniture of the new city.

The reality of the new landscape took shape as a vast park, rationalized horticulturally and in plan. It was not so much designed as "engineered"; Fred Hoerger, a landscape engineer in the service of Carl Fisher, established the outlines of the new natural scenery. The naked plain of the city was planted as a field of Bermuda grass, and the future avenues and streets were outlined with Australian pines and, less frequently, royal palms. The oceanfront strand of coconut palms was reinforced with the addition of a sufficient number of similar trees to give the place the sense of a grove. The Bermuda grass was designed to hold down the sand, while the fast growing pines were a tree of convenience: their instant maturity lent brand-new Miami Beach an air of antiquity. A pair of Japanese gardeners, Kotaro Suto and Shigezo Tashiro, executed more elaborate plantings; however their flowering palate of plants, bushes and trees, including bougainvilleas, orchids, poincianas, hibiscus, oleanders, coconuts, oranges, grapefruits and avocados were largely enhancements to the purely private realm. In Miami Beach, the landscape tradition would henceforth serve primarily individual utopias, less so the public realm.

Perhaps the reformulation of landscape can be seen as an attempt to perfect Florida's environment in the manner of the English landscape ideal — to "render actual and evident, that which is potential and inevident."[12] Promotional materials of the period support this view, emphasizing that the climate and native soil appeared capable of, in fact ideally suited to, supporting the most exotic tropical foliage. Idealized nature quickly replaced raw nature; tropical flora and fauna extrinsic to South Florida were introduced onto the fresh land and thrived, creating a horticultural metamorphosis. The success of the venture was seemingly confirmed when colorful butterflies invaded the city.[13] The flourishing beauty of Miami Beach kept reinforcing this ideal.

A darker view is that the reformulation of landscape utterly reinvented the terrain, obliterating the intrinsic. Landforms and nature were groomed to imitate a commercially conceived scenic ideal. The glamour of the scenery was tied to its nearly immaculate conception according to the latest fashion. In either case, idealized nature was pursued as an instrument of urban planning. It is worth noting, in this context, that the

quality of nature envisioned for the public realm was rudimentary. A comparison between Miami Beach and the development of Coral Gables reveals the much richer use of landscape in the latter.[14] In practice, the lack of any comprehensive landscape plan placed emphasis on the careful integration of individual efforts, a situation that paralleled the similarly laissez-faire architectural and urban development of the city.

In any case, more than exotica was imposed on the soil of Miami Beach. The promise of a sporting life enriched the vision of the ideal landscape. Residential areas of Miami Beach were largely designed around one of the most extensive agglomerations of golf courses, polo fields and water frontage available anywhere in the United States. The manicured landscape of polo fields and golf courses, fragments of the English and Scottish countryside, organized and gave character to surrounding residential streets.

---

12 Emile Benton MacKaye, *The New Exploration* (University of Illinois Press: Urbana, 1962), 148, quoted in Francesco Dal Co, "From Parks to the Region: Progressive Idealogy and the Reform of the American City," Giorgio Ciucci et. al., *The American City: from the Civil War to the New Deal* (London; New York: Granada, 1980), 183.

13 Fisher, 118.

14 Ann Armbruster, *The Life and Times of Miami Beach* (New York: Alfred A. Knopf, 1995), 25.

above:
Advertisement for Miami Beach showing before and after images, as well as the equipment used in the transformation. From brochure, *The Call of Miami Beach, Florida.* c. 1923. Archives and Special Collections, Otto G. Richter Library, University of Miami.

The creation and grooming of fresh land, indeed the remaking of Miami Beach, was evidence of a comprehensive faith in technology among industrialists characteristic of the early twentieth century. Carl Fisher, the main protagonist of the dredge and fill operation, was in fact influenced by the example of Robert Ingersoll, an agnostic republican who "elevated man's industrial achievements to the level of religion."[15] Fisher and his friends, the beneficiaries of automotive wealth, were the city's first residents and developers. Capital earned in the automotive industry was thrust into the creation of land and infrastructure, making this progressive venture one of the first to benefit from automotive wealth and production.[16]

Fisher, a believer in the machine age that would later inspire the modern architects of the 1930s, established Miami Beach's fundamental relationship between landscape and machine. It was a city built for the automobile (as well as the motor boat and airplane, other Fisher interests), although not necessarily designed around it. As early as 1918 it was accessible by car, the terminus of "more than 600 miles of perfect roads radiating in every direction from Miami Beach."[17] The most important of these was the Dixie Highway, a network of roads assembled by Fisher and opened in 1915, connecting Florida to various points in the Midwest. The Dixie was modeled on the Lincoln Highway, Fisher's first effort at trailblazing and America's first transcontinental highway. In Miami Beach, the car was linked to the landscape through a web of parkways, causeways, broad avenues and commercial streets designed to be pleasurable to the driver. The automobile featured prominently in early poetic descriptions, such as *A Little Journey to Altonia*, a paean to Carl Fisher's Miami Beach written in 1918 by John Oliver LaGorce, Fisher's friend and then Associate Editor of *National Geographic*. LaGorce told the reader that "to motor slowly along the Ocean Drive and watch the multi-hued waters caress the beach is a wondrous thing."[18] He described Miami Beach as a network of roadways "bordered by tall, graceful Australian pines, so pleasing and restful because of their distinctive feather-like foliage, standing shoulder to shoulder with thousands of glorious palms…Through these eye-delighting scenes the motorist motes or the horseman rides, catching glimpses through the Brazilian rubber trees and Spanish laurel of the fragrant orange blossoms and the mimosa…"[19]

A Little Journey to Altonia was perhaps the first of a number of small books and brochures that exalted Miami and Miami Beach with poetic descriptions and literary detail. For instance *The Town that Climate Built*, a book by Victor Rainbolt, mixed historical documentation with myth, cultural commentary and promotion, as can be discerned in chapter headings like "The City of Youth and the Garden of Eden," "The Cosmopolitan Ostend of the Western World" and "Paradise of Perpetual Summer." As Miami Beach emerged as a national phenomenon, a series of authors perpetuated this literary genre into the 1930s and beyond, including Charles Edgar Nash's 1938 book *The Magic of Miami Beach*, Howard Mehling's 1960 chronicle *The Most of Everything: The Story of Miami Beach* and Irving Zieman's 1954 collection *Miami Beach in Rhyme,* that recounted the history and culture of the resort in verse.

The tabula rasa was soon an important real estate commodity. In a state rapidly developing around the theme of exotic attractions,[20] the fabrication of new waterfront real estate created valuable and unique assets. The "improved" landscape was a stage setting for the imposition of the unique homes and expressive architectural landmarks that were planned. Indeed, the first buildings on Miami Beach appeared as follies within this garden landscape. To the author John Dos Passos, Florida appeared "fabulous and movie-like," a place where whole cities were built in three months.[21] The rapid construction of the city reinforced the pervasive stage-like quality that remained an important feature through the 1940s.

---

15 Rothchild, 38-42.

16 Carl Fisher's fortune came from his purchase and later sale of Prest-o-Lite, the company that controlled the patent for carbon-filament automobile headlights.

17 Brochure, *The Call of Miami Beach, Florida,* c. 1923.

18 John Oliver LaGorce, *A Little Journey to Altonia: The Lure of a Clockless Land Where Summer Basks in the Lap of Winter* (Indianapolis, Indiana: Carl G. Fisher, 1918), unpaginated.

19 Ibid.

above:
Ocean Drive with palm trees. c. 1913. Photograph by Matlack. Courtesy of the Historical Museum of Southern Florida.

20 Brochure, *Florida at the NY World's Fair*, 1939, The Mitchell Wolfson Jr. Collection, The Wolfsonian-Florida International University. The brochure notes that Florida had more exotic attractions than any other state in the country.

21 John Dos Passos, *USA: The Big Money* (Boston: Houghton Mifflin Co., 1937), 231. Dos Passos described Florida as an Eden without a serpent, and Miami Beach as a paradise.

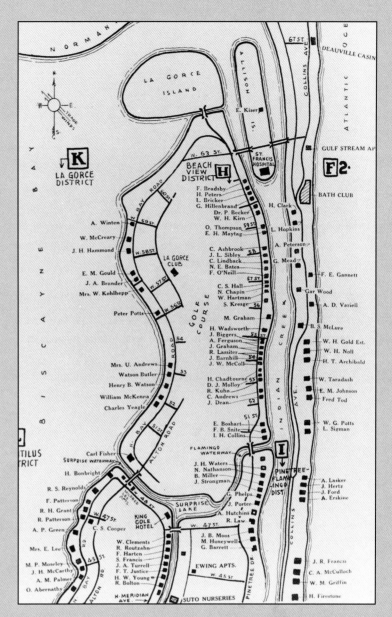

top left:
Map, "Southern Half of the Town of Miami Beach." From *Ocean Beach Realty Map*.
1915. Courtesy of the Historical Museum of Southern Florida.

top right:
Map of Miami Beach (indicating the homes of well-known industrialists) c. 1920. Courtesy of
the Historical Museum of Southern Florida.

Layer Two: The Multiple Inventions of a Leisure Suburb

Within a few months the new flowering forest did indeed shade a mushrooming metropolis – golf courses, houses, roads of glittering white coral, even hotels. So rapid was its building, outsiders doubted its durability as a building project. Its fantastic loveliness made Miami Beach seem more like a stage set than a city.[22]

The *raison d'être* for the makeover of Miami Beach was to fulfill its vocation as a leisure city. However, competing notions about how to develop the city caused the "leisure city" to be a somewhat unstable concept in Miami Beach, subject to ownership patterns, shifting ideals and the will of the economy. The city developed as a collection of independent communities representing a range of planning ideals. Thus the resort hotel in the garden, the public bathing beach fronted with a terrace of hotels, the gridiron of the urban resort, the grand boulevard, the picturesque parkway and the garden suburb all cohabited the island in the early 1920s. Each, perhaps, was a discreet utopia built upon separate American planning traditions and connected to contemporary culture in different ways. Eventually the distinct "colonies" met, causing a collision of design ideals from which a new multifaceted utopia of leisure emerged.

The different urban patterns imposed on the new landscape reflected in part the independent planning of at least three distinct real estate development firms. In South Beach, the Ocean Beach Realty Company assembled the traditional elements of a seaside resort city: an oceanfront "boardwalk" as the setting for an architectural promenade; "bathing casinos" built along the ocean; an entertainment pier and a mix of homes, hotels and boarding houses. To the north, in the area that became known as Collins Park, the Miami Beach Improvement Company planned an oceanfront community of hotels and houses beyond the limits of a functioning farming district maintained by developer John Collins. South Beach and Collins Park were similar in many respects, including the use of the gridiron and the early dedication of oceanfront parks that in both cases served not only as broad public spaces, but as the urban "front yard" of the city. With little ambition toward civic grandeur, however, no other areas were initially set aside for civic functions or public spaces. Miami pioneer Marjory Stoneman Douglas's idea of a "great boulevard along the ocean beaches"[23] was dis-

carded in favor of private oceanfront real estate throughout most of the city. Landmarks of both civic and commercial dimension were left to develop after the fact on Lincoln Road as well as on Washington Avenue, the line of division between the oceanfront and the rest of the grid.

Contrary to the more urban gridiron of South Beach, the city taking shape along the north and west sides of Miami Beach adhered to the model of a picturesque garden suburb. Here was an assemblage of homesites organized along the new bayfront edge as well as along canals, lakes, artificial islands, recreational amenities and parkways. Probably influenced by the contemporary Parks Movement and Frederick Law Olmsted's picturesque plans for urban parks and garden cities, this area of private villas was anchored by a series of grand hotels that were linked to the city's amenities, and by the shopping district of Lincoln Road. The combination of garden suburb, grand hotel, golf course and elegant shopping district established a model of development that would be repeated throughout Florida. In Coral Gables, for instance, the picturesque residential streets anchored by the Biltmore Hotel and its golf course on the one hand and Coral Way on the other exhibited the same interdependence of elements.

In order to facilitate residential development, pattern books of house designs were developed specifically for Miami Beach. Fisher's Alton Beach Realty Company published "Winter Homes for Southern Florida" (c. 1915), fifteen home designs fashioned around the theme of the Florida Villa. The guidebook noted that "varying climates have produced varying types of homes the world over" and that the Florida Villa combined the best "time tried and enduring styles of architecture" with practical innovations peculiarly its own.[24] The stylistic variations stretched from Italianate to Prairie Style and American Colonial, reflective of American eclecticism and the casting about for an appropriate architectural style. However, there is no record of any model homes being built, and they had little effect on the stylistic development of Miami Beach. Most modest new structures were vernacular in construction and conception. The prevalent tradition was the wood vernacular bungalow that was well adapted climatically and conveyed a relaxed image. It had large windows, deep porches and wide eaves, and was sometimes faced with local oolitic limestone.[25] In a 1940 retrospective, the *Miami Herald* noted that bungalows were popular "because of increasing orientation toward outdoor living."[26] Another pattern book of homes, published around 1920 by a consortium of the major developers,

---

22   Fisher, 118.

23   Marjory Stoneman Douglas, quoted in Armbruster, 25.

24   Brochure, *Winter Homes for Southern Florida: A Book of Design*, Historical Museum of Southern Florida.

25   Ivan A. Rodriguez, Margot Ammidown, Emily Perry Dieterich, Bogue Wallin, *Wilderness to Metropolis* (Miami: Metropolitan Dade County Office of Community Development, Historic Preservation Division, 1982), 79.

26   *Miami Herald*, 21 April 1940.

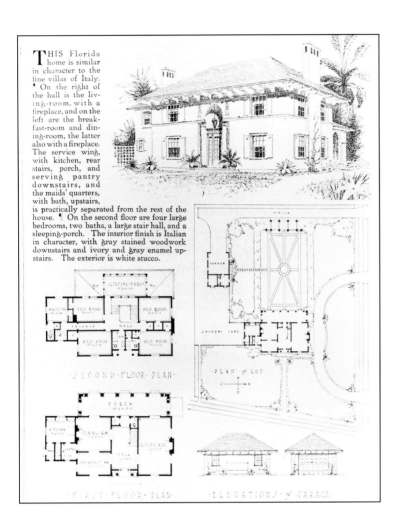

THIS Florida home is similar in character to the tine villas of Italy. ¶ On the right of the hall is the living-room, with a fireplace, and on the left are the break-fast-room and dining-room, the latter also with a fireplace. The service wing, with kitchen, rear stairs, porch, and serving pantry downstairs, and the maids' quarters, with bath, upstairs, is practically separated from the rest of the house. ¶ On the second floor are four large bedrooms, two baths, a large stair hall, and a sleeping-porch. The interior finish is Italian in character, with gray stained woodwork downstairs and ivory and gray enamel up-stairs. The exterior is white stucco.

illustrated recently built homes.[27] This time, however, the variety of models was characteristic of Florida's progress in evolving a palate of regional styles, featuring mainly vernacular and Mediterranean Revival examples. Notwithstanding the understandable narrowing of architectural vocabulary, the model homes produced for Miami Beach were perhaps the first appearance of a liberal eclecticism that was a defining feature of the city. Moreover, they may have influenced the later development of theme villages in Coral Gables built between 1924 and 1926.

Grand hotels set the tone of the garden suburb areas of Miami Beach, and in some ways for future hotel developments. The first grand hotel was the Flamingo (1921), built by Carl Fisher and designed by Philadelphia architects Price & McLanahan. Constructed between Fisher's motor boat speedway and his polo fields, the Flamingo occupied a compound whose central element was a stepped tower crowned with a colored glass dome capable of beaming light across Biscayne Bay to Miami. Conceived around the theme of the exotic bird that inhabited the Bahamas, it established a precedent for the artistic celebration of the "tropical" in Miami Beach hotels. Sources for the architecture can be found in the tradition of American holiday hotels, as well as in the rail-road hotels that established the resort character of the region. However, it is interesting that the Flamingo abandoned both the wood vernacular tradition of hotels like the Royal Palm (1896) in Miami, as well as the broad palatial massing of hotels like the Ponce de Leon (1888) and Alcazar (1889) in St. Augustine by Carrère and Hastings. In spite of its garden setting, the Flamingo's tall vertical massing, plain exterior wrappings, elaborate silhouettes and lavish lobbies recall the American commercial skyscraper, perhaps reflecting the popularity of that emerging building type in the 1920s.

top left:
Sample house plan based on the villas of Italy. From brochure, *Winter Homes for Southern Florida: A Book of Design.* c. 1914. Courtesy of the Historical Museum of Southern Florida.

bottom left:
Coral Rock House, corner of Collins Avenue and 9th Street, Miami Beach. c. 1914. Courtesy of the Historical Museum of Southern Florida.

27   Brochure, *Homes "Miami Beach" Florida,* c. 1918, Historical Museum of Southern Florida. A consortium of The Miami Beach Ocean View Company, United Companies Realty Corporation, Miami Beach Improvement Company and Alton Beach Realty Company likely published this brochure.

Flamingo Hotel and grounds, east front view from Bay Road, Miami Beach. 1934. Courtesy of the Romer Collection, Miami-Dade Public Library.

Lincoln Gate, view looking east along Lincoln Road toward intersection with Alton Road, Miami Beach. c. 1920. Courtesy of the Historical Museum of Southern Florida.

The Flamingo was the first of a generation of hotels that are primarily significant for their siting. The uninspired towers of the Fleetwood (1925) and Floridian (S. D. Butterworth, 1925) hotels, as well as the palatial Nautilus (Leonard Schultze & Fullerton Weaver, 1924), joined the Flamingo along the undulating west edge of Miami Beach where, dominating Biscayne Bay, their massive silhouettes were visible from Miami.[28] Inland, the Lincoln (August Geiger, 1917) and Boulevard (William Francis Brown, 1925) hotels were located facing golf courses, while the King Cole (Kiehnel & Elliott Architects, 1925) was strategically located on Surprise Lake, between polo fields and a golf course. The grand hotels were landmarks and icons of Miami Beach's real estate development, but they were also elements of a real estate strategy of forfeiting the worst land as recreational green space and selling the best land around it. These grand hotels, usually implanted on the emptiness of a newly created subdivision, helped launch the residential development of particular districts. As one brochure described it, hotel builders "selected a point far from the developed sections, moving materials and men to the point, proceeded to build first the grounds, then the building, sometimes a half-million dollar project — oftentimes more, and then awaited the building of the city around the hotel."[29] Strategically, the hotels generated demand for the single-family homes and estates which were the intended product. It is notable that, in contrast to similar schemes today, although developers took great pains to bring tourists, they did not build the houses. The subsequent construction of houses spanned many years and architectural styles; coupled

with variations in lot size and orientation, whether by chance or by design, the diversity yielded a mixed and rather democratic American suburb whose character in many ways mirrored the denser housing districts of the city.

Along with the grand hotels, Lincoln Road was an important component of Carl Fisher's plan of developing a resort image centered on themes of leisure, exclusivity and cosmopolitan worldliness. Lincoln Road was designed to accommodate the nation's most elegant boutiques, galleries and showrooms, and it succeeded at this. Described as the "Fifth Avenue of the South," its shops offered the latest fashions in clothing, furs, jewelry and automobiles. Symbolic of a city that mixed business and pleasure, its sidewalks were designed in two zones: one for pedestrians on the move and the other for window shoppers who wished to stroll. A row of coconut palms, forming a median between the walking lanes, lined either side of the street. At its west end, an overarching decorative gate, made of coral rock and steel assembled to form a gigantic trellis, introduced an element of civic art appropriate to the de facto symbolic heart of the city. In fact, Lincoln Road developed an important civic presence. It was the location of the Community Church (Walter De Garmo, 1921) and the office-tower of Carl Fisher's real estate empire (August Geiger, 1924), and soon became home to at least four cinemas. Stretching from the Atlantic Ocean to Biscayne Bay, it also formed the most important east-west connector in Miami Beach and thus its central meeting place. Located at the northern end of the gridiron of South Beach

28 Armbruster, 26.

29 Florida Editors Associated, *The Book of Florida: An illustrated description of the advantages and opportunities of the State of Florida and the progress that has been achieved with a biographical record of those citizens whose endeavor has produced the superb structure (commercial, industrial, agricultural and political) which comprises the strength of this charming section* (Florida Editors Association, 1925), 67-68.

Residence and studio of Henry Salem Hubbell, Dade Canal, Miami Beach. Schultze & Weaver, 1925. Courtesy of the Historical Museum of Southern Florida.

Brown's Hotel, Collins Avenue and 2nd Street, Miami Beach. Architect unknown, c. 1914. From *Ocean Beach Realty Map*. 1914. Courtesy of the Historical Museum of Southern Florida.

and the southern end of the picturesque suburbs to the north, Lincoln Road evolved in the 1930s as the social melting pot of the city.

The constituent pieces of the city, created by separate development interests, were joined in 1915 to form the Town of Miami Beach. Nevertheless, a bipolar structure that concretized divisions of class and ethnicity would become a permanent feature of the city. Below Lincoln Road was the rational grid, a fragment of the democratic subdivision of America. It would naturally evolve to accommodate a dense district of housing. To the north, free-flowing streets and open spaces delineated an Anglo-American suburb synonymous with wealth and privilege, low in density, and exceedingly well equipped with recreational facilities. Here, in a typical instance of paternal intervention, Fisher limited the availability of building lots in order to maintain price levels. Ethnicity was also restricted to Caucasian gentiles. The merging revealed Miami Beach to be a functionally zoned and even segregated modern city.

As proof of this emerging differentiation, small apartment hotel buildings were built among the scattered homes within the gridiron of South Beach. The first hotel on Miami Beach was in fact Brown's Hotel (1915), a two-story wood structure in a simple vernacular wood-clad style. Its mass largely filled its narrow site, although it was maintained freestanding by the provision of setbacks. It was a deep rectangular structure, bisected by a corridor along its entire length, with apartments arrayed into the depth of the lot and facing sideways. Its façade articulated a narrow street frontage, while the provision of a front porch and front yard as the main public focus of the building maintained both the original suburban feeling of Miami Beach and the primacy of the avenue as an urban space. Brown's Hotel was the archetype for the modest class of housing that subsequently urbanized South Beach. The basic pattern of freestanding building, front yard and frontal progression from the avenue persists today. Derived in plan from the tenement, multi-unit dwellings like Brown's provided modest hotel amenities for middle class tourists, often in the informal lifestyle of an apartment.

The construction of Brown's Hotel among a fabric of houses, while well adapted, points to the lack of control that was an early feature of the city. As a consequence of its loose foundational plans and vision, a lively and largely uncontrolled development sector arose. Driven mainly by small entrepreneurship, new housing shaped by market forces became an important factor in the development of Miami Beach. The Florida Land Boom of the 1920s soon swept the city, stimulating even more activity and change. A 1925 advertisement by the Miami Beach Chamber of Commerce carried a call to contractors and builders: "Take Notice!! 100 more hotels and 300 more apartment houses needed now."[30] Although the boom and its related phenomenon of mad speculation are often ascribed to market hype, they were also reflective of the real market forces of rapidly expanding immigration from the North. As John Christian Kofoed postulated in *Moon over Miami*, the boom was not as crazy as it seemed in retrospect.[31] It matched population increases that were dramatic, and was proof of the nation's unquenchable thirst for leisure and land.

30 Brochure, advertisement from *The Call of Miami Beach*, 25 August 1925, Historical Museum of Southern Florida.

31 John Christian Kofoed, *Moon Over Miami* (New York: Random House, 1955).

Layer Three: Making the City Mediterranean

[Miami Beach] …is Florida's booming catholic pleasure dome, looming low and broad against the Atlantic sky. Coconut and royal palms, hibiscus, croton, flame vines, night-blooming jasmine shroud mile upon serpentine mile of streets and lanes and waterways…The creamy, orange, blue and yellow palaces, villas, cottages are of concrete blocks beneath their stucco (to guard against "the next hurricane"). Their open patios, loggias, halls and broad window spaces are designed for life and ease in the sun.[32]

The desire to transform Miami Beach into a Mediterranean city corresponded with the ascendancy of the Mediterranean Revival style in Florida. This regional expression derived partially from nineteenth century eclectic traditions, but its appearance in Florida was contemporary with the Spanish Colonial style popular in the early twentieth century and evoked notably at San Diego's 1915 Panama-California Exposition. San Diego demonstrated two important aspects of the Spanish Colonial style: first, the success of style and civic art in creating a sense of identity and place; second, the appropriateness within a certain territorial, climatic and cultural context of Spanish Colonial architecture as a regional style. Architects and developers working in Florida were quick to see the value of imposing the template of a stylistically unified and regionally appropriate civic art onto its growing new cities. The Mediterranean Revival defined the style of the 1920s in Miami Beach, and because it also embodied new planning paradigms, set the stage for the modern city of the next decade.

Compared to the wood vernacular structures that had begun to define the character of Miami Beach, the Mediterranean Revival was a less modest and more romantic vision of South Florida development. It was immediately used in the elaborate villas built for the industrial elite that began to favor Miami Beach in the early 1920s; mansions in the choicest waterfront areas soon competed with Addison Mizner's Mediterranean vision in Palm Beach. Even more importantly, the Mediterranean Revival introduced a more urban paradigm that included formal frontages and courtyard-type buildings. If its masonry walls and closed courtyards were less climatically sensitive, scenographically this architecture began to tap the potential that tropical Miami Beach could provide. Many buildings featured an asymmetrically juxtaposed façade massing, some with watchtower motifs. The style's aged look conveyed the instant pedigree of ancient architecture on the new city.[33]

View looking west along Española Way, Miami Beach. Date unknown. Robert Taylor, c. 1925. Courtesy of the Historical Museum of Southern Florida.

The Mediterranean Revival contributed three important influences to the urban structure of Miami Beach: the implantation of a sophisticated urban ensemble, the refined elaboration of the grand hotel type and the "stagey" and more urban development of the small apartment building type. The thematic Spanish Village of Española Way deployed, more than any other project before it, the image-making and city-building potential of a unified civic art. Built inside the block structure of South Beach, it is virtually a city within the city, sited to flow from west to east, toward the beach. First conceived of as a series of houses and cottages,[34] the project was redesigned only a year later under the control of Newton Baker Taylor Roney (who would later develop the famed Roney Plaza Hotel) as a parade of six hotels, two of which were built.[35] As completed under the guidance of architect Robert Taylor, the complex is a self-contained artists' colony in the guise of a narrow Spanish street. Its thematic architecture, appearing purposefully haphazard and unplanned, defined a sophisticated urban layering of functions, combining gallery frontages on the street, workshops above and artists' residences behind. The *Miami Daily News* equated the project with the goal of creating an "ambiance" unique to South Florida. It purportedly was originated by New Yorkers visiting Miami: "they mentioned that with all the tropic surroundings of the Beach, there was no place where an artist would feel the same atmosphere as he would in Greenwich Village in New York or in the artist quarter in Paris."[36]

32 "Pleasure Dome," *Time,* 19 February 1940, 18.

33 Beth Dunlop, "Inventing Antiquity: The Art and Craft of the Mediterranean Revival Architecture," *The Journal of Decorative and Propaganda Arts* 23 (1998): 190-207.

34 Howard Kleinberg, *Miami Beach: A History* (Miami: Centennial Press, 1994), 91.

35 Ibid.

36 *Miami Daily News*, February 1926, quoted in Kleinberg, 90.

Perhaps, like Addison Mizner in Palm Beach, Roney wished to provide artistic and artisanal foundations for Miami Beach. In fact, Miami Beach preservationist and historian Barbara Baer Capitman (1929–1983) cites Roney's Spanish Village as the likely inspiration for Addison Mizner in the construction of Worth Avenue and the adjacent shopping district via Mizner.[37] The thematic and associational intentions of Española Way were echoed in the architectural evolution of Lincoln Road as a Mediterranean "paseo," and in the reconstruction of Collins Bridge and connecting Collins Canal according to a "Venetian" theme. Regardless of stylistic specificity, the idea of a thematic definition of space would powerfully influence architects of the 1930s.

It was within the urban grid that the Mediterranean Revival achieved a new level of sophistication. D. Kingstone Hall's Blackstone Hotel (1929) and Martin Luther Hampton's Miami Beach City Hall (1927), exploited the peculiar grid shift along Washington Avenue to monumental effect with towers that rose from lower wings. The grand Roney Plaza Hotel, developed by Roney just before the crash of the land boom in 1926, marked the crest of Mediterranean Revival in Miami Beach. It also marked the definitive transformation of the grand hotel type toward a more urban syntax, a transformation important to later hotel design. The Roney was located on one of the most geographically significant sites of the city: a narrow isthmus between the ocean and a natural lagoon, near the end of the Collins Canal that cut Miami Beach into north and south sections. Roney chose Schultze & Weaver to design what would be the city's grandest hotel. The New York architects designed a monument similar in importance to their other Miami projects, the Coral Gables Biltmore Hotel (1925) and the Miami Metropolis Building in downtown Miami (1926). The Roney Plaza incorporated the same stepped tower element executed in platoresque detail that emulated Sevilla's towering Giralda. Schultze & Weaver laid out the hotel as a simple L-shape, sheltering on its ocean side a large garden incorporating a pool and cabana deck that stepped down to a boardwalk along the beach. The urban correlation of façade and streets on both sides of the "L" impacted at the corner, where the tower was monumentalized. With its front to the city and its back to the ocean, it was a resort of urban impact. Whereas earlier development was related more to gardens, the Roney Plaza announced the importance of being "on the ocean" as well as within the city, an imperative that would become critical in the 1930s.

The Mediterranean Revival marked the first intensive urbanization of South Beach following the Great Florida Land Boom of the mid-1920s. During this period, the character of the southernmost section, South Beach,

top:
Aerial photograph of Miami Beach looking northeast, showing the Blackstone Hotel and the Miami Beach City Hall. c. 1930. Courtesy of the Historical Museum of Southern Florida.

above:
The Roney Plaza Hotel, Collins Avenue and 23rd Street, Miami Beach. Schultze & Weaver, 1926. Courtesy of the Historical Museum of Southern Florida.

37 Barbara Baer Capitman, *Deco Delights: Preserving the Beauty and Joy of Miami Beach Architecture* (New York: E.P. Dutton, 1988), 65.

began to shift from houses to apartments, and a new culture of housing appeared. The pressure of the boom accelerated the transition to new housing types that were characteristic of the modern city. Not surprisingly, the hotel and apartment types popularized in New York during the 1920s were a significant influence. Low-rise apartment blocks and towers, emblematic of the urban development of Manhattan and its outer boroughs, became the preferred housing prototypes.

The Mediterranean Revival style also coincided with the introduction of new urban forms and spaces, especially the courtyard patio. Many buildings were still simple rectangular structures built in the space of one lot and bisected by a corridor, yet others expanded to two lots in order to incorporate a patio. Architecturally the courtyards emulated Mediterranean and Caribbean models, with an ornamental mixture of paving, landscaping and fountains. An example was the eclectic Casa Casuarina (1930), which was built like an urban palace. The Parkway Apartments (1936), slightly larger, was more representative of a hacienda. The Ester Apartments (1933, p. 75), one of Lawrence Murray Dixon's first buildings, elaborated a well-defined urban patio surrounded on three sides by apartments and on the fourth by a low garden wall directly on the street. Smaller structures explored the spatial theme of the Spanish *callejón*, or alley.

Notwithstanding the interest in Mediterranean housing types, most apartment buildings were transitional structures that remained tied to Anglo-American architectural and urban traditions. Typically, the formal articulation of freestanding building mass to make courtyards produced U, C, L and O-shaped forms that developed an interior focus. The patio thus created was largely scenographic in nature, working independently of the building organization, which remained tied to internalized corridor systems. Furthermore, courtyard spaces supplemented, but did not replace, the importance of the suburban front yard.

The dichotomy between the reticular grid of South Beach and residential developments with more picturesque and contemporary curvilinear patterns immediately to the north may have influenced the southern area's more urban development. As the first part of Miami Beach to be developed, South Beach always had a less exclusive "feel." Limitations on multi-unit dwellings in other neighborhoods and exclusive (as well as racially restrictive) purchasing privileges forced the less luxurious lodgings to unrestricted areas like South Beach, where they became the dominant building type.

top:
"Hotels and Apartments at Miami Beach." From brochure *The Lure of Miami Beach, Florida.* 1928. Published by F. S. Benedict, official publication of the Miami Beach Chamber of Commerce. Courtesy of the Historical Museum of Southern Florida.

above:
Casa Casuarina, Miami Beach. Henry LaPointe, 1930. From *Florida Architecture and Allied Arts.* 1938. Courtesy of the Otto G. Richter Library, University of Miami.

Layer Four: The Residential Scale of the Modern City

The Great Land Boom of the 1920s catapulted the urban development of Miami Beach's southern districts. Yet the city was still in its adolescence at the beginning of the 1930s. From an airplane or from the heights of the Blackstone Hotel, the view was of a city under construction. The aggregate effect of boom-time construction was diluted by the large open spaces of the incomplete city. Yet the number of open lots rapidly diminished during the next ten years; by 1941 Miami Beach had nearly completed its urban fabric. New lodgings were shaped by an influential modernizing trend in housing design, emphasizing efficient domestic arrangements and a new aesthetic for the Machine Age.

One impetus for new housing models was the increasing population density of South Beach. Another was the process of infilling, which diminished the amount of open space in the city. With increasing physical and population density came alternative models for the urbanization of the block designed to preserve usable physical space. Ignited by a national housing shortage and war-era reform programs, the progress of European housing and the German *Siedlungen* model in particular were introduced to Americans in the late 1920s and early 1930s by writers like Catherine Bauer and Henry Wright, as well as by exhibits such as the Museum of Modern Art's 1932 International Style Exhibition. In an article called "The Modern Apartment House" (1929), the urbanist Henry Wright lamented that fifteen to thirty percent of floor area built in 1928 was wasted on halls, corridors, and lobbies. He articulated a set of basic requirements for apartment plans which included space-saving walk-up apartment access, two-room-deep units with multiple exposures, and formal articulation of the building mass in relation to open area in order to define a public realm.[38] The ideas were further elaborated by the Housing Division of the Public Works Administration, which built low-cost housing after the Depression: in 1935 it codified and published model plans and type configurations.[39] These *Unit Plans* provided a kit of parts from which the designer could arrange spatial compositions.

In contrast to comparable national and international housing developments, the arrival of new housing types in Miami Beach was not connected to a program of social improvement through housing reform. In fact, mirroring the speculative conditions prevailing during the 1920s boom (albeit in a less frenzied manner), the city was once again a big

top:
The Public Works Administration's "kit of parts" approach to housing design. From "Unit Types of Plans for Low-Rent Housing Projects," *Architectural Record* (March 1935).

above:
Aerial view of Großsiedlung Britz toward northwest. c. 1931. Bruno Taut, 1926. From *Vier Berliner Siedlunger der Weimarer Republik.* © Archive GEHAG.

38   Henry Wright, "The Modern Apartment House," *Architectural Record* (March 1929).

39   The Housing Division of the Public Works Administration, "Unit Types of Plans for Low-Rent Housing Projects," *Architectural Record* (March 1935).

above:
Residential quarter, Cité Industrielle. Tony Garnier, 1917. Rendering from *Tony Garnier, Une cité industrielle: étude pour la construction des villes* (New York: Princeton Architectural Press, 1989).

right:
The rue Mallet-Stevens, Paris. Robert Mallet-Stevens, 1927. Photograph from Jean-Francois Pinchon, *Robert Mallet-Stevens: Architecture, Furniture, Interior Design* (Cambridge: MIT Press, 1986), 114. Courtesy of Delegation à l'Action Artistique de la Ville de Paris (DAAVP).

Apartment building types evolved toward models of low-cost worker housing. A hybrid structure, called the apartment hotel, accommodated the more modest seasonal tourist in domestic accommodations. However, modern types quickly lost their association with housing reform and were transformed by individual capitalists in the language of resort architecture. Economic distribution of interior space eliminated corridors and lobbies; most circulation was effectively removed from the interior thickness of the building. The two-room-deep units reduced the transverse thickness of housing blocks from forty feet to about thirty-five feet, allowing enough space for a garden court as well as for entryways, balconies or galleries in the sideyard of a single lot. The reduced building coverage, from about seventy to fifty-five percent, improved standards of space, light and air. The additional open space was important, because the increasing density and the disappearance of open space in South Beach made courtyards a significant amenity.

The thinner, smaller buildings of the 1930s produced an urbanism that unwittingly mirrored urban projects of the early twentieth century. For instance, Miami Beach's freestanding, garden-style building configuration, coupled with the scale of its architecture and open spaces, seemed related to Tony Garnier's project for *Une Cité Industrielle*, first exhibited in Paris in 1904 and developed for publication in 1917. The two cities reflected radically different ideals and conditions, since Miami Beach represented the densification and functional diversification of an American suburban landscape using an adaptation of vernacular, Mediterranean and modern housing prototypes; Garnier's ideal industrial city, on the other hand, was notable within its context for its decreased density. Perhaps the similar urbanism produced reflected an international consensus regarding the correct scale and density of new towns.

In South Beach, the tight green zones between parallel rows of linear buildings thus expanded to form passage-like garden courts that bisected the traditional street structure of Miami Beach in a perpendicular fashion. The passageways formed an informal space toward which all units were oriented. This orientation improved the closeness and accessibility of each unit to open space. The strategy of urbanizing the centers of urban blocks, with buildings composed around cul-de-sac passageways treated as something between a street and courtyard, recalls the rue Mallet-Stevens of 1927 and other Parisian squares. Like the rue Mallet-Stevens, this urban scheme synthesized the bar-types of the workers' *Siedlungen* with the internal focus of courtyard types.[41] The quality of the passages emphasized their continuity with the streets and their spatial qualities. The edges joining one space and another often swept seamlessly in a curve, or stepped out toward the street. The entry corner

capital market, spurring investment and reinvestment by locals and visitors. Government policy merely promoted housing development through Federal Housing Administration (FHA) loans. Housing progress was seen in Miami Beach prior to the acceptance of the modern style. Efficient walk-up type units, for instance, appeared in buildings designed in the Mediterranean Revival style. These new types reflected a commercial consciousness about state-of-the-art domestic architectural design, which often superceded issues of style. As a visiting architect reflected to the *Miami News*, "although America has not yet developed a distinct type of architecture….Our homes are the last word in the world today for comfort, utility, beauty and general efficiency."[40]

40 "Architect Predicts Sky Cities: Beach Visitor Say Towering Buildings will be Communicated with by Airplane Taxis," *Miami News*, 17 March 1938.

41 Fernando Montes quoted in Jean-Francois Pinchon, *Rue Mallet-Stevens: Architecure, Furniture, Interior Design* (Cambridge: The MIT Press, 1990), 114.

was almost always designed as a curve or chamfered, usually with wrap-around windows. In most locations the courts became virtual streets, continuous from the avenue to the alley. The rear apartment generally projected into the garden sideyard, in order to visually terminate the courtyard space. Wrapping into the enclosed patio also increased the number of rooms with good frontage.

In concept, orienting bar-shaped buildings toward semi-private passages would allow all units to receive the same orientation. In reality, the location and continuities of the passages were never rationalized or systematized. Arbitrary or contextual spatial approaches were preferred to the technical concerns of orientation demonstrated by Ernst May and Walter Gropius in their *Standarte Zeilenbauweise*. Neither the dynamic planning of the Deutsche Werkbund exposition at the Weissenhof Siedlung of 1927 nor the repetitive system of the *Siedlungen* could be integrated into the rigid plan structure and autonomous development of South Beach.

Although most hotels and some apartment buildings retained a traditional corridor organization, new apartment types evolved providing access to units through walk-up stairwells or exterior galleries (catwalks). Walk-up types, derived from the row-house model, had a limited number of units being served by a common entry stair. Arriving at one's apartment door directly emphasized domesticity or homelikeness. A series of stair halls connected the units to the garden, becoming vertical extensions of the semi-public passageway. Within the garden court, the entry to each stair hall was set upon a stoop and articulated as the main feature of the façade. The practicality and amenity of the typical unit were also improved. More closets, modern kitchens, and beds folding into walls or sliding under shelves enhanced livability. Every living room faced the courtyard. Corner windows, often located in small articulations of the building façade, allowed more light and air circulation.

Following the already established patterns and restricted by site constraints, modern apartment buildings and hotels incorporated letter-shaped massing configurations on single and double lots. Yet their thinner massing and reduced circulation spaces transformed those types, and allowed new types — such as double-bars, triple-bars and J-shaped buildings — to evolve. Letter-shaped buildings benefited from larger courtyards, but the transformation of single-bar types was most significant. Walk-up and catwalk type single-bars were thinner and could thus be reorganized asymmetrically to face and activate one side-yard, providing a public entry frontage in the long direction. The other side of the building, always secondary to the main façade, was for services. Double-bars, formed by the mirroring of two single-bars, maximized the potential to define the resulting passageways.

Dixon Apartments, 740 Meridian Avenue, Miami Beach. 1941. Photograph by Moser & Son. Collection of the Bass Museum of Art. Gift of Lawrence M. Dixon Jr.

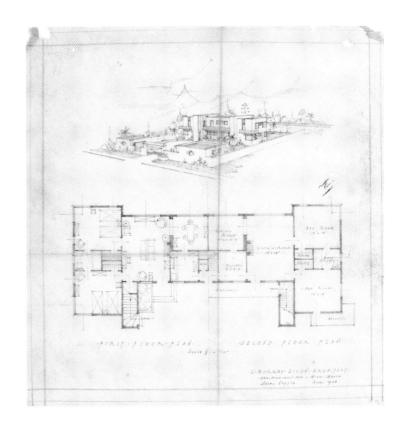

Prototype apartment building. Lawrence Murray Dixon, 1934. Sketch looking from street. Graphite and crayon on tracing paper, 18 x 21." Illustrator unidentified. Collection of the Bass Museum of Art. Gift of Lawrence M. Dixon Jr.

top:
The Fairview Apartments, 1205 Meridian Avenue, Miami Beach. Lawrence Murray Dixon, 1937. Photographer unidentified. Collection of the Bass Museum of Art. Gift of Richard B. Dixon.

above:
Howard Court, 700-708 Meridian Avenue, Miami Beach. Lawrence Murray Dixon, 1937. Photograph by Moser & Son. Collection of the Bass Museum of Art. Gift of Richard B. Dixon.

right:
The Joy Apartments, 1262 Pennsylvania Avenue, Miami Beach. Lawrence Murray Dixon, 1937. Photograph by Moser & Son. Collection of the Bass Museum of Art. Gift of Lawrence Murray Dixon Jr.

bottom right:
Norma-Lee Apartments, Euclid Avenue, Miami Beach. Lawrence Murray Dixon, 1939. Photograph by Moser & Son. Collection of the Bass Museum of Art. Gift of Lawrence Murray Dixon Jr.

According to the *Miami Daily News*, it was Lawrence Murray Dixon's Harriett Court Apartments (1935) that set the style of cross-ventilated apartments on Miami Beach.[42] Dixon later designed the even more advanced Central Apartments (1939, p. 114). The Central was thoroughly cross-ventilated by means of projected windows, so that every apartment had three exposures. Experimental kitchens that "incorporated innovations of industrial designers" were also included. At the Rhapsody Apartments (Dixon, 1939), every unit had access to a balcony. Others, like the Pinecrest Apartments (Dixon, 1936, p. 84-86) and the Flamingo Terrace (Dixon, 1940, p. 117), included at least one swanky duplex apartment. At the Pinecrest, the two-story living room was over-arched by a pecky cypress ceiling.

Other building groupings of the 1930s were notable. Bungalow court hotel and apartment complexes, typically grouped formally around common structures like a laundry or sun deck, or even the owner's house, were built within the gridiron of South Beach. Dixon's Forde Ocean Apartments (1936), built along the Atlantic Ocean on a narrow lot, offered an innovative solution to the problem of views; the staggered building masses provided every unit a view of the sea. Located closest to the beach, a maisonette with a two-story living space faced the ocean. The mix of such duplex units into buildings of more modest character, while rare, illustrated the relative absence of social hierarchy within the South Beach districts.[43]

The role of the tropical landscape was integrated carefully into the overall architectural expression. Planters were always attached to the building, allowing the architecture to mold the landscape, or the landscape to serve as architectural ornament. The integration also accommodated spatial constraints, especially in the passageways, which were sometimes no wider than ten feet. Canvas pavilions provided shade and the design of the ground plane included pathways, patios, and elaborate dance platforms, often paved in terrazzo, as places for activity and movement. In spite of the emphasis on semi-private passageways and courtyards, the traditional front yard space and avenue-facing façade were strictly maintained and highly articulated with regard to the street. The front yard often included low walls and hedges that defined the space of a small seating patio, providing screening and incremental privacy from the street.

AERIAL VIEW OF FORDE OCEAN APARTMENTS AND ITS BEAUTIFUL SURROUNDINGS   MIAMI BEACH, FLORIDA

top:
Forde Ocean Apartments, 6605 Collins Avenue, Miami Beach. Lawrence Murray Dixon, 1936. Postcard. Collection of Allan T. Shulman.

above:
The Rhapsody Apartments, 730 15th Street, Miami Beach. Lawrence Murray Dixon, 1939. Photograph by Moser & Son. Collection of the Bass Museum of Art. Gift of Lawrence Murray Dixon Jr.

42 "Advanced Type Apartment Under Construction at Beach," *Miami Daily News*, 28 May 1935.

43 This important issue deserves additional research, as demonstrated by the discovery of the rental archives of the Lincoln Terrace Apartments at 1602-6 Meridian (private collection of Joel Hoffman and John Stuart).

Layer Five: The Metropolitan Scale of the Modern City

Lying alongside the rolling Atlantic like a scintillating jeweled necklace,
Miami Beach is set deep in the American tropics—almost 300 miles farther
South than Cairo, Egypt. Most cosmopolitan of New World resorts, this
streamlined south sea island is ablaze with inimitable tropical beauty…
Yet Miami Beach is a modern Southern city: efficiently operated hospitals,
a complete library, nine churches, exclusive shops…[44]

Miami Beach achieved the paradigm and proportion of a city during
the 1930s. As post-Depression building evolved into a full-fledged
boom, a large number of skyscraper hotels were built, particularly along
the largely undeveloped oceanfront. The activity was so great that,
describing the rapid completion of forty-one oceanfront hotels in 1939,
Architectural Forum noted that the "chatter of riveting machines compete with the roll of the surf along Miami Beach."[45]

The transformation toward a more urban Miami Beach was determined by a number of factors. The first factor was changes in the urban
structure of the city. Hotels and apartment buildings replaced the intimate scale of houses. Previously empty lots filled in, making the fabric
of the city continuous. Other changes were part of a social transition that
brought a rising population density, changing patronage and new notions
about tourism. Finally, the image of the highrise American city, particularly New York, became the preeminent urban, architectural and artistic
paradigm of development.

Miami Beach's oceanfront streets and park frontages, particularly
along Lummus Park, left underdeveloped in the original scheme of the
city, were transformed into an urban façade of considerable breadth and
were the terrain onto which the metropolitan image could fix. This stylistically integrated façade on the park became an important component
of an emerging civic ideal, achieving an almost classical relationship of
city to open space. The rapid urbanization of Miami Beach's oceanfront
with tall residential structures was not an isolated phenomenon. The
evolution of Ocean Drive from private homes to hotels recalls the nearly
contemporary and analogous transformation of avenues bordering
Central Park, particularly in the relationship of the building façade to
civic space and the variations of its skyline. The sudden tower elements
breaking Miami Beach's formerly consistent three-story baseline was

top:
View looking south along Collins Avenue. c. 1941. Photograph by Samuel H. Gottscho.
© Doris Schleisner. Courtesy of the Historical Museum of Southern Florida.

above:
View looking south along Fifth Avenue, New York City. c. 1935. Photograph by Samuel H.
Gottscho. Courtesy of the Library of Congress, Prints and Photographs Division, Gottscho-
Schleisner Collection. © Doris Schleisner.

44 "Miami Beach is Calling You," *Miami Beach Hotel and Apartment Book, Season*
1940–1941 (Miami: Miami Beach Chamber of Commerce, 1940), 3.

45 "Boom Over Miami Beach," *Architectural Forum* (December 1940): 10.

especially remindful of Central Park West, where a similar effect was produced by the Multiple Dwellings Law of 1929.[46] Across the bay in Miami, the contemporary construction of towers along Biscayne Boulevard, the coastal esplanade fronting the city's important bayfront park, produced a similar effect. In Miami Beach, however, it is particularly striking that the change occurred within only ten to fifteen years of its initial development.

The American skyscraper was a genuine American building type whose influence in the early twentieth century radiated from New York, Chicago and other large commercial cities to influence resort hotels, like the boardwalk inns of Atlantic City. The "adoration" of skyscrapers and the impulse to build them soon transformed Miami Beach, which grew an impressive skyline in the mid-1920s. The towers of the Flamingo, Fleetwood and Floridian hotels, arrayed along the shore of Biscayne Bay at measured distances, were particularly striking. This linear arrangement of skyscraper hotels, as well as their park-like settings with regard to the waterfront, exerted a strong fascination on the Russian architects Moisei Ginzburg and Andrei Burov, who visited the city in the early 1930s. They translated this visual imagery into their plan for the reconstruction of Yalta.[47] Inland, the slender Blackstone Hotel and the City Hall tower, as well as the monumental corner tower of the Roney Plaza, contributed their profiles to the early manifestation of a metropolitan silhouette. During the 1930s, this evolution accelerated as new towers were built along the ocean frontage of the urban grid. They not only became actors in the landscape, but played an increasingly important role in shaping the resort's modern urban life.

Towers were, of course, partly a product of the congestion and density of urban cities. However they were quickly becoming important symbols of a new residential architecture. Architects, like Ralph Thomas Walker, saw them as models of living in the Machine Age. In an address at New York University, Walker focused on the skyscraper as a means of living: "The skyscraper, to my mind, is the only means, and I am making that very broad, of living in this age of the machine. It is a perfect example as an expression and a reflection of the age. It is built by probably the finest organization outside of the automobile industry, a cooperative effort that is amazing to everybody from the other side who comes here and sees it."[48] In Miami Beach, tower hotels quickly reflected this "new way of life" and expressed it in a strikingly modern streamlined imagery.

Rooftop solarium of the Abbey Hotel, 300 21st Street, Miami Beach. Albert Anis. 1940. Courtesy of the Historical Museum of Southern Florida.

Towers also were an expression of prosperity, futurism and metropolitan fantasy, inheritors of the "decade of unrestrained urban optimism,"[49] the 1920s boom that was largely killed by the Great Depression in 1929. The dramatic renderings of Hugh Ferriss, who delineated ideal tower forms as well as towers in a futuristic city planning context, were particularly influential in defining the metropolitan landscape.[50] The daring height of skyscrapers and their relationship to both city and landscape were illustrated dramatically by the commercial photographer Samuel H. Gottscho, whose famous views of New York's idiosyncratic building groupings became the sources of inspiration for developers and architects in other cities. Gottscho photographed the new tower hotels of Miami Beach as well, portraying them in dramatic day and night views the way they were undoubtedly conceived: as elements of a modern metropolis.

Skyscraper hotels sprouted up along the oceanfront, demonstrating the financial feasibility of this type of structure in the post-Depression era. Although towers were already a feature of the city, the new construction responded to new issues and a different set of values. These were not the monumental set-piece towers of the 1920s, but rather the infill of the American urban landscape. The Tides (1936, p. 90-93) and

46   Robert A.M. Stern, Gregory Gilmartin and Thomas Mellins, *New York 1930: Architecture and Urbanism Between the Two World Wars* (New York: Rizzoli, 1987), 403.

47   Jean-Louis Cohen, *Scenes of the World to Come: European Architecture and the American Challenge 1893–1960* (Paris: Flammarion, 1995), 162.

48   Ralph Thomas Walker, "The Relation of Skyscrapers to our Life," *Architectural Forum* (May 1930): 691.

49   Carol Willis, "Drawing Towards Metropolis" in Hugh Ferriss, *The Metropolis of Tomorrow* (New York: Princeton Architectural Press, 1986), 148.

50   On Hugh Ferriss, see note 49 and also Jean Ferriss Leich, *Architectural Visions: The Drawings of Hugh Ferriss* (New York: Whitney Library of Design, 1980).

Project for a tower on the ocean. Kiehnel & Elliott Architects, c. 1936. Rendering. From *A Monograph of the Florida Works of Kiehnel & Elliott, Architects* (Miami: 1938). Courtesy of the Historical Museum of Southern Florida.

the Victor (1937, p. 98-101) hotels, for instance, towered seven and eight stories over Ocean Drive and provided increased amenities, including large vertical lobbies and restaurants. Yet they fit into the weave of lower-scaled buildings by incorporating larger setbacks or by providing entrances scaled to the neighboring buildings.

Along the ocean, towers incorporated important sequences of spaces designed to mediate between the avenue and the water. Their massing provided more room for garden, pool and terrace on the ground level, while a narrow or tapered silhouette reduced their massiveness above. The vistas of their articulated tops, mixed in a landscape of smaller buildings, realized perhaps better than in any other American municipality the city form envisaged by Hugh Ferriss (see p. 213).

The tower motif became important in smaller hotels as well. Although the 1930s produced a modern architecture fundamentally freer of detail, it frequently produced buildings that monumentalized basic utilitarian residential structures. The technique hid the mundane character of the buildings. The monumentalizing trend was perhaps a manifestation of what the critic Talbot Hamlin called the "frustrated monument complex,"[51] an aspect of mounting civic and national pride mixed with the impact of the great architectural phenomenon of the 1930s: the world's fairs. Like monuments, the resort architecture of Miami Beach developed a solid and sculptural appearance. The appearance of the tower motif along with the vertical thrust of nearly every tall building was significant. In smaller buildings, turrets, pylons, masts and other similar elements suggested the presence of a tower. Often tower elements were the pivot or crown of typologically complex building forms. More common were buildings like the Clevelander Hotel (Albert Anis, 1937), where the stepped skyscraper motifs were found not only in the façade but even in the details of the door surrounds.

Programmatic complexity was a hallmark of modern skyscraper hotels, and was an impetus to increase their size and height. Hotels of at least one hundred rooms, like the Tides and Victor on Ocean Drive, or the Raleigh, Grossinger Beach and Atlantis further north, incorporated a lobby, dining rooms and cocktail bar, the three programmatic features considered critical to the social life of the hotel. Their roofs were equipped with luxurious penthouses and solaria, replacing ground floor

51 Talbot Hamlin, "The Frustrated Monument Complex," *Pencil Points* (October 1941).

areas used up by construction while offering privacy and a view. They featured small amenities like news and cigar stands, and oceanfront dining and dancing terraces. Oceanfront cabana colonies extended the realm of the hotel onto the sand and all the way to the water's edge.

The pressure to compact an ever greater amount of uses onto the small lots of Miami Beach propelled the development of mixed-use buildings, particularly at the intersections of commercial and residential streets. On Lincoln Road, for instance, the Lincoln Center Hotel and Office Building (p. 179) coupled an ordinary commercial block containing ground-floor shops and two additional floors of offices (never built), with a hotel that wrapped the other three sides of the property to form a shared patio court. The synthesis, designed by Igor Polevitzky[52] and Thomas Triplett Russell, paid homage to Miami's legacy of courtyard buildings, but the Lincoln Center was a new mixed-use building type. The grander Albion Building, designed two years later by Polevitzky & Russell, was an even more ambitious exploration of the same hybrid patio scheme, wrapping a retail wing, offices, a seven-story 110-room hotel, lobby, restaurant, bar, pool, artificial beach and cabana colony around a terrazzo-paved patio (p. 183; 184-5). These hybrid types marked the apex of the urban hotel in Miami Beach, as well as the birth of a new genre of all-inclusive resort hotel. After World War II, this type flourished under architects like Morris Lapidus, who would build his "flabbergast hotels" upon the foundations of the post-Depression hotel.

The 1930s, largely characterized by phenomenal construction, also marked years of planning progress in Miami Beach. The advent of zoning in 1933 was seen as important to the development of more coherent planning and architectural guidelines. Probably responding to the example of New York City's landmark 1916 zoning laws, Miami Beach's zoning prescribed high and low intensity districts, and regulated setbacks and density. In a 1938 essay, *Architectural Forum* compared the construction of the mid-1930s boom with the earlier 1920s boom: "when building began again about four years later, new building laws provided a sounder basis for construction but the resort character remained and today the fad is modern. It is a modern that is far too often a mere grafting of a new type of skin on the same old frame, and as such will probably follow its predecessors. In the growing understanding of the nature of modern planning, however, there is the basis for an architecture in Florida that is both local in character and contemporary."[53] Henry Hohauser, a local architect, was more optimistic, "The consummation of a well planned community, Miami Beach has emerged from the status of a testing ground to a full-fledged, well-planned city in its own right."[54] The new zoning ordinance helped to standardize the urban realm in the 1930s, although it was remarkable how its very standards were largely a formalization of the accepted building practice informally upheld by the city's architects since the 1920s.

In essence, although Miami Beach was assembling all the trappings of a modern metropolis — modern housing, state of the art hotels and skyscraper buildings in the latest style — it was structurally no more "modern" than the modernity of its foundations on the suburban grid of 1912. By the 1930s, its development was taking place against the backdrop of attacks on the nature of traditional cities. The "question of the city" was actively debated, most notably by architects like Frank Lloyd Wright and Le Corbusier. Predictions of the doom of the city — Wright's Disappearing City — and alternative models — such as Le Corbusier's *Ville Contemporaine pour trois millions d'habitants* — were symptomatic of the crisis of the city and the search for alternatives. Even the urban themes of the 1939 New York World's Fair, otherwise so influential in Miami Beach, proposed a future urbanism based on the car. In light of the prevailing discourse, the fidelity of a progressive Miami Beach to traditional town development notions, the maintenance of vernacular traditions, and the success of the city economically, socially and architecturally is all the more striking.

52 For more information on Igor Polevitzky, as well as the Lincoln Center and Albion buildings, see Allan T. Shulman, "Igor Polevitzky's Architectural Vision for a Modern Miami," *Journal of Decorative and Propaganda Arts* 23 (1998): 334-359.

53 "Florida Architecture: An Outstanding U. S. Resort Center Turns to Modern for Its New Residences and Commercial Buildings," *Architectural Forum* (December 1938): 449.

54 "Henry Hohauser, Architecture," *Miami Beach Building Journal* (April 1947). From the scrapbook of Henry Hohauser, courtesy of the Mitchell Wolfson Jr. Collection, The Wolfsonian-Florida International University.

Layer Six: The Role of Ethnicity and Class

Although Mediterranean and modern influences are undeniable, demographic forces may also explain the emergence of a more urban city and culture, and of the courtyard type in particular. The tremendous twentieth century expansion of wealth in America and advancements in transportation made Miami Beach increasingly a seasonal satellite of America's great industrial centers. The rising middle class, mainly urbanites, quickly appropriated the ideal of a tropical vacation, expanding the number of tourists. The destination of this new class of tourists was also the focus of Miami Beach's development activity in the 1930s: the gridded district south of the Collins Canal. Here were the "swarming thousands of thrifty folk,"[55] as *Time* magazine described them, the tourists who spent two weeks in a room costing five to seven dollars, close to the dog track and near the public beach. As early as the 1920s, the construction of numerous small hotels, apartment buildings and rooming houses had consolidated this area as a working class resort. Highly stylized and built in an intensely compact fashion, these resort hostelries became urban icons. Their repetitive and self-referential forms, spaces, organizational structures and façades were partly the evidence of post-Depression social cohesion, political stability and domestic harmony. In fact they represented a unifying civic culture increasingly linked to the roles of class and ethnicity as defining characteristics of the growing city.

The influence of class and ethnicity was especially manifested in the appearance of the "garden apartment," which was implicitly linked to models of worker housing. Garden apartments were a model of suburban development not related to single family houses; instead they were "people's palazzos" that exuded monumentality and a sense of metropolis. In New York, they were first built by social cooperatives and philanthropic groups as improved worker housing, and were significant for the presence of a garden as a feature of the building.[56] The garden decreased lot coverage while increasing access to light and air, and became synonymous with social reform. It also served to reinforce notions of collective living. Typical were the housing projects in New York created by Jewish collective organizations, such as Herman J. Jessor's Worker's Cooperative Colony (1927) and Springsteen & Goldhammer's Amalgamated Clothing Worker's Union Housing (1930); the central feature of both was a large internal courtyard that became

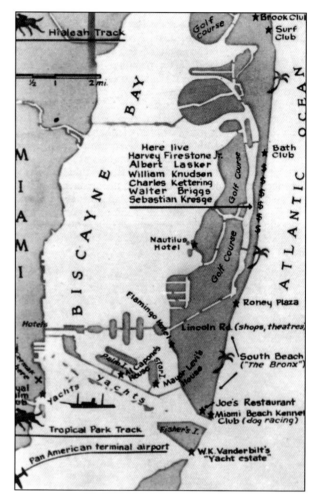

Map of Miami Beach indicating the homes of the mayor and Al Capone, South Beach (as "The Bronx"), Lincoln Road and Millionaire's Row. From "Pleasure Dome," *Time*, 19 February 1940, 19.

Noonan Plaza, The Grand Concourse, The Bronx, New York. Horace Ginsbern, 1931. Rendering from *Building a Borough: Architecture and Planning in the Bronx 1890–1940* (New York: The Bronx Museum of the Arts, 1986).

55 "Pleasure Dome," *Time Magazine*, 19 February 1940, 19.

56 Richard Plunz, *A History of Housing in New York City* (New York: Columbia University Press, 1990), 122-163.

the focus of communal identity. The garden apartment soon appeared on the Grand Concourse, the Eastern Parkway and other axes of middle class resettlement in the Bronx and Brooklyn during the 1920s and 1930s. An excellent example was Horace Ginsbern's landmark Noonan Plaza (1931), located in the Bronx. Ginsbern applied the garden apartment ideal to the creation of a 15,000 square foot interior garden whose entry, framed between twin towers, was a monumental portico. Inside, the garden was scenographically elaborated with mosaic walkways, fountains and a pool stocked with water lilies, goldfish and swans.[57]

Through the garden apartment type, the urban structure of New York's outer boroughs became stamped on South Beach, and signified an acceptance of increasing density. In fact, the type arrived in Miami Beach in conjunction with the immigration of large numbers of residents from the outer boroughs of New York. The phenomenon of increasingly dense housing development, even in a resort, ran against the grain of mainstream American middle class culture, which was better represented by contemporary suburban developments. The predisposition toward density, or "urbanism as a way of life"[58] could be partially attributed to issues of class and ethnicity and its associated lifestyles. South Beach served a first generation of patrons who emigrated from Northeast urban ghettos and middle class garden apartment districts and sought to retain the sense of proximity which defined those areas, albeit in a garden setting.

Synchronized with its growth and densification, Miami Beach became the chosen location for a community of middle-class city dwellers. Records of building construction and occupancy during the 1930s indicate that the construction of the city during those years was also a "Jewish phenomenon," a fact that is of some significance in the development of the metropolitan equation of the city. Miami Beach's hotel owners, builders and guests were overwhelmingly Jewish. The Jewish life of Miami Beach had roots in the segregation of resort tourism that was a feature of the early twentieth century and that excluded urban Jews, especially the working class, from fashionable resorts like Saratoga Springs in upstate New York. Whether enforced or by commonality, many Jews came to frequent a specific resort geography, an archipelago whose northern stations were New York's Catskill Mountain resorts and certain cities along the New Jersey shore (Atlantic City), and whose southern anchor was Miami Beach. The segregation and ghettoization of Jewish resorts mirrored the

lifestyle depicted by architect and theater designer Joseph Urban when he described his project for the Jewish Theater in New York City: "Jewish life in a big city is still somewhat a neighborhood life — owing, partly at least, to the tradition which makes it desirable to live within easy reach of the synagogue."[59]

The previous development of the Catskill resorts provides some perspective on the role of ethnicity and class in the development of Miami Beach. Close to New York City, the Catskills were the resort paradigm for a generation and class of Jewish Americans. The mountains provided an antithesis to, and even a redemption from, New York's urban life: rustic living, fresh air and wholesome exercise. Hundreds of small hotels and lodges competed for guests, catered to a variety of tastes and functioned as a community away from home; a culture of entertainment, including dancers, singers and comedians, flourished. Idealized as a "Jewish Eden" and parodied as the "Borscht Belt," the Catskills represented a summer resort culture whose winter equivalent became Miami Beach. The communal culture of a getaway from the city, the confederation of hundreds of small hostelries and entertainment as the center of communal life were reproduced along South Florida's barrier island beaches.

Resort owners from the Catskills, whose early development predated Miami Beach, expanded south in the 1930s. Thus the Haddon Hall and Beacon hotels were built by the owners of the famed Catskills resort Kutshers. The Plymouth (1940) and Adams (1938) hotels belonged to the White Roe, the Lord Balfour (1940) to Blum's Hotel, the Avalon (1941) to the Olympic and the Marlin Hotel (1939) was an extension of the Tamarack Lodge.[60] The connection was more explicit in the case of Grossinger's, the largest and most beloved of Catskills mountain resorts. In Miami Beach, the Grossinger Beach Hotel opened in 1940, claiming to be "new and modern in everything but the Grossinger traditions of comfort, hospitality, service, informality and warm friendliness."[61]

Unfolding in Miami Beach was a cultural phenomenon of urban life in a twentieth century American city. For Jews, the resort of Miami Beach became a cultural Eden whose expression was paradoxically one of assimilation and integration into American life. It was significant that Jews played all the roles in the development of the city, as owners, developers, architects and patrons. In that sense, Miami Beach was itself an expression of that assimilation, and its architecture and architects were

57 Donald Sullivan and Brian Danforth, *Bronx Art Deco Architecture* (New York: Hunter College, City University of New York, 1976).

58 Louis Wirth, "Urbanism As A Way of Life," *American Journal of Sociology* 44 (July 1938): 1-24; quoted in Plunz, 132.

59 Joseph Urban, *Theatres* (New York: Theatre Arts Inc., 1929).

60 Phil Brown, *Catskill Culture: A Mountain Rat's Memories of the Great Jewish Resort Area* (Philadelphia: Temple University Press, 1999).

61 From a postcard, c. 1947, collection of Allan T. Shulman.

the tools of its realization. Howard Mehling, in *The Most of Everything: The Story of Miami Beach*, broached the question of ethnic character in a chapter titled "Is Miami Beach Jewish?"[62] Here, after signaling the complexity of the question, he distinguished Jewish content from Jewish character; in other words, Jewish patronage did not necessarily add up to a Jewish resort. On the other hand, the writer Isaac Bashevis Singer felt at home in Miami Beach. He depicted the Jewish dimension of South Beach during the early-post-war era in the introduction to *My Love Affair with Miami Beach*: "Alma would take me into all the hotels, just to see the lobby. You could go any day into the lobby of a hotel and just sit down. And I saw all kinds of people; I'd hear all kinds of Yiddish dialects. And by recognizing the Yiddish dialect, I could tell where they came from. And I saw them playing cards and making jokes that I had already heard many times before. And some were intimate and called each other 'darling.' Others acted like strangers. I saw again a piece of home…For me, a vacation in Miami Beach was a chance to be among my own people."[63] Jewish life, metropolitan Jewish life, was an unstated sub-theme of Miami Beach, a paradigm that held sway until the 1970s when the dilapidated buildings became a mere stand-ins for a Jewish home for the aged.

It is also significant that this almost Mediterranean land, risen from the sand, was populated nearly synchronously with "Jewish Palestine," producing, whether by chance or design, a similar aesthetic and urbanism. Like Tel Aviv, the Jewish metropolitan center of Palestine, modernism as the architectural idiom of progress permeated the culture of Miami Beach. The parallel must have been appreciated by visitors to the Jewish Palestine Pavilion at the 1939 New York World's Fair, dedicated by Albert Einstein on May 28, 1939 and devoted entirely to issues of progress. "Conceived in the age-old Mediterranean tradition yet executed in a straightforward modern technique, with a simple white building group centering about a landscaped courtyard,"[64] the Palestine Pavilion and the development of Palestine itself mirrored the construction of Miami Beach. The Jewish presence in Miami Beach suggested a kind of "urban Diaspora" — the reconstruction of an urban culture on new soil — while also, in its links to a nascent Jewish state, reflecting the parallel for a "return from Diaspora."

top:
The Palestine Pavilion at the 1939 New York World's Fair, Flushing Meadows, New York. Arieh El-Hanani, Norvin R. Lindheim, Lee Simonson and J. J. Levinson, 1939. Rendering from Meyer W. Weisgal, ed., *Palestine Book: Official Publication of the Jewish Palestine Pavilion at the New York World's Fair 1939* (New York: American Committee for Jewish Palestine Participation at the New York World's Fair for the Benefit of the Jewish Palestine Building Fund, 1939), 18.

above:
View of Dizengoff Circle, Tel Aviv. c. 1939. Photograph from Meyer W. Weisgal, ed., *Palestine Book: Official Publication of the Jewish Palestine Pavilion at the New York World's Fair 1939* (New York: American Committee for Jewish Palestine Participation at the New York World's Fair for the Benefit of the Jewish Palestine Building Fund, 1939), 73.

62 Howard Mehling, *The Most of Everything: The Story of Miami Beach* (New York: Harcourt, Brace and Company, 1960), 129.

63 Isaac Bashevis Singer, introduction to *My Love Affair with Miami Beach* by Richard Nagler (New York: Simon & Schuster, 1991), vi-vii.

64 Meyer W. Weisgal, ed., *Palestine Book: Official Publication of the Jewish Palestine Pavilion at the New York's World's Fair 1939* (New York: New York American Committee for Jewish Palestine Participation at the New York World's Fair for the Benefit of the Jewish Palestine Building Fund, 1939).

Layer Seven: The Overlapping of Layers or Miami Beach as "Urban Assemblage"

Architecture, attesting to the tastes and attitudes of generations, to public events and private tragedies, to new and old facts, is the fixed stage for human events. The collective and the private, the society and the individual, balance and confront one another in the city. The city is composed of many people seeking a general order that is consistent with their own particular environment. The changes in housing and in the land on which houses leave their imprint become signs of this daily life.[65]

Miami Beach was the product of its many layers and the interaction of those layers. The layers motivated the development of distinct building types that defined public space in characteristic ways. These types evolved to address an increasingly urban condition, and reflected an architectural consciousness that was the final layer of pre-World War II Miami Beach. Hotels and apartment buildings responded to their restrictive context by using strategies that transformed empirically. In Miami Beach, the articulation of building masses to form public spaces, and the relationship of buildings to spaces, affirmed a tradition of cohesion. At the level of the city, the urbanism of Miami Beach became an assemblage of types.

Hotels and apartment buildings made up the majority of buildings in the urban districts, and thus functioned as the chief definers of public space. In spite of the fact that almost all were freestanding, the extremely tight proximity of buildings (the interval between buildings was normally ten to twenty feet) allowed them to define closed street spaces as well as compose common spaces between them. These spaces were organized by the public façades that addressed them. The buildings formed a legible network of avenues and streets, as well as a connective tissue of interstitial garden spaces that ran through the grid of the urban plan. As modern housing prototypes like garden apartments, *Siedlungen* models and towers, were adopted, these too were increasingly tailored to the compression of these spaces, an evolution that was particular to Miami Beach. In this hybrid environment, even modest hotels became highly articulate instruments of a complex urban world in which individualism and harmony were balanced.

Space-making was reinforced by a formal unity of the work of many eras: common building setback, height and width were features that made the streetscape consistent and unified. Building placement was controlled by the reticular structure of the American grid, and modulated by a neat regularity of building forms and styles, which produced a unified streetscape of closely spaced buildings and tight urban spaces. Regular rhythms and thematic harmonies contributed to a feeling of overall aesthetic cohesion, congruity and accord.

The urban environment of South Beach was a product of incremental infill, the result of natural accretions and the evolution of design idioms. The regular planning of the American grid structure was not only the point of departure, but also the stabilizing factor, for this complex urbanism. The figure-ground relationship between the grid and the architecture was analogous to the model of scaffold to event proposed by Colin Rowe.[66] It became the framework that allowed contingencies to develop naturally and chronologically. This landscape was inherently decentralized and flexible, allowing for multiplicities. The pattern of the street grid and the rules governing the relationship of buildings to the street were offset by the almost irrational, spontaneous and organic secondary spaces that developed on corners, between buildings, and in courtyards. The Miami Beach block was a gridiron of passages permitting labyrinthine circulation. An informal network of semi-private spaces wove through the block and around the buildings in a direction running from ocean to bay. The proximity and horizontal continuity of façades integrated the whole.

Within this pattern, hotels were both monuments and fabric, creating an alternation between urban and suburban forms and structures. Building types may be read as detached objects in a continuous system of such pieces. On the other hand, they may be viewed as the texture that defines a continuity of voids. The relationship of mass and open space in South Beach was not that of a traditional space-oriented urbanism, but neither was it really modern. The street, with its horizontal continuity of building masses, was like the closed and defined outdoor spaces of traditional urban patterns. The spaces between buildings, pieces of continuous courtyards linking street and alley, belonged to the open and flowing space of the modern movement.

Strategies of type usage emerged within this system. Larger and more complex building types were used primarily on corner sites, while simpler bar-shaped types were more common on interior lots. Nevertheless, there was a random quality to the interrelationships of hotel and apartment building types in Miami Beach. The potential combinations of type and the possibilities for complex urbanism were almost without limit. The fronts of two buildings may have faced each other, making a combined court. But fronts often faced backs, and so on.

Together the building types prevalent in pre-war Miami Beach can be analyzed as elements of a "typology"; this typology had as its most important elements the organizational models and form types prevalent throughout the city. Three organizational models can be noted in pre-1960s

---

65 Aldo Rossi, *The Architecture of the City* (Cambridge: MIT Press, 1982), 22

66 Colin Rowe, *As I Was Saying: Recollections and Miscellaneous Essays,* ed. by Alexander Caragonne, (Cambridge: MIT Press, 1996).

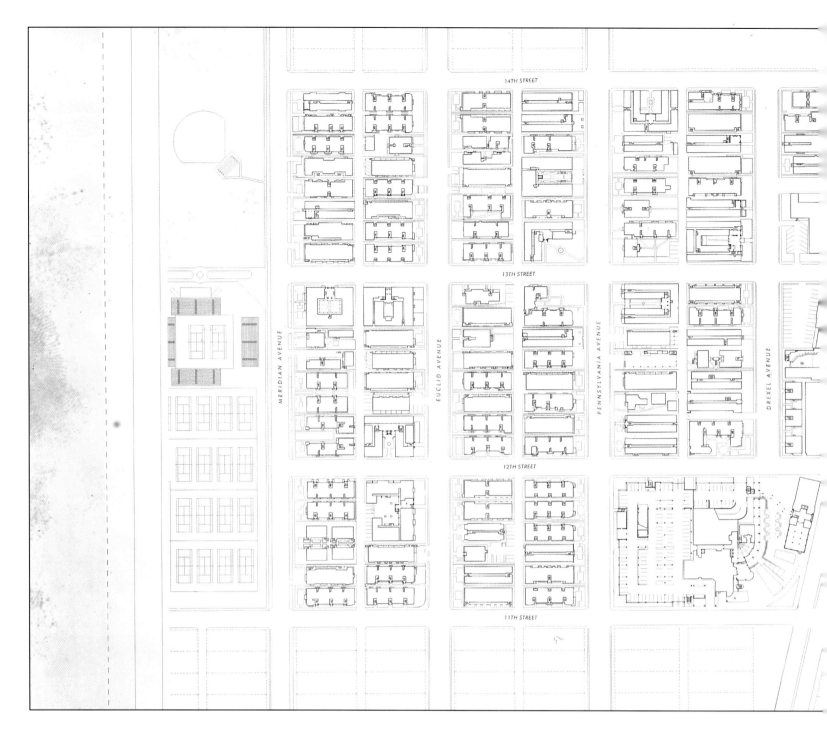

Typological Map of Miami Beach. Research and drawing by Allan T. Shulman. © Allan T. Shulman.

South Beach: the double-loaded corridor type, the walk-up type and the gallery access (catwalk) type. Building form variations included single, double and triple bars, U-, C-, L-, O- and J-shaped forms. A catalog of local building types can be gathered from the most common variations of building forms and organization found in Miami Beach. The intersection of organizational types and forms produced almost every possible variation. Part of what was characteristic about South Beach was the repetition of typologies and their variation and integration on any single block. Each building represented a random fragment in an unpredictable but strictly ordered whole.

Although coordination between architects is never explicit, an "echo effect" is often discernable in the work of competing architects. The overall consistency of forms and details between all the architects

of the era is remarkable. More explicitly, buildings often evolved in deference to their neighbors. The suite of L-shaped buildings that occupied the northeast corners of several street intersections on Collins Avenue is an example. The first was Henry Hohauser's Essex House (1938, p. 181), an L-shaped building organized with a continuous building mass along Collins Avenue, and an open courtyard facing the side street. The building design resolved several challenges by presenting a continuous façade along its most important street frontage, providing an important corner feature in the guise of a rounded façade topped by a pylon, and stepping back the building mass on the side street to provide a maximum number of room views. In addition, the main mass of the building was raised on pilotis, so that the ground floor was recessed at the corner, providing a generous porch entry. The model was so rational it was the prototype for

Lawrence Murray Dixon's subsequent Tudor House (1939, p. 181), Tiffany (1939, p. 180) and Senator (1939, p. 104, demolished) hotels, as well as Albert Anis' Bancroft Hotel (1939). These buildings, mainly topped with spires on their rounded corners, found other echoes in the spires of the nearby Kent (1939, p. 181) and Palmer House (1939, p. 106) hotels, among others. Another notable collaborative moment was found at the intersection of 13th Street and Pennsylvania Avenue, where Dixon's Norma-Lee (1939, p. 26) and Joy (1937, p. 26) apartments, an L-shaped building and a J-shaped building that mirrored each other across a street intersection, collaboratively formed a space across the street.

Limited by both small lot sizes and the financial constraints of the Depression, most Miami Beach hotel and apartment buildings of the 1930s were not large. As compensation, they frequently aspired to monumental effects, appearing like miniaturized grand hotels. This quality of miniaturization produced toy-like results, objects that dominated spaces of equally miniature scale. Sculpted with precision as if by industrial designers, they evinced a maximum of thematic economy while eschewing "pretensions to infinity, sublimity and the artistic."[67] They were, in fact, follies referent to contemporary culture, to great monuments or simply to lyrical themes; whatever the case, they never forfeited their urban qualities or aspired to be entirely object buildings.

67   Ibid., 13. These are the qualities that Rowe ascribes to the plan of Austin, Texas in his analysis entitled "Program versus Paradigm: Otherwise Casual Notes on the Pragmatic, Typical, and the Possible." Rowe attributes these criteria to Claude Levi-Strauss's characterizations of the "miniature."

The product was a grand "little" urban vision, an assemblage of small monumental buildings. Strung out along broad avenues, each a compact and self-sufficient resort, they produced a concentrated landscape of interrelated urban landmarks. They comprise a miniature metropolis, a city devoted entirely to leisure. The urban implications were most apparent in the continuous seafront terrace of hotels that was Ocean Drive, which brings to mind the similar urban façade of hotel façades in Montreux, Vevey and Ouchy, as well as the contemporary development of Copacabana. However, in its most lyrical guise, it rather appeared, as Colin Rowe once remarked, like "a city as imagined by Babar."[68]

Miami Beach is both a case study of American urban development and a unique incident, a circumstance of time, place and character. As it progressively incorporated and adapted alternative models of development, including the most significant urban and architectural trends to influence Florida's development, the resort laid the foundation for future historic districts that would be urbanistically coherent, for its future as a depository of design heritage. The American gridiron, the Garden City movement, the picturesque tradition of the American Parks movement and the City Beautiful movement were all significant in its early planning. Later, vernacular, Mediterranean and modern architectural traditions were superimposed on the plan of the city.[69]

Yet, Miami Beach's origins as a resort destination have produced a tradition of transience and an easy susceptibility to change. In spite of its heritage of planning traditions, Miami Beach's urban and architectural development was essentially unplanned, left to the forces of speculative interests. The plurality of its founders fostered an initial ambiguity about the character of the city that eventually produced varying interpretations. These traditions were often competitive, setting the stage for an alternation between suburban and urban experiences. They were expressed in the process of building and rebuilding that has entered the architectural ethos of Miami Beach.

Within a period of only thirty years from its conception, Miami Beach was transformed from its intrinsic natural foundation into a leisure suburb, a romantic resort, and finally a sophisticated, populous and multi-cultural city. Its developmental layers were distinguishable, but often overlapped and collided with the city's underlying planning. This was particularly visible in South Beach, where the irresolute urbanity of the gridiron structure allowed the city to redefine itself so frequently. Bridging separate and often opposing planning and design traditions, the layered process of Miami Beach's development represented an evolutionary model of American town planning that corresponded neither to the urbanism of traditional planning approaches nor to the opposing canons of the revolutionary modernists that sought to dissolve the city. In this hybrid, adherence to any one type or style was less important than the value of various traditions and devices as economic tools, as symbols of culture and in creating a sense of place. They were left to interrelate as best they could, partially blended of course, by the effect of thickening plant life.

The analogy of layering is particularly appropriate to the developmental history of Miami Beach. The paradigm of boom, bust, invention, reiteration, transformation and recombination has continued to the present day. Miami Beach's wartime role as a training and convalescent center segued into a post-war boom whose patrons included former trainees. A generation of larger and more glamorous hotels climbed north along the coast during the 1950s and 1960s, while older areas of the city became the haunt of retirees. The South Beach area briefly welcomed a new generation of immigrants, before it was renovated and gentrified as a result of its nomination to the Department of Interior's National Register of Historic Places in 1979.

Miami Beach never belonged to Florida's expansive tradition of thematic cities. It is, rather, a loosely knit city of opportunity, open to the changes characteristic of fast moving trends in America. Miami Beach has proven particularly sensitive and adaptable to changes in American lifestyle, transportation and technology. Rather than problematic, its ability to absorb new urban and architectural models was the necessary prerequisite to its evolution of a unique urban identity in so short a time. In spite of its ambiguities, and perhaps because of them, the urbanism of Miami Beach works.

---

68 Conversation between the author and Colin Rowe in Miami Beach, 1998. The monarch Babar the Elephant was created in 1931 by French author Jean de Brunhoff.

69 The vernacular, Mediterranean and modern traditions parallel the analysis of Andres Duany and Elizabeth Plater-Zyberk in "The Three Traditions of Miami," although for the purpose of this discussion, their development was particular to Miami Beach.

opposite:
Miami Beach housing types. Research and drawing by Allan T. Shulman. © Allan T. Shulman.

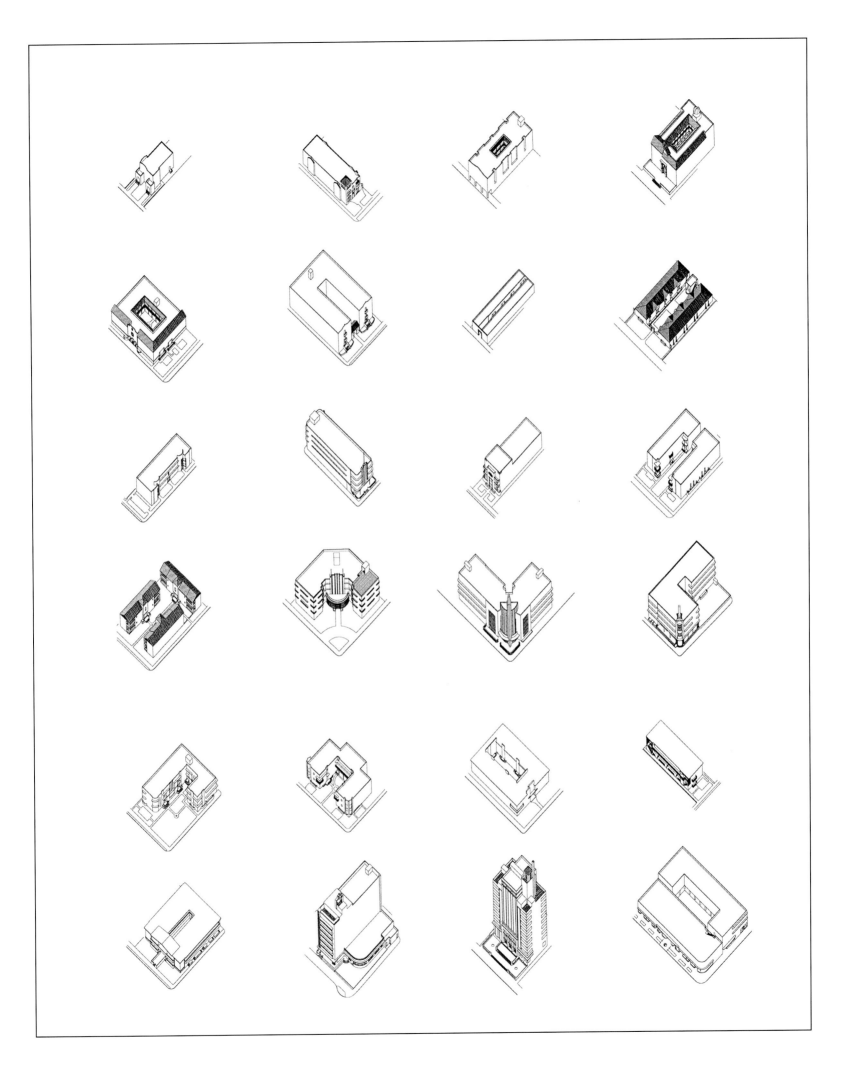

MIAMI BEACH BETWEEN WORLD'S FAIRS: THE VISUAL CULTURE OF A MODERN CITY

Allan T. Shulman

Along about the year 1936 there will sprout in the U.S. a second building boom. It will probably be less of a boom than its predecessor. Its mother will be necessity, not the stock market. Its wage scales may be lower, its silk stockings skimpier, and its automobiles more battered than the wage scales, silk stockings and automobiles of the decade before. But its architecture, by and large and with all proper allowance for the intransigence of millionaires and the caution of speculative real estate developers, will surpass the architecture of the school of Coolidge. For the characteristic (though not necessarily the most common) architecture of the boom of the thirties (and the forties) will be inventive, not imitative, rational, not faked. The characteristic architecture of the thirties, in other words, will be Modern.[1]

It was during the 1930s, a period of national fascination with the "American way of life,"[2] that Miami Beach synthesized its own modern culture. Its look was strongly shaped by the city's *raison d'être* as a resort city and destination of the newly empowered urban middle class. Its architecture and planning were also remarkable for their distinctly urban character, which corresponded to an "alternative" American notion. In opposition to the image of middle class freedom and wealth represented by the popular "Williamsburg" house in the suburb, Miami Beach exulted in the modern, the streamlined, the exotic and the glamorous. It romanticized urban life; it idealized the urban values of holidays spent at the beach, the domesticity of garden apartment living and the romance of grand — and small — hotels. Miami Beach's iconic modern architecture and cityscape are the reflection of these thoughts. They represent elements of an ideal city expressed through a visual culture designed to be accessible to the average citizen.

This essay will focus on four themes fundamental to the development of a visual culture on Miami Beach. First, it will explore the role of exhibition architecture, the showcases of progress that have consistently influenced the city's urban and architectural evolution. The romantic ideals of the Spanish Colonial style, so critical to the development of Florida's Mediterranean Revival, derived from world's fair design. The

progressive introduction of modern design, and Miami Beach's modern design vocabulary in particular, can also be attributed to the exhibitions. In fact, the world's fairs of 1933 in Chicago and 1939 in New York were bookend events that galvanized the resort's style during its Depression-era construction boom. Mirroring, and even emulating, the spectacles of these two world's fairs, Miami Beach emerged as a paradigm of progress, stylistic innovation and urban spectacle.

Second, Miami Beach will be interpreted as an incubator of modern architectural trends, from which a unique and regionally adapted style evolved. The stratum of the city constructed between 1933 and 1942 incorporated a spectrum of American modernism, reflecting the eclectic and evolving preferences of patrons, clients and architects. While the modernizing and monumentalizing influences of modern classical culture were considerable, the tremendous impact of machine age culture exerted a contrary futuristic thrust to modern developments. An evolving regionalism, influenced by issues of building vernacular, climate and landscape, set the stage for a local expression of modernism. The monumental, the machine and the tropical symbolize the mixed metaphors of a hybrid modern architecture evolved specifically on Miami Beach.

Third, the prominent — almost indispensable — role of ornament in the elaboration of modern design will be examined. Miami Beach deployed an extraordinary measure of decoration in the creation of its modern image. This "Art Deco" side of Miami Beach reflects a face of American modernism that was demonstrative, exuberant and synthetic — contrary to the pure and doctrinaire canons of the International Style movement.

Fourth, interrelated with the role of ornament in architecture, Miami Beach's visual culture will be shown to have evolved increasingly around the idea of Florida's uniqueness and its potential for the exotic. The natural, the ideal and the picturesque were not just sources, they became the thematic generators of new ornament. The celebration of local themes appeared in the ornamental details of buildings, transforming them into paeans to the distinctive character of South Florida.

---

1   Catherine Bauer, "The House That Works," *Fortune* 12 (October 1935): 59-65, 94, reprinted in Warren Susman, ed., *Culture and Commitment 1929–45* (New York: George Braziller, 1973), 279.

2   David Hillel Gelernter, *1939: The Lost World of the Fair* (New York: The Free Press, 1995), 49. The author connects images of "the American way of life" to the influence of films, recordings and paintings.

Miami Beach Fire Station No. 3, 2300 Pinetree Drive, Miami Beach, view of the tower. Robert Law Weed, 1938. Courtesy of the Miami Beach Fire Department.

The New Visual Culture

Viewed historically the selection of "style" is, of course, not an arbitrary matter, left in the hands of individual architects; on the contrary, it evolves with the necessity of a natural event. The progress of this evolution is of the highest importance for all civic art, as "style" is the basis of harmony without which no strong civic art is possible.[3]

Style is neither a reliable nor an inclusive measure of the characteristics of Miami Beach's buildings; these are better defined by their form and space-making strategies. Yet, style is expressive of the "cosmology" of the resort, reflecting a world of values, meanings and intentions. It is also, as Werner Hegemann and Elbert Peets noted, a critical element in the foundation of a civic art. Miami Beach, above all, is about the definition and continuous redefinition of a sense of harmony and civic art.

Although the Mediterranean Revival had held sway in Miami Beach since the 1920s, the Depression-era building boom triggered a significant re-imaging of its resort architecture. The architecture of Miami Beach moved inexorably, if cautiously and with certain idiosyncrasies, toward the expression of modernism. Perhaps there was, as Erich Mendelsohn proposed, an intuitive urge to express the "will of the era."[4] Mendelsohn saw the era as symbolized by the machine, which he elevated as an element of a newly ordered life. The idealist urban delineator Hugh Ferriss instead saw the skyscraper as the "avatar of the era."[5] Miami Beach was actualized during these years of optimistic modernism, a process that transformed the very fabric of the city.

First detectable in the commercial buildings of the city — as Richard Kiehnel noted, "modern business demands modern architecture"[6] — the modern style soon spread to hotels, apartment buildings and finally houses. Distinct from European modernism, which at that time was consolidating a functionalist rigor and purist aesthetic, a more synthetic approach took shape.

3   Werner Hegemann and Elbert Peets, *The American Vitruvius: An Architects' Handbook of Civic Art* (New York: Architectural Books Publishing, 1922), 107.

4   Erich Mendelsohn, "The International Consensus on the New Architectural Concept, or Dynamics and Function" (1923). Published in Erich Mendelsohn, *Erich Mendelsohn. Complete Works of the Architect: Sketches, Designs, Buildings* (New York: Princeton Architectural Press, 1992), 24.

5   Hugh Ferriss, *The Metropolis of Tomorrow* (New York: I. Washburn, 1929; reprinted by Princeton Architectural Press, 1986), 16. Ferriss wrote: "Admire or condemn as you may, yonder skyscrapers faithfully express both the characteristic structural skill and the characteristic urge — for money; yonder tiers of apartments represent the last word in scientific ingenuity and the last word but one in desire for physical comfort."

6   "Plans are Completed by Nunally Company for $200,000 Store Building: Construction Work Will Start At Once," *Miami Herald*, 2 June 1935.

An element of this modern visual culture was continuity with past traditions. It has generally been accepted that modernism replaced the Mediterranean Revival emblematic of Miami Beach's previous era of development. However, the gradual transition between styles suggests instead, an evolution. The perpetuation of masonry construction, traditional building forms and spatial types — patio, porch and loggia – indicates a succession of architectural themes. Further, the modern style maintained the decorative impulse of the 1920s, particularly the attention to the plastic qualities pertaining to the façade and the development of skyline. The monumentality of Mediterranean Revival architecture was, if anything, magnified by the modern.

Like Renaissance architects, the modern builders of Miami Beach were conscious of creating both the stage and the city; it was in the public realm of urbanism that style became effective. Style was seen as a wrapper used to identify the public faces of residential buildings, with embellishment making a noble façade for an urban avenue and ennobling interior public spaces such as lobbies. Style thus served to create scenography, vistas and perspectives as the backdrop to the theatrical movements of the tourists. Tourists were made actors, whether sitting in front of buildings, moving through lobby and patio spaces, or promenading on the street.

Within the spatially restrictive and competitive urban context of South Beach, style was also a form of advertising, allowing apartment buildings and hotels to distinguish themselves from their neighbors. The uniqueness of individual structures within the grid was highlighted in pastel-tinted linen postcards, an important record of Miami Beach's architecture through the 1950s (p. 152-3). These images show buildings as isolated objects, juxtaposed against a landscape that is flat, but ornamented with features more emblematic of Miami Beach and the tropics than reality. The postcards, used as advertisements, were inherently idealistic, reveling in a vision of a landscape removed from spatial dimensions.

top right:
Saks Fifth Avenue, interior view, 701 Lincoln Road, Miami Beach. Polevitzky & Russell Architects, 1939. Photograph by Samuel H. Gottscho. © Doris Schleisner. Courtesy of the Historical Museum of Southern Florida.

bottom right:
Burdines Store, Lincoln Road and Meridian Avenue, Miami Beach. Robert Law Weed, 1936. Photograph from *Florida Architecture and Allied Arts, 1937 Yearbook* (Miami: Florida Architecture and Allied Arts, 1937), unpaginated.

Many historians have speculated that style was an important battleground of the 1930s, and the nature of competing and evolving styles in Miami Beach affirms this thesis. The modern classical quality of many buildings reflected the new civic grandeur of the decade and, perhaps, even the need for common social action in the collective revitalization of Depression-era America. The modernist face of the city was somewhat referent to the Bauhaus movement and models of socialist housing in Europe. In fact, this modernist face may have been a distinct reaction against rigid modern classicism. As Siegfried Giedion noted in his essay, "The Dangers and Advantages of Luxury", "An obvious danger is the suppression of modern architecture in most (and soon, very likely, in all) totalitarian countries. To satisfy our need for luxury, splendor and beauty, we must create for our own 'optical vision.' "[7] The move, during the 1930s, away from classicism and toward machine-type architecture, can be viewed as a revolt against both fascism and communism — in a direction toward the development of an American aesthetic. In practice, the battle of the styles was engaged and resolved within each building.

The modernity of 1930s Miami Beach was partly grounded in social interests. Rejecting an architecture of inside-out functionalism, its buildings were urban citizens. The serial pattern found in the repetition of modest buildings in the grid suggested a democratic nature. Within a congested urban context, buildings achieved the critical success of being modern without a loss of urbanity, meaning, identity or civic grandeur. They represented a society whose parts were efficiently organized, well articulated and equal.[8]

The critic Lewis Mumford, whose column in the *New Yorker* documented the development of New York, explored this quality in the metropolitan architecture of the 1930s. In 1937 he wrote, "the chief question one should ask about a new building is not 'Does it stand out?' but 'Does it fit in?' Is it another ruffle on the surface of chaos or is it something firm enough to be carried further, with appropriate modifications, in the next building? Every new structure, if it is really well designed, should be capable of becoming the nucleus of a whole city."[9] The significance of Miami Beach is that the stylistic treatment, as well as typological development, of its individual buildings was guided by a collective pattern, a comprehensive "dream city."

The hundreds of hotel and garden apartment type buildings built during the 1930s were the foundation for the development of a pecu-

liarly public and modern way of life. A distinct monumentalizing and modernizing trend, already well established in the design traditions of American hotels, found new significance. Corresponding to a reprise of classical consciousness in America, Miami Beach hotels were increasingly conceived as architectural landmarks according to an American tradition whose archetypes were probably Isaiah Rogers' Tremont Hotel in Chicago (1827–30) and the Astor House in New York (1832–36).[10] The newfound recognition of the American hotel's inherent modernity was also important; as early as 1908, the architectural journalist Joseph Lux, a follower of Otto Wagner, defined the hotel as a kind of *machine for living*: "a synthesis of hospital, wagons-lits and machinery."[11] The hotel was thus a temple to mobility and symbol of modernity, fashion and avant-garde trends in residential architecture. It is not surprising that Miami Beach's resort culture, centered around the life of its many hotels, was so comfortably modern, nor that this modernity would have such a global impact on the cityscape.

An important element in the development of Miami Beach hotel culture was the trend toward ever larger, more glamorous and sophisticated structures. The Astor House and The Metropolitan in New York, nineteenth-century paradigms of luxury in the grand style, set the stage in the late 1920s and early 1930s for an even larger and more complex class of grand hotels, surpassing their predecessors in height and often breadth. Embracing the tower as a model, metropolitan hotels incorporated new programs, conveniences and unprecedented levels of luxury on their spatially restricted urban lots. The imagery of the emerging metropolitan hotels was particularly significant; depictions of the Plaza group, which included the Sherry-Netherland Hotel (1926) and Hotel Pierre (1930), became visual icons of the period. They exercised a powerful influence in Miami Beach where skyscraper hotels, albeit small ones, were built in increasing numbers. Their imposing silhouettes, monumental entrances and grand lobbies imposed a glamorous metropolitan scale on the city.

The grand hotel type achieved critical definition with the completion of Schultze & Weaver's soaring forty-one-story Waldorf-Astoria Hotel (1931) in New York. The Waldorf combined a glamorous lobby, a variety of entertainment and social spaces, luxury and convenience in both the public and the private realm. Its two-towered silhouette, sculpted by Lloyd Morgan, achieved the status of a landmark. Schultze & Weaver had previously introduced the tower motif to Miami, in their

7   Siegried Giedion, "The Dangers and Advantages of Luxury," *Architectural Forum* (May 1939): 348.

8   Barbara Haskell, *The American Century: Art & Culture 1900–1950* (New York: Whitney Museum of American Art/W. W. Norton & Company, 1999), 150.

9   Robert Wojtowicz, ed., *Sidewalk Critic: Lewis Mumford's Writings on New York* (New York: Princeton Architectural Press, 1998), 174.

10   Nikolaus Pevsner, *A History of Building Types* (Princeton, N.J.: Princeton University Press, 1976), 175-176.

11   Joseph Lux, quoted from O.A. Graf, *Die Vergessene Wagnerschule* (Vienna: 1969) as quoted in Pevsner, 192.

Waldorf Astoria Hotel, 50th Street façade, New York. Schultze & Weaver (Lloyd Morgan, designer), 1931. Courtesy of The Mitchell Wolfson Jr. Collection, The Wolfsonian-Florida International University.

Radio City Music Hall, Rockefeller Center, New York. View of the lobby showing Ezra Winter's mural *The Fountain of Youth*. Associated Architects, 1932. Photograph by Samuel H. Gottscho. Courtesy of Library of Congress, Prints and Photographs Division, Gottscho-Schleisner Collection. © Doris Schleisner.

designs for the Biltmore Hotel in Coral Gables, and the Nautilus and Roney Plaza hotels in Miami Beach. Although a mere eight stories tall, hotels like Lawrence Murray Dixon's Tides and Atlantis incorporated the classic stepped-tower configuration, as well as a continuous suite of grand public rooms.

The pretension to fashion, elegance and sophistication inherent in Art Deco were visible at every level of Miami Beach's construction. Again, the landmarks of New York City provided sources for emulation and even extraction. For instance, the interior of Radio City Music Hall at Rockefeller Center (1934), designed by industrial designer Donald Deskey, was highly influential in Miami Beach.

Considered by historian Bevis Hillier as "the Art Deco shrine,"[12] Radio City's interior synthesized the theatrical and aesthetic qualities that would become the archetype of Miami Beach's hotel lobbies: the marquee entry, the two-story lobby with wrap-around balcony, wall

murals, decorative metalwork and lighting. The lobbies of Dixon's Atlantis, Tides, Victor and Grossinger Beach hotels, as well as Polevitzky & Russell's Shelborne (p. 188) and Albion hotels, were all designed around this principle. In the most elaborate instances, such as at the Shelborne, there was even the idea of the grand sweeping stair rising to the mezzanine, an idea that would be carried further in the postwar era by Morris Lapidus in his famous "stairs to nowhere" in the Fontainebleau Hotel. The theatrical ambiance was reproduced in smaller hotels as well. Dixon's Fairmont Hotel (p. 94-95) and Henry Hohauser's Colony (p. 56) were both equipped with signage marquees, locally redefining the relationship between buildings and the urban theater.

Perhaps in the shadow of the larger and more glamorous hotels, an equally powerful trend in low-density housing was also appearing in Miami Beach. Samuel H. Gottscho's courtyard photograph of the Lincoln Terrace Apartments (p. 41), for instance, perfectly captures the humanism,

12   Bevis Hillier, *The World of Art Deco* (New York: E. P. Dutton and Co., Inc., 1971), 21.

domesticity and intimacy that were fundamental aspects of residential Miami Beach. Here, sunshine illuminates the stucco walls, shadows fall from concrete "eyebrows," out-flung metal windows catch the breeze and the geometric textures of glass block and wood screen doors are captured in the rich natural texture of keystone. The studied complexity of the faceted façade forms a backdrop. Outside the camera's eye, one can easily imagine the "average" people who make use of the city. Gottscho's photo makes an important point about the visual culture of Miami Beach: the pursuit of enchantment and sensory delight were the organizing principles of an extraordinary eclecticism to which the application of style was often little more than a subtext.

The Modern City as Exhibition Architecture

When you come right down to it, a great World's Fair is the architect's form of the good old American custom, the Binge. He can cut loose and let down his hair and eat wild honey and do what he always wanted to do ever since he was able to draw parallel lines. He can work in the realm of almost pure fantasy, without worrying much about his client's idea of how a building ought to look, because he is using (perhaps happily) impermanent materials, and because his real client is the general public, and what the general public wants is not utility, but romance and beauty and drama.[13]

above:

Panama California International Exposition, San Diego, 1915. Entrance approach taken from across canyon. Cram, Goodhue & Ferguson. Photograph from *Bertram Grosvenor Goodhue, Architect and Master of Many Arts* (New York: DaCapo Press, 1976), plate cxxi.

13   Paul Conant, "Never-Never Land in San Francisco: First Showing of Designs for the 1939 Fair," *Pencil Points* (June 1937): 377.

While Depression-era Miami Beach evolved through a process of infill development into urban reality, its architects and patrons were inspired by the "otherness" of festival architecture: the world's fairs, which were the popular ideal cities of the 1930s. Expositions were archetypal leisure cities, offering a wide range of spectacle and entertainment through their architecture and planning. Like a world's fair, Miami Beach rose quickly and inexpensively from open land, producing a cohesive and thematically harmonious environment. Exposition architecture, imbued with social and cultural meaning, found new application in resort architecture.

Expositions played a critical role in the early development of twentieth century modernism in America. They were symbolic events tied to the industrialization of the country that began in the 1850s and paralleled the country's material growth and economic expansion. President McKinley, who was assassinated at the Pan-American Exposition in Buffalo (1901), declared that "expositions are the time-keepers of progress. They record the world's advancement."[14] Fairs also marked important transitional stages in the forging of American architecture. They were battlegrounds and arbiters of the great twentieth century debates of classical versus modern, nationalism versus internationalism and progressive versus traditional.[15] Exhibitions were visited and commented on by millions of ordinary people, making them a powerful source of "popular" culture in post-Depression America. Their important educational role — they were often referred to as the "world's universities" — gave the fairs a manifold influence on American culture and the arts. From the stage of these world exhibitions, the spirit of a unified and modern design permeated America's popular culture. Exhibitions became a primary source of inspiration and imagery for the building of cities like Miami Beach. New building systems, forms and finishes, the popular use of pylons, synthetic materials, structural signage, lighting techniques and more can all be traced to the fairs.

Even before the 1930s, the link between exhibition architecture and the development of civic art was noted by Werner Hegemann and Elbert Peets in *The American Vitruvius*. They emphasized the role of exhibitions, particularly the World's Columbian Exposition in Chicago (1893) and the Panama-California International Exposition in San Diego (1915), in demonstrating the power of stylistic unity and coordinated building typology. It was precisely these ideals, what Hegemann and Peets referred to as the "older motives" of *beaux-arts* planning principles,

14   President William McKinley as quoted in Robert W. Rydell, *All the World's a Fair: Visions of Empire at the American International Expositions, 1876–1916* (Chicago: University of Chicago Press, 1984), 4.

15   Erik Mattie, *World's Fairs* (New York: Princeton Architectural Press, 1998), 190.

that influenced Miami Beach early on, in its self-conscious desire to create architectural and urban cohesion.[16]

The World's Columbian Exposition in particular, called the "birthday of civic art in America,"[17] established a pattern of influence between exhibitions, architecture and the city that would hold sway until World War II. At Chicago, the central feature was the formal arrangement of monumental classical buildings around a spectacular court of honor, an arrangement that stressed the harmony of individual parts and their relationship to the entire composition. Coordinated in style, height and even color, the so-called "White City" of Daniel Burnham was the measuring stick for all future American exhibitions and the aesthetic foundation for an ideal about urban America that would propagate itself as the "American Renaissance." The San Diego Exposition referred to the classical mold of Chicago 1893 in terms of urban conception (its focus was a monumental urban court), however its buildings were elaborated, under the hand of the eclectic architect Bertram Goodhue, in a regionalized "Spanish Colonial" manner.

Florida's Mediterranean Revival is an inheritor of the American Renaissance tradition by means of the Spanish Colonial style. Although traditionally linked to dreams of the nearby Caribbean, and to the inspiration of Florida's Spanish roots as diffused through the old Spanish city of St. Augustine, the Mediterranean Revival was indeed exhibition architecture. Its rigorously consistent application, used to scenographic and theatrical effect, created both civic art and a sense of place. The stylistic hegemony of Florida's Mediterranean Revival unified Miami Beach early on during its boom era of development.

One of the most important elements in this new scenographic urban architecture was the use of stucco. After an initial phase of steel and glass halls, exhibition architecture turned toward stucco, a cheap and easy-to-render material capable of a variety of effects. Stucco permitted the qualities of lightness, experimentation and fashion that were important in exhibition design. It could be elaborated as a kind of continuous wrapper, more or less textured, and was capable of rendering large flat wall surfaces with sufficient detail. Introduced into Miami Beach through the Mediterranean Revival, a new stucco and masonry vernacular replaced wood and coral rock as the cosmetic "foundation" of modern Miami Beach. Stucco architecture created an urbanism of sustained drama in the incomplete but rapidly evolving city of Miami Beach.

The Exposition Internationale des Arts Decoratifs et Industriels Modernes in Paris (1925) and the later Stockholm Exhibition (1930) were the first to propel the advance of modern architecture from the avant-garde to popular acceptance, and both had a major influence on American developments. The Paris Exposition, promoted by the French government in order to demonstrate French leadership and progressiveness in the decorative arts, convincingly established the link between modern architecture and the decorative arts, a theme that would become a major motif of the period.

The Exposition was also significant for transforming the city of Paris into a phantasmagoric experience through elaborate nightlighting and water displays on the Seine. Full of what historian Bevis Hillier called "plundered references to modern culture,"[18] the Paris Exposition assembled and diffused numerous decorative themes, including the stepped skyscraper profile, pylons, zig-zag geometric motifs, symbols of speed and power, sunbursts and fountains, waves and nautical themes. The exposition's nearly instantaneous and revolutionary impact on America was described by the Franco-American architect Paul Cret in "Ten Years of Modernism." Cret noted that one year after the Exposition, "earnest attention was given to the experiments pursued abroad toward the creation of a new style."[19] According to Robert Stern, the Paris exhibition was "the decisive event in America's move toward architectural modernity."[20] The Stockholm Exhibition, orchestrated five years later by Gunnar Asplund in a comprehensive modern vocabulary, further opened the floodgates of modernism in exhibition architecture.

above:
Exposition Internationale des Arts Decoratifs et Industriels Modernes, Paris 1925. Porte de la Concorde. From Bevis Hillier & Stephen Escritt, *Art Deco Style* (London: Phaidon Press, 1997).

16   Hegemann and Peets, 99-109.

17   The quote is attributed to Ralph Adam in Hegemann and Peets, 100.

18   Bevis Hillier, *Art Deco of the 20s and 30s* (London: Studio Vista/Dutton Pictureback, 1968), 24.

19   Paul Philippe Cret, "Ten Years of Modernism" *Architectural Forum* (August 1933): 91.

20   Robert A. M. Stern, Gregory Gilmartin and Thomas Mellins, *New York 1930: Architecture and Urbanism Between the Two World Wars* (New York: Rizzoli, 1994), 27.

In the United States, exhibitions in museums and at fairgrounds were equally important to the introduction and diffusion of modernism. The New York Machine Age Exposition (1927), the International Style Exhibition at the Museum of Modern Art (1932) and the Exhibition of Contemporary American Industrial Art at the Metropolitan Museum of Art (1934) were seminal displays that introduced modern trends to a wider audience. However, it was the world's fairs, launched in almost every part of the country, that brought modernism to the larger public: A Century of Progress in Chicago (1933), the California Pacific International Exposition in San Diego (1935), the Texas Centennial Exposition in Dallas (1936), the Great Lakes Exposition in Cleveland (1937), the World of Tomorrow in New York (1939) and the simultaneous Golden Gate International Exposition in San Francisco (1939). Interestingly, world's expositions themselves were the subject of an exhibition at the Museum of Modern Art in 1936.

According to its chronology, the enterprise of developing post-Depression Miami Beach intertwined with the two greatest of these Depression-era expositions: A Century of Progress and the World of Tomorrow. These were significant because of their size and scope, as well as their cultural proximity to Miami Beach. Over forty million people visited each fair, making them perhaps the most important cultural happenings of the 1930s.

A Century of Progress Exposition, held on the Chicago lakefront in 1933, was the first entirely modern American exhibition. It incorporated and translated the advances of Paris 1925 into the American context, comprising novel structural solutions, a modernistic look and decorative surface treatments in new materials. It was also significant for its parallel emphasis on showmanship, including visual effects orchestrated by industrial and set designer Norman Bel Geddes, and scenographic effects of color and light by Viennese architect Joseph Urban. The scenography of the fair was highly successful, though not successful enough to redeem the exhibition pavilions, which most saw as uninspiring.

Such was the trajectory of modernism, reinforced by the fair's theme of "progress," that eminent, evolutionary modern architects like Paul Philippe Cret, Daniel Burnham Jr., John A. Holabird and Edward H. Bennett, all members of the Exhibition's Architectural Commission, set themselves the goal of making modern buildings. The result was generally classical and formal in plan, and experimental in form and imagery. The interplay of flat and curved surfaces and the gridded texturing of planes fit into a new pattern that emphasized volume, while

The Hall of Science at A Century of Progress Exhibition, Chicago, Illinois. Paul Philippe Cret, 1933. Rendering from *Architectural Forum* (August 1932).

de-emphasizing ornament and mass.[21] Experimenting with the skin of the buildings, most were realized as sculptural sheds. "Consider the architecture of the buildings. Wonder, perhaps, that in most of them there are no windows. Note curiously that these structures are for the most part unbroken planes and surfaces of asbestos and gypsum board and plywood and other such materials on light steel frames, rather than a parade of sculptured ornamentation."[22]

Historian and critic Henry-Russell Hitchcock, Jr. inferred from the Chicago Fair that "modernism in America seemed still to permit, if not to call for, every vagary of composition and ornament."[23] Yet these "vagaries" had an undeniable impact on Miami Beach. Modern classicism, the less-than-pure alloying of modern trends into classical discipline, became, from 1935 forward, the foundation of Miami Beach modernism. Furthermore, the genre of modernism introduced in Paris and translated in Chicago — namely the meshing of modern decorative arts into modern architecture, was the inaugural and persistent modern prototype for the Miami Beach building.

As at the Paris Exposition, progress in the uses of electricity and illumination were also highlighted at the 1933 World's Fair. Although the official guidebook, with its emphasis on scientific progress, showcased practical uses like "light hygiene, ray therapy and food irradiation," it also expounded eloquently on the use of night lighting: "Should you gasp with amazement as, with the coming of night, millions of lights flash skyward a symphony of illumination, reflect again that it is *progress* speaking with exultant voice of up-to-the-second advancement."[24]

By the mid-1930s, colored neon tubes became an immutable feature of new construction in Miami Beach. Neon was used for the decorative highlighting of architectural features like eyebrows and medallions. Recessed planes, such as the vertical band of the Raleigh Hotel, created an indirect mood lighting. The vertical pylons of the Essex House, the Palmer House, as well as the Kent, Senator and Tudor hotels were illuminated. Neon was also used as concealed lighting in ceiling coves and behind glass block panels. Most commonly, it was threaded in stainless steel or aluminum channel letters in signage, creating of the nighttime streetscape a glamorous and lyrical collage of color and light. Night lighting was captured in period postcards, as well as in Samuel H. Gottscho's dramatic photography (p. 71; 184-5). In the 1940s it was Miami Beach's brilliant silhouette that formed a backdrop for U-boat attacks on Atlantic shipping.

Florida Tropical Home featured in the Home and Industrial Arts Group at A Century of Progress Exhibition, Chicago, 1933. Robert Law Weed. From "The Modern Houses of the Century of Progress Exposition," *Architectural Forum* (July 1933): 58.

Florida chose to represent itself at the Chicago Fair both with an exhibition pavilion and a model home. The Florida Pavilion projected an image of the state tied to the more romantic Mediterranean Revival style. However, the Florida Tropical Home, featured in the Home and Industrial Arts group, was a thoroughly modern creation. A one-story concrete home with a breezy mezzanine designed by Robert Law Weed, it contained the seed of a yet unfertilized vision of a modernism tempered to the tropics. It featured airy two-story living spaces; the idea of living on rooftops expressed in nautical roof decks; porches and loggias covered by thin concrete slabs supported on pipe columns or cantilevered concrete beams; large windows protected by projecting concrete canopies (termed "eyebrows"); and a smooth appearance, which veiled the building's structural logic. The Florida Tropical Home was widely emulated by all the modernist architects of Miami Beach. More importantly, it helped define Florida's regional modernism. The exhibit home illustrated and advocated the modern style as useful and appropriate to "modern living" in general, and more importantly, as uniquely conditioned to the landscape and climate of Florida.

The New York World's Fair of 1939 was held in the heyday of construction on Miami Beach, and thus had an even more significant impact on the city than Chicago's in 1933. The "World of Tomorrow" illustrated the ascendancy of industrial designers, who took the spotlight as the new imaginators of the nation's future. The two most important features of the fair, Democracity in the Perisphere and General Motors' Futurama, were

21   Jennifer Frehling, *Henry Hohauser: Miami Beach Moderne 1935–48* (Master's thesis, School of Architecture, University of Virginia, 1994), 22-23.

22   "Style of Buildings," *Official Guide Book of the Fair* (Chicago: A Century of Progress, 1933), 22.

23   Henry-Russell Hitchcock, Jr. quoted in "The Pattern Palls... And Is Reexamined" *Architectural Forum* (September 1936): 186.

24   *Official Guidebook of the Fair*, 25.

designed by Henry Dreyfuss and Norman Bel Geddes, who also designed other pavilions. Walter Dorwin Teague, Raymond Loewy and others were similarly involved. Industrial designers gave a prototype look to the fair's exhibition pavilions that was readily assimilated in Miami Beach. Forty years later, Barbara Baer Capitman, the woman who is credited with having saved Miami Beach from certain destruction and who was also connected to industrial designers, wrote: "The realization that such industrial commercial designs belonged in the realm of art history and serious study was most welcome to preservationists in Miami. It was a major tool for persuading the public that our modest pop-culture little hotels were an aspect of the aesthetic achievement of machine-age America. It was now much more possible for design critics to elaborate on the 'beauty' of the District."[25]

The other major contribution of the New York World's Fair is that it offered a "kaleidoscopic array of innovative architecture."[26] Again, light played an important role in the theater of place-making: "By day the buildings are a little seedy, for strong sunlight is unkind to most temporary materials, but at night it is entirely a different matter. As darkness falls, a dream world becomes reality. Then the buildings one by one awake with color and light; then the Perisphere is a blue moon hovering over the water; then the tower of the Glass Center shines crisply and the blue flanges of the Petroleum Building spread outward like an inverted pagoda…The effect becomes just what a carnival should be — a splendid riot…Here is the architecture of light, projected in a way that makes Broadway seem pallid and feeble."[27]

The 1939 World of Tomorrow Exhibition was well publicized even before its opening. Interest began to grow in Miami Beach around both the theme and its attractions. The *Miami Herald* and *Miami Daily News* noted the presence of a "1939 World's Fair Exposition trend" at Henry Hohauser's Essex House Hotel (1938),[28] whose pylon-like illuminated sign capped a streamlined body comprising sweeping lines and nautical motifs. The Essex's spire, repeated at the Tudor, Senator and Tiffany hotels, marked the corners of South Beach. The proportion of these spires to the building mass behind probably reflected the influence of the trylon and perisphere, symbols of the "World of Tomorrow" Exhibition. The vertical accentuation was viewed by at least one critic, Lewis Mumford, as "the tamest and most bourgeois American formula."[29]

World of Tomorrow Exhibition, Flushing Meadows, New York, 1939. View of the Trylon and Perisphere. Photograph by Samuel H. Gottscho. Courtesy of the Library of Congress, Prints and Photographs Division, Gottscho-Schleisner Collection. © Doris Schleisner.

above:
The Plymouth Hotel, 336 21st Street, Miami Beach. Anton Skislewicz, 1940. Rendering. Courtesy of the Romer Collection, Miami-Dade Public Library.

25 Barbara Baer Capitman, *Deco Delights: Preserving the Beauty and Joy of Miami Beach Architecture* (New York: E. P. Dutton, 1988), 54.

26 Stern, 727.

27 Wojtowicz, 236.

28 "Hotel in Miami Beach Reveals World's Fair Influence: Essex House Project Will Cost $145,000," *Miami Daily News*, 18 September 1938. See also the *Miami Herald*, 18 September 1939.

29 Wojtowicz, 82.

The Barclay Plaza Hotel. View from Washington Avenue, Miami Beach. Kiehnel & Elliott, 1935. From *A Monograph of the Florida Works of Kiehnel & Elliott, Architects* (Miami: 1938).

Nevertheless, Art Deco's vertical emphasis — the smoke-stack-like stair towers of the Claire Apartments or the signage pylons and marquis that soar above the Albion building — was universally applied. At Anton Skislewicz's Plymouth Hotel (1940), a dramatic corner pylon housed the elevator shaft and was a sort of prow, crashing through the prismatic and elliptical volume that was the volumetric extension of the space of the lobby.

The Albion building (1939), a sophisticated mixed-use structure, enthusiastically dubbed itself the "Hotel of Tomorrow." Incorporating constructivist signage pylons that projected over its streamlined corner, it distinctly reflected the fair's architecture. However, it was the built-in bed-side radios, awning windows and trick beds, features that were introduced in advance of their appearance at the fair, that captured the most attention in the press. One critic found the hotel's courtyard, an open space surrounded by the pin-wheeling elements of the building, reminiscent of the "street intersection" at General Motors' Highways and Horizons Pavilion.[30]

Indian themes were visible in many details of the city, including the tall decorative headdress of the Helen Mar (p. 153), and the ziggurat motif in the upper parapet of Kiehnel & Elliott's Barclay Plaza Hotel (1935). They were also apparent in the stepped profiles of Dixon's small apartment building series of 1941, like the Lawrence, the Herbshire and the Fletcher Apartments (p. 126-8). Corbelling, typical of Mayan walls, appeared in the interiors of hundreds of Miami Beach apartment buildings, where they formed arches that divided rooms.

The legacy of the world's exhibitions in Miami Beach was the civic art of coordinated place-making. However, their influence extended to the art of making theater through architecture. The elements of civic art and theater are most evident in the elaboration of façades, which are the prosceniums of the city, and in public interior spaces like lobbies, which are the stages. The lobby, in particular, was the quintessential social space of the Miami Beach hotel, the place where the theater of the city was acted out. According to Harold Mehling, a historian of the resort, lobbies were the scene of Miami Beach's most dedicated and social pastime — sitting.[31]

Detail of the tower of the Albion Hotel, Lincoln Road and James Avenue, Miami Beach. Polevitzky & Russell Architects, 1939. Photograph by Samuel H. Gottscho. © Doris Schleisner. Courtesy of the Historical Museum of Southern Florida.

---

30 "Albion at Beach Called Hotel of Tomorrow" caption to article "Albion Hotel is Completed on Beach Site: Modern Trend is Featured in New Resort on Lincoln Road," *Miami Daily News*, 10 December 1939. On the subject of the World's Fair influence, see also "$250,000 Hotel to Open Today on Miami Beach: Royal Palm, at 1545 Collins Avenue, Contains 73 Rooms," *Miami Daily News*, 17 December 1939.

31 Harold Mehling, *The Most of Everything: The Story of Miami Beach* (New York: Harcourt, Brace and Company, 1960).

Three Modernisms:
The Monumental, the Machine and the Tropical

Three streams of modernism were fundamental to the architectural culture of Miami Beach in the 1930s. First, modern classicism was a transitional vocabulary, linking the *beaux-arts* sources of Miami's Mediterranean vernacular with evolutionary trends of American modernism. Second, a new sensibility, influenced by European modernism but specifically referent to American industrial culture, influenced the development of a futuristic architectonic style. Third, a regional perspective, inspired by Miami's unique climate and fed by both *beaux-arts* doctrine and modernist discourse transcended formal design idioms, evolving them into the vernacular "tropical modern."

Modern classicism was the framework for the evolution of modernity in Miami Beach, a kind of scaffold upon which subsequent stylistic trends were layered. The style evolved from the liberal traditions of the Ecole des Beaux-Arts, the system under which most of Miami Beach's architects were trained. It responded to the practical, technical and even moral challenges of the International Style by rationalizing yet maintaining the elements of the classical language. The progressive flattening, thinning and abstracting of classical façade elements, the suppression and control of decoration and the use of empty wall surfaces as elements of composition were hallmarks of this new classicism. The severity and order of the style, which swept America in the 1930s, crystallized the spirit of the era and the sentiment of the nation. The critic Talbot F. Hamlin recognized this ubiquitous modern classicism, affecting all building types, as an evolved American style.[32] Capable of projecting ample public grandeur, modern classicism offered a form of evolutionary modernism applicable to the decorum of an urban resort.

Modern classicism's synthetic outlook was moreover a critique of contemporary ahistorical movements, and offered an alternative to the white functionist modernism of the International Style. In the classical tradition, it emphasized character development as conveniently detachable from the problem of content, which was the realm of a consistently typological approach. Regional issues of climate, construction technique, materials and customs assumed larger importance.

Miami Beach Library and Art Center (now Bass Museum of Art), Collins Avenue and 22nd Street, Miami Beach. Russell Pancoast, 1930. Collection of the Bass Museum of Art.

The Miami Beach Library and Art Center (now the Bass Museum of Art), designed by Russell Pancoast in 1930, was Miami Beach's archetypal modern classical building. The library was reminiscent of Paul Philippe Cret's Folger Shakespeare Library, a critical source of America's modern classicism built one year earlier (1929) within the monumental core of Washington D.C.[33] Fashioned from native quarry keystone and incized with bas-relief ornament, the Library had two wings positioned on either side of a higher central mass fronted with a monumental entry loggia.

Applying the aesthetic of modern classicism, Miami Beach's Mediterranean Revival style was "modernized" in the early 1930s, producing a flattening and abstracting of its characteristic quoins, projecting balconies, arches, cornices, niches and entrance surrounds. Lawrence Murray Dixon and Henry Hohauser, leaders of the group of designers that built post-Depression Miami Beach, both adopted this transitional Mediterranean style in their early work. For instance, Dixon's Ester Apartments (1933, p. 75), a C-shaped residential patio, and the later Harriet Court Apartments (1935), a mirrored double-bar structure, in fact the first buildings to incorporate modern domestic plan arrangements, illustrated a hybrid style, blending clay tile roofs and abstracted quoins with clean modern lines. Henry Hohauser's Edison Hotel (1935) suggested a Mediterranean palazzo, comprising a rather plain volume built over rusticated arches that wrapped around the corner. On closer inspection, its elements were revealed to be paper thin, and the overlapping play of its simple lines and flat spaces emphasized volume, not mass. Moreover, the vertical extension of the arched window bays over the front entrance hinted at Hohauser's roots designing commercial buildings in New York City.

32   Talbot F. Hamlin, "A Contemporary American Style: Some Notes on its Qualities and its Dangers," *Pencil Points* (February 1938): 99-106. "It is a style that sometimes, recognizing its classical basis, adopts frankly classical mouldings, cornices, or conventional proportions, but it avoids the use of the orders and is usually free from historical precedent. It accepts the freedom of steel constructions, but it never considers the expression of structure as more than a minor factor. It believes in the greatest restraint in the use of architectural ornament, but it welcomes richness of decoration in well applied sculpture and in the lavish treatment of metal grilles, window and door frames, and other minor features; and it loves broad surfaces of rich materials. Usually, though not always, it seeks for axial symmetry and definite monumentality."

33   Richard Guy Wilson, "Modernized Classicism and Washington, D.C.," in Craig Zabel and Susan Scott Munshower, eds., *American Public Architecture: European Roots and Native Expressions*, vol. 5 of *Papers on Art History from the Pennsylvania State University* (University Park, Pa.: Pennsylvania State University, 1989), 272-86. Wilson notes that Cret's Folger Library, along with Bertram Grovesnor Goodhue's National Academy of Sciences building, became "prototypes for a vast range of public buildings that appeared in America in the 1920s, 30s and 40s. They gave a new face to American governmental architecture."

Hotel Edison, 960 Ocean Drive, Miami Beach. Henry Hohauser, 1935. Courtesy of the Romer Collection, Miami-Dade Public Library.

The Cavalier Hotel, 1244 Ocean Drive, Miami Beach. Roy F. France, Inc., 1936. Photograph courtesy of *The Miami Herald*, 6 September 1936.

By 1935, modern classical components like loggias, pillastrades and tall attic fronts emerged from the Mediterranean vernacular. Monumental façade arrangements could be found in countless smaller buildings like the Cavalier Hotel, designed by Roy France (1936). Here, a three-story façade was monumentalized as a kind of triumphal arch that celebrated the lobby entrance. Its tripartite organization was elaborated in the taut plasticity and abstracted classical detailing of fluted pilasters, figural bas-relief panels in quarry keystone and a signage band. The fronts of Dixon's Atlantis and Tides hotels were even more dramatic; a pillastrade loggia comprising deep stone portals soared three stories high. Above, the recessing of window bays and spandrels to emphasize the intervening pilasters delivered a powerful vertical surge. The Atlantis, molded to its site and program, exhibited a rather typical lack of formality; entered off-axis, its frontal asymmetry was diffused by a series of setbacks while in back the building was bent to capture more oceanfront views. One cannot help comparing this monumental architecture of contingencies, designed in response to the landscape and the city, with the work of Ely Jacques Kahn in New York. Kahn was the commercial architect of important utilitarian buildings that historians Francoise Bollack and Tom Killian described as follows: "They completed the city, giving this city of merchants a solid, savage presence. One cannot imagine New York, the Metropolis, without this architecture."[34] Something of this celebration of circumstance, visible in the localized occurrences of monumental impulses, was present in almost all of Miami Beach's other imposing towers, and in its smaller apartment-hotels as well.

Modern classical elements were frequently denatured from their roots and used for purely symbolic value. The upper façade of Dixon's Beach Plaza Hotel (1936, p. 97), with its weave of stepped pilasters, window bays and recessed spandrels, was an example of this fragmentation. Designed to emulate the skin of a modern office building, its verticals did not reach to the ground but were instead planted on the horizontal plane of a projecting concrete slab that was held aloft on narrow pilotis. Below, reflecting a programmatic shift, was the recessed void of the wrap-around porch that opened the life of the street into the public space of the ground floor. At the Palmer House Hotel (1939, p. 106), Dixon counterbalanced continuous horizontal windows strips and eyebrows that wrapped around the corner with a modern classical

34   Francoise Bollack and Tom Killian, *Ely Jacques Kahn, New York Architect* (New York: Acanthus Press, 1995), vii.

composition at the entrance area. Here, the entry surround was veneered in green textured keystone, framed by fluted pilasters and balanced by an oval aperture that framed a delicate arabesque of metalwork. In a vertical composition that began at the oval, the façade developed vertically into an aedicule — an emblem of a larger building. Emerging from the regular mass of the building, the façade transformed itself into a stepped tower element — a miniature skyscraper — topped by a romantic lantern. It was a strategy that Dixon would repeat, most notably at the Adams Hotel (1938, p. 105). By selectively and rather creatively applying the Modern classical vocabulary until 1942, Dixon demonstrated a pattern of synthesis and continual recombination that allowed new themes to develop while maintaining consistency and continuity.

The extensive public works projects of the New Deal, which nationally were an important vehicle for the transmission of modern classicism, had a different impact in Miami Beach. Here, modern structures built by private initiative generally predated and vastly outnumbered public work. The Public Works Administration (PWA), instituted in 1934, instead contributed civic structures that were models for the careful integration of public facilities and civic grandeur into the grain of the city. Robert Law Weed's Fire Station No. 3 (1938), built with PWA assistance, was one of Miami Beach's most modern structures. Weed, the designer of the progressive Florida Tropical Home at the 1933 Chicago World's Fair and a local architect with a reputation as a serious modernist, designed a hybrid structure so well adapted to its residential surroundings that it was featured in the *Miami Herald* under the headline: "Yes, Sir, It Is A Fire Station."[35] Small, residentially scaled

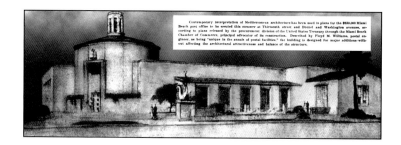

top:
Miami Beach Fire Station No. 3, 2300 Pinetree Drive, Miami Beach. Robert Law Weed, 1938. Rendering courtesy of the Miami Beach Fire Department.

above:
Miami Beach Main Post Office, 1300 Washington Avenue, Miami Beach. Howard L. Cheney, 1939. Courtesy of *The Miami Herald*, 2 May 1937.

wings trimmed with traditional shutters balanced a larger central block whose alignment with the bridge that crossed the Collins Canal elevated the station to a minor urban monument. The center block was consummately modern; it featured a semicircular colonnaded portico flanked by garage doors on the ground floor, and a horizontal projecting window screened with climatically appropriate louvers above. Behind soared the "drill tower," a streamlined pylon that featured long vertical lines of glass block and a wrap-around balcony.

Like Weed's fire station, Howard L. Cheney's Miami Beach Main Post Office, a PWA project of 1939, articulated a careful balance between civic and residential features. Dominating the corner of Washington

35 "Yes, Sir, It Is A Fire Station," *Miami Herald*, 25 December 1938.

Avenue and 13th Street was the main hall, a cylindrical drum capped by a lantern. Low wings projected on either side, and the one that faced the avenue was fronted with a modern-classical loggia that connected to a gabled wing. A raised plaza in front of the loggia on Washington Avenue provided the first entirely public urban patio in Miami Beach. The Post Office is also significant for its integration of public art, directed by the Section of Painting and Sculpture of the Works Progress Administration (WPA), created in 1935. Inside the cylindrical drum, below the Dome of Heaven sunburst that adorned the ceiling, rows of bronze boxes were arrayed under a forty-foot-long mural by Charles Russell Hardman. Hired as the result of a regional competition, Hardman originally proposed locally meaningful themes of golf or agriculture, but the WPA rejected these.[36] Instead his mural depicted scenes from Florida's history.[37]

The most ambitious modern classical structures were commercial, not public in character, and built on Lincoln Road. Albert Anis's Mercantile Bank Building (1941), was a vast commercial office building that comprised two lower wings that spanned an entire block and that swept at their center toward a "tower" element. The provision of a miniature *cour d'honneur* mirrored the hieratic design of Kiehnel & Elliott's Nunally Building (1936) and Victor Nellenbogen's renovation of the Sterling Building (1941). The Mercantile assembled the elements of the PWA aesthetic, monumental massing, rich materials, sober detailing and public art to a degree impossible in hotel architecture. Entirely clad in keystone, like the Public Library, its façade included fluted metallic spandrels under the windows and a continuous base of black vitrolite as the only decoration. Its murals, painted in 1947 by Leo Birchansky, celebrated America's rise to prominence through industry, power, opportunity and agriculture, and were directly referential to the themes of the WPA. In the adjacent Liggett's Drugstore, other murals told the story of the development of medicine through the ages. The murals hovered over the drug counter, as well as over the lunch counter, imported "bodily" from the San Francisco World's Fair, on which orange squeezing machines were deployed. The counters were the setting for what *Life* called a "new standard of pharmaceutical elegance."[38]

A second modern tradition, increasingly conspicuous since 1935, was the acceptance of a more revolutionary and futuristic aesthetic based on European modernism. A desire for "newness" began to pervade Miami Beach architecture, reflecting the progress and promise of America's industrial culture, as well as the city's own recent vintage. Perhaps influenced by the contemporary emphasis on hygiene, visitors seemed to want a world that was newly fresh and clean.[39] The preference

top:
The Nunally Building, 924 Lincoln Road, Miami Beach. Kiehnel & Elliott, 1936. From *A Monograph of the Florida Works of Kiehnel & Elliott, Architects* (Miami: 1938).

above:
Soda fountain and mural in Liggett's Drugstore, Mercantile Bank Building, 420 Lincoln Road, Miami Beach. Albert Anis, 1941. Photograph from *Life*, 24 February 1941, 77.

36 "56-Year-Old Mural Still Inspires Fans," *Miami Herald*, 13 June 1996.

37 Hardman's murals depict the encounters between Ponce de Leon and native Americans, their battle with Hernando De Soto and finally the signing of a peace treaty.

38 "Miami Beach Shops On a Luxury Lane." *Life*, 24 February 1941, 77.

soon revealed itself in the local newspapers, which displayed a near compulsion to use terms such as "modern," "ultra-modern," "new," "progressive" and "unique" to describe almost anything vaguely modern-looking. The power of newness soon amalgamated with the salubrious image of a sun-washed resort. By the late 1930s the architects of Miami Beach adopted modernism not just as the most appropriate natural consequence of the era, but as the "manifest destiny of the tropics."[39]

The International Style, launched during the eponymous exhibit at the Museum of Modern Art in 1932, became the most important purveyor of modernist ideas in the United States. It first entered the mainstream of Miami Beach architecture as an affirmation of modern trends in housing reform, and later infiltrated the elaboration of building façades. Notwithstanding its traditional tile roof, Dixon's Royal Arms Apartments (1934, p. 74) was functionally modern; incorporating a walk-up unit arrangement, it was a low-slung building where the doors and windows were laid out to emphasize horizontal repetition, not hierarchy. Dixon's later Forde Oceanfront Apartments (1935, p. 87-89) was another hybrid. The plan of each unit comprised neo-classical circular and capsule-shaped rooms, however the stepped-plan arrangement of the overall design betrayed an awareness of similar stepped housing projects, like those of Hans and Wassili Luckhardt in Germany.

Although there were few "avant-garde modernist" architects in Miami Beach, the International Style soon manifested itself in a thousand details. Henry Hohauser's Colony (1935) was an early temptation toward modernism. Designed as a regular block, it was elaborated with continuous window bays that entirely wrapped the front of the structure. The continuous eyebrows above and sill below reinforced the impression that the building was composed of cantilevered trays, a false impression since a recessed structural column in the face of the wall provided support. The ground floor lobby had enormous windows that were screened from the strong tropical sun by thin horizontal louvers. The Colony's cinematic marquee fin and canopy, integral elements of its iconic image, were on the other hand elements of Miami Beach's theatrical architecture of commercial design.

The architectonic principles of the International Style found quick application, often through scenographic treatment of a building's stucco envelope. The challenge was that the expression of volume, the thematic use of cubist massing, as well as a reductionist aesthetic and "mecanomorphic" design representative of the machine age were interpreted into the masonry vernacular. Intersecting geometries of precise, smooth, volumetric masses were flattened and abstracted into shallow step-backs with variations in relief. Planar offsets were used to create

The Colony Hotel, 730 Ocean Drive, Miami Beach. Henry Hohauser, 1935. Rendering. Courtesy of The Mitchell Wolfson Jr. Collection, The Wolfsonian-Florida International University.

the illusion of cubist variations, or in order to achieve graphic effects, presenting the building in a structural context distinct from the flat exterior walls of the 1920s. Offsets also allowed for the introduction of sensuous colors and materials that were nonetheless integral with its planar surfaces. Ornament was applied in a rhythmic fashion to accent volumes and planes with sculptural relief, or simply as a pattern in the abstract geometric of terrazzo floors. Dixon's Pinecrest Apartments (1936, p. 84-86) illustrated how a relatively straightforward L-shaped building mass was elaborated as a collage of projecting and recessing planes distinguished by material changes and even stylistic alternation: note the modern classical quality expressed in the volume of the duplex apartment.

The structural implications of modern construction in concrete and steel had architectonic ramifications, even if these systems were rarely used. Thus, while the tradition of masonry and wood-frame construction, established during the Mediterranean Revival, was maintained, the plastic possibilities of new structural systems were explored through small articulations of building façades. Even within a single façade plane, a building's stucco envelope was often "modeled" as a compressed sculptural field through which incised lines could be traced. Henry Hohauser's Adelphia Hotel (1941) developed a fiction of multiple overlapping planes in which the windows appeared as recessed voids.

39 Lawrence Murray Dixon Jr., "L. Murray Dixon's Tropical Architecture," typewritten manuscript provided by Lawrence Murray Dixon Jr., unpaginated and undated.

Adelphia Hotel (currently Port Washington Hotel), 1020 Washington Avenue, Miami Beach. Henry Hohauser, 1941. Rendering. Courtesy of The Mitchell Wolfson Jr. Collection, The Wolfsonian-Florida International University.

in various ways, most explicitly in the radiator-grill-like fins that adorned rooftop elevator machine rooms and stair bulkheads. Compositionally, there was the illusion of volumetric progression in the crisp intersection of simple masses. This sense of movement, as well as the classicizing order that underlied the structural integrity of its masonry construction, were elements that related this work to another artistic source, the Precisionist painters, who were active in the 1920s and whose interest in themes of architectural and machine culture is well documented.

The evolution of Miami Beach modern pivoted on an increasingly bold and plastic use of form as ornament after 1938, and a gradual abstraction of building components into volumes, surfaces, patterns and lines. Architects like Lawrence Murray Dixon, Henry Hohauser, Anton Skislewicz and Roy France became bolder in elaborating buildings as component masses, highlighting precise elemental volumes that appeared timeless, universal and pure. Special emphasis was often placed on the corner, as with the use of a drum or pylon at the intersection of building masses. Hohauser's Hoffman's Cafeteria (1939), illustrated the thematic superimposition of cylindrical and planar forms, which rose to monumental proportions at the angle. The counterpoising vertical and horizontal thrust of the elements was exaggerated by fluting the vertical drums and incising the horizontal wings with speed lines. Two central pylons flanking the entry absorbed and neutralized the building's contrary vertical and horizontal thrusts. A continuous projecting concrete canopy tied the composition together, and offered a pedestrian scale. The corner of Dixon's Senator Hotel (1939, p. 104) incorporated a sophisticated play of convex glass nested in a concave wall form, a plasticity he would repeat in his South Seas Hotel (1941, p. 130), where the center bay of the tripartite façade billowed out.

It was a curious yet rather typical mix of modern classical and modern features, illustrating one phase of the Miami Beach dialectic between monumentality and horizontalism; the ground floor was a tripartite façade with solid corners and a center bay that was vertically projected by a series of events: a signage band mounted on a projecting canopy, a vertical pylon entirely clad in glass block and a flagpole mounted on a stepped pedestal. Above the continuous projecting concrete canopy that divided the lower and upper parts of the building, the second floor was a modernist collage. Corner windows cut the building corners, resulting not only in a cantilevered appearance that seemed to suppress mass, but also in better sunlight and ventilation in the rooms.

The evocation of platonic volumes in the architecture of this era reflected, as many have pointed out, the dominance of the machine in American life and culture. The aesthetic ascendancy of the machine, evoked in Margaret Bourke-White's quote "dynamos are more beautiful than pearls,"[40] was no doubt intertwined with the contemporary evocation of machine culture in art and photography. The documentation of skyscrapers, dams and dynamos by Bourke-White, Alfred Stieglitz and Walker Evans, and of grain silos by Charles Sheeler and Charles Demuth were thus important agents of interpreting the Machine Age. Miami Beach buildings were exemplars of this modern industrial culture

The notion that skyscrapers, giant machines unto themselves, were the most important architectural achievement of America,[41] may have influenced the development of this type as a significant post-Depression housing model. Dixon's Victor Hotel (1937, p. 98), borrowing from Howe & Lescaze's PSFS building in Philadelphia, was a first tentative step toward designing a truly modern tower. Polevitzky & Russell's Shelborne Hotel, considered the most progressive hotel in Florida when built, was an essay on the blending of the International Style into local traditions.[42] Situated on a narrow oceanfront site, the hotel was located at the center of a sequence of spaces leading from the street to the Atlantic Ocean and shot up as a thirteen-story skyscraper. The approach sequence swept from the street to the glass front of the lobby in the form of a concrete canopy on steel columns. Bordering the canopy was a drive court,

40 Richard Guy Wilson, Dianne H. Pilgrim and Dickran Tashjian, *The Machine Age in America* (New York: Brooklyn Museum in association with Abram, 1986), 30.

41 Thomas Tallmadge quoted in ibid., 30.

42 See Allan T. Shulman, "Igor Polevitzky's Architectural Vision for a Modern Miami," *Journal of Decorative and Propaganda Arts* 23 (1998): 334-359.

and the sweep of the canopy was in fact defined by the automobile circulation. Yet the centerpiece of its innovative planning was its acknowledgment of the front-to-back asymmetry of the site. The functional schism between the east, which faced the ocean, and the west, which faced the city, was elaborated in the different massing of each façade. The west one was frontal while on the east side the compact mass of the tower eroded, providing an ocean view and terrace to a maximum of rooms. This dichotomy between modernist and modern was crystallized in the competing imagery of the two sides. The west façade was inherently compositional, mitigating the building's apparent volume with a combination of projecting canopies, decorative tile treatment and corner windows. In addition, there was the dynamic diagonal connecting the twist of the projecting glass-enclosed entry with the dramatic sky-sign, which spelled the hotel's name in cast-concrete letters (the "S" was twenty-eight feet high). On the east side, the building was rendered in the idiom of the International Style. One of the few steel-framed structures on Miami Beach at the time, its façades were actually block curtain walls, a system which revealed itself in Miesian balcony trays and continuous horizontal window treatment.

The architecture of Miami Beach avoided structural and functional rationalism. Bound to a conventional masonry vernacular, no building followed the principles of the International Style as displayed at the Museum of Modern Art in 1932. Yet, these more traditional buildings exhibited some of them. An example is Dixon's Senator Hotel (p. 104). Here, pilotis were cleverly used at the corner to create a wrap-around porch joining Collins Avenue with the garden. Below the hovering body of the upper floors, the mainly glassed-in lobby took its own shape. Further, an attitude and construction technology that allowed the convenient divorce of the façade from the function of the building facilitated the expression of a style or commercial message. The façade, disconnected from the interior program and composed from a purely pictorial point of view, could clearly mask the true nature of the building. The concept of living on the rooftop was also elaborated in the tradition of roof deck and penthouse solarium. Other buildings achieved an almost industrial aesthetic. Dixon's Phillard Apartments (1939), perhaps more than any other building, explored the expression of a frankly industrial architecture. The main feature was a vertical block that was highlighted in white in the beautiful perspective rendering from Dixon's office (p. 149).

top:
"My Egypt." Charles Demuth, 1927. Oil on composition board. Collection Whitney Museum of American Art.

above:
Hoffman's Cafeteria, Collins Avenue and Española Way, Miami Beach. Henry Hohauser, 1939. Rendering. Courtesy of the Romer Collection, Miami-Dade Public Library.

top:
The Shelborne Hotel, view from the ocean, Collins Avenue, Miami Beach. Polevitzky & Russell Architects, 1939-40. Photograph by Ernest Graham. Courtesy of the Historical Museum of Southern Florida.

left:
The Shelborne Hotel, view from the street, 1801 Collins Avenue, Miami Beach. Polevitzky & Russell Architects, 1939–40. Photograph by Samuel H. Gottscho. From *Architectural Record* (July 1941).

Streamlining came into Miami Beach's stylistic repertoire toward the end of the 1930s, breaking down the hegemony of cubic forms. Arriving from a variety of sources, the architectonics of streamlining softened and smoothed the gridded city with its powerful combination of curves and horizontality. As historian David Gebhard pointed out, the origins of streamlining were both popular and technical. Its visual imagery connected with the world of science fiction, like Jules Verne's *Twenty Thousand Leagues Under the Sea* (1870), and the popular comic strip of the 1920s and 1930s, "Buck Rogers."[43] On the other hand, streamlining evoked the influence and products of industrial designers like Bel Geddes, the utopian industrial designer whose book *Horizons* (1932) evoked the power and usefulness of industrial landmarks. It was embedded in the rise of hygenics,[44] and in the notions of Raymond Loewy, whose published drawings indicated the evolutionary streamlining of almost everything. There was also the futurist love of speed, translated to Miami Beach through streamlined trains such as the Silver Meteor and airplanes such as the McDonnell Douglas DC-3, both sheathed in polished lightweight metal and familiar to travelers as relatively inexpensive, efficient and exciting.

Architecturally, the streamlining of Miami Beach refers to the work of expressionist architects, particularly the German Erich Mendelsohn, who espoused the "horizontal tendency," claiming it by nature more appropriate to a democratic industrial society with its "parallel connections of elements."[45] However, it was the sweeping curves of his architecture that were most influential. Speed grooves, continuous eyebrows and rounded columns are probably referent to his work. The continuous horizontal fins of the Colony Hotel, as well as its rounded marquee, illustrated these horizontal forces.

On the narrow lots of Miami Beach, and especially where buildings were constructed right up to the street, streamlining introduced building corners in stucco or glass that swept around or were cleanly radiused. At the Goldwasser's Shops on Lincoln Road (1937, p. 102-3), the entirely glass corner not only swept around the corner, but in on itself. The curves conveyed a sculpted, molded, even "mecanomorphic" appearance; they were de facto industrial products of the machine age.

The New Yorker Hotel (1940) exhibited Henry Hohauser's mastery of the architectonics of streamlining. The front of the hotel referred almost directly to the modern classicism of his earlier Park Central, a detached tower element that soared vertically like an Indian headdress. Complete with corner windows and a large entry portal topped with a semi-circular

43   David Gebhard, *The National Trust Guide To Art Deco in America* (New York: John Wiley and Sons, Inc., 1996), 13.

44   Hillier, 21.

45   Mendelsohn, 23.

projecting canopy, it maintained volumetric autonomy. Sweeping from the trunk of the tower, the main hotel body rolled back in repetitive steps, rounding the front corners and then telescoping into space as it receded, echoing the Shelborne Hotel. A similar but reverse telescoping effect, creating a streamlined garden court, was achieved at Dixon's Haddon Hall Hotel (1941, p. 129). The mixture of streamlining and modern classicism was also picked up as a minor note in Dixon's Marlin Hotel (1939, p. 107), whose streamlined body was carried over the recessed porch typical of its Collins Avenue location.

The New Yorker, the Haddon Hall and the Marlin hotels reflected the important fact that horizontal streamlining was almost without exception balanced against the residual interest in the vertical development of modern classicism. In fact, the more dramatic the horizontal emphasis, the more arresting was the counterbalancing verticality. This play of horizontals and verticals achieved its greatest sophistication in Kiehnel & Elliott's Carlyle Hotel (1939). The Carlyle's streamlining included radiused corners — the building presented almost no square edges — and strong horizontal banding, emphasized by the eyebrows that ran almost continuously around the structure. Moreover, its courtyard façade billowed out in a convex bow. The counterbalance was pro-

vided by three powerful pylons, like the virtual entry to some World's Fair. Across the street, the similarly streamlined Cardozo Hotel (1939), named in honor of America's first Jewish Supreme Court judge, Benjamin N. Cardozo, echoed the Carlyle's sweeping corners.

Tropical modernism was the third trend of modernism on Miami Beach. It represented the evolution of a new regional vernacular from the modernist vocabulary and from elements of Florida's building tradition. It reflected a consciousness about tropical architecture encouraged by the ascendant regionalism of the 1920s and 1930s. Regarding this consciousness, the Mediterranean Revival was already critically concerned with making an "appropriate" architecture for Florida. Nevertheless, it was the modern, lacking meaningful associations with other places and times, that nurtured "tropicalism" to the point of generating a new style. William Orr Ludlow, an officer of the American Institute of Architects, visited South Florida in 1939 and equated the achievements of Florida's architects toward a new expression as a step toward a new national style: "We shall have an American style not copying Spanish or Italian renaissance, or even our New England or Virginian colonial."[46]

Certainly, the unique urban and regional conditions of South Florida, including its landscape and tropical climate, imposed variations on the standard modern formulas. What made tropical modern truly regional was its emphasis on conceiving an image and lifestyle unique to the environment of South Florida, a concept that derived directly from Robert Law Weed's already described Florida Tropical Home. The house's visually striking and practical features (eyebrows, roof-decks, expansive window areas) became fundamental elements of the tropical modern style in hotels and apartment hotels. Its adaptation of vernacular elements, like patios and porches, was further proof of its regional roots.

Dixon's Central Apartments (1940, p. 114) demonstrated the synthesis of tropical modern in residential architecture. The main leg of the J-shaped structure faced a sideyard garden. The relationship of the building to the garden was gracefully articulated, with broad steps and embracing planters around each modern classical entry. Its windows ran in continuous bands, often projecting out of the volume of the building, which gave every apartment three exposures. Projecting windows captured a maximum of views and air, but were sheltered from the sun by a continuous eyebrow that swept the entire length of the structure. Above the second floor was a vented attic, while at the rear, a screened concrete wall concealed the rooftop sundeck and garden. At the Rhapsody Apartments (Dixon, 1939, p. 27), every unit had access to a balcony,

46 "Florida Architecture Praised After Inspection of this Area," *Miami Herald*, 5 March 1939.

top:
Carlyle Hotel, 1250 Ocean Drive, Miami Beach. Kiehnel & Elliott, 1941. Rendering. From *Florida Architecture and Allied Arts*, 1942.

The Penn Terrace Apartments, 1211 Pennsylvania Avenue, Miami Beach. Henry Hohauser, 1936. Rendering. Courtesy of *The Miami Herald*, July 1936.

The New Ornamentation

Each time has its own compulsion, which becomes apparent in art, revealed in the creations of tone, of speech, of color, and form. Whoever perceives compulsions feels them to be the same in all their varied manifestations. It is that which charms him in contemporary performance as possessing life. It is the rhythm of a period.[47]

Although polemical modernists are traditionally considered to have had a decisive "cleansing" impact on architecture in the 1930s, the vital role of ornament in Miami Beach proves that modern decorative arts were still in the program of prewar American modernism. Miami Beach architects found synthesis in ornament that was eclectic, inspired by the modern era and related to its natural environment. The collage of decorative features in the public spaces of the city, indeed the idiosyncratic relationship of space, ornament, material and symbols, became emblematic of Miami Beach resort architecture.

Miami Beach's modern ornament is commonly attributed as a regional variant of Art Deco, the ubiquitous style of 1930s America. Although it is a sweeping and contemporary interpretation, Art Deco is a useful term as it applies to Miami Beach architecture. It emphasized the broad implications of the style, including the search for, and the formation of, a "modern style." Likewise it implied the necessary and beneficent presence of decorative arts, the assimilative face of modernity, and the merging of diverse trends into a laissez-faire modernism. As Bevis Hillier noted in *Art Deco of the 20's and 30's*, the first major work published on the subject, Art Deco was "the last of the total styles."[48] It permeated all arts to effect a general aesthetic. This interdependence between art and architecture, and the collaboration of diverse artists, was a defining characteristic of Miami Beach's own version of Art Deco.

Art Deco transformed Miami Beach's Mediterranean Revival ornamental language so completely because its image-making value was equivalent. It arrived in Miami Beach as a coherent style nearly ten years after its synthesis at the Exposition Internationale des Arts Decoratifs et Industriels Modernes in 1925. During the intervening years, its polyglot and synthetic language became an important inspiration for American modernism. It already reached its zenith in a multitude of New Deal civic buildings, and in the commercial buildings that played an increasingly important role in the expression of public grandeur in

while at the Forde Ocean Apartments (1936, p. 86-89) every unit had either a terrace or a roof deck. Similarly, Henry Hohauser's Penn Terrace Apartments adapted Miami Beach's prototype single-lot apartment building type to accommodate front balconies. The use of exterior walkways and brise-soleil panels, like at Dixon's Norgate Apartments (1940, p. 116) and Flamingo Apartments (1940, p. 117) respectively, were indicative of the same innovative trend.

The tropical modern indulged nautical motifs like pipe railings and ships' ladders, indicative of life at sea. It preferred concrete, not only as a "modern" material but as a material which, because of its moldable plasticity and resistance to rot and insects, was particularly suited to Florida. Native quarried keystone, used extensively during Miami Beach's Mediterranean Revival, was rendered "new" by filling and dyeing; the result was a polished stone commonly colored red, green or yellow. Native pecky cypress wood was used in the construction of ceilings and in wood paneling.

The adaptations of tropical modern attested to one of the most comprehensive twentieth century attempts to reconcile environment and architecture, and to merge them in a regional expression. The "tropical modern" found its full expression between 1945 and 1960 in the thematic and almost scientific experiments of Miami architects like Igor Polevitzky, Rufus Nims, Alfred Browning Parker and others, who reinterpreted vernacular building types in a modern vocabulary and evolved sheer and transparent building skins.

47 Fritz Schumacher, "Trends in Architectural Thought," *Architectural Forum* (April 1931): 399.

48 Hillier, 9.

Skyscraper bookcase. Paul Theodore Frankl, c. 1926-30. Painted plywood, wood, brass hardware. Courtesy of The Mitchell Wolfson Jr. Collection, The Wolfsonian-Florida International University.

Markowitz & Resnick, 1214 Biscayne Boulevard, Miami. Lawrence Murray Dixon, 1936. Photograph by Samuel H. Gottscho. © Doris Schleisner. Collection of the Bass Museum of Art. Gift of Richard B. Dixon.

America.[49] New York's skyscraper boom and everyday commercial establishments like restaurants, cinemas and drugstores, built throughout America in the 1930s, were generators of Art Deco. These origins made Art Deco perfectly appropriate to Miami Beach, a city of commercial spectacle based on themes of leisure, entertainment and mobility.

Given the intimate relationship between Art Deco and the skyscraper, it is not surprising that building tops became a favored area for demonstrative civic art toward the end of the 1930s. The skyline of Miami Beach was punctuated with an array of features, from the cupola of the National Hotel (Roy F. France, 1940) to the stepped tower of the Grossinger Beach Hotel (Dixon, 1940, p. 119), reminiscent of Josef Hoffmann's Palais Stoclet in Brussels (1905–11). On the tallest buildings, these elements concealed rooftop elevator machine rooms and water tanks. They were also found on ordinary smaller buildings as corner markers, as the central feature of a pyramidal composition or as the terminus of an axis. The metallic crown of Dixon's Royal House Apartments was an example. Together, the vertical projections helped counterbalance the tight horizontal continuity of the urban fabric.

In Miami Beach, architectural progress was influenced by the role of ornamentation and the reform of decoration, indeed the "new ornamentation," initiated in Europe and conveyed to America after the Paris Exposition of 1925. Through the medium of its demonstration pavilions, as well as in contemporary projects like the rue Mallet-Stevens, French architects like Robert Mallet-Stevens and Pierre Chareau offered a model for the integration of "modern" decoration into an increasingly cubic, abstracted and functional architecture. The Paris Exposition also opened the door through which other European ideas would soon influence American design. The immigration of European designers, mainly Austrian, was particularly notable. Josef Urban, Paul Theodore Frankl, Josef Frank, Bernard Rudofsky, Richard Neutra and Rudolf Schindler, among others, brought Viennese avant-garde decorative arts and a modern architectural sensibility to America. Collectively, they counteracted the purist trends of European modernism, offering a middle ground that accepted synthesis and decoration.

A particularly Viennese influence was evident in the decorative and patterned use of materials like stone, terrazzo and glass. Dixon's Markowitz & Resnick store (a showroom for plumbing equipment) was remarkable for its syncopated window modulation, which was framed by a marble façade. Similar qualities were found in the interiors of Henry Hohauser's

49 Stern, Gilmartin and Mellias, 29-30. Stern states that in the Era of Commerce and Convenience, "public grandeur became largely a by-product of commercial enterprise."

Hoffman's Cafeteria, where the checkerboard floor was the stage, while oversized Art Deco floral patterns formed wall pillars behind.

The influence of the Austrians extended to the fundamental role of ornament in architecture. For instance, Joseph Urban's work at the Chicago Fair, and his designs for theaters and theater sets, especially his application of scenographic techniques, inspired an evolution in Art Deco toward the making of "urban theater." In addition, Paul Theodore Frankl wrote some influential books that addressed the role of the decorative arts in architecture. These included *New Dimensions*, a survey of recent work published in 1928 with a foreword by Frank Lloyd Wright. In that book, which perhaps echoed Wright's own ideals, Frankl declared that "America today is the only country in the world that may be said to be creating a modern architecture that is distinctive and expressive of its people."[50] In *Form and Reform*, published in 1930, Frankl proposed that contemporary expression in the decorative arts was the logical and necessary outcome of a new spirit manifested in every phase of American life.[51] Another important text coming from Austria, Josef Frank's *Architecture as Symbol* (1931), criticized the Bauhaus and De Stijl's ideal that buildings and interiors should be aesthetically integrated as *Gesamtkunstwerke* or "total works of art."

Among the eclectic modernizing trends of the late 1930s, Miami's newspapers made reference to the "Swedish modern" style in the description of buildings as diverse as Albert Anis's Winterhaven (1939, p. 183) and Dixon's Tudor (1939) hotels. In the absence of any explicit interpretation, the Swedish modern poses several interesting possibilities. It may refer to the established traditions of stylized Scandinavian classicism, illustrated in the work of Eliel Saarinen, whose arrival in the United States in 1923 may have propelled the popularity of this style. It may also refer to the success of modernism at the Stockholm exhibition of 1930 by Gunnar Asplund, who also toured the United States lecturing on problems of Swedish architecture. In fact, subsequent Swedish pavilions were noted for their advanced modernity. Finally, it may refer to the historical process of modernization of Swedish arts and crafts that by the 1930s yielded the design style called Swedish Modern. For instance, the Swedish decorative arts and interior furnishings designed by Svenskt Tenn, a collaboration between Joseph Frank and Estrid Ericson, were richly colored and patterned designs for furniture, materials, lamps

The Tudor Hotel, 1111 Collins Avenue, Miami Beach. Lawrence Murray Dixon, 1939. Rendering. From *Miami Herald*, 14 May 1939.

and appliances based on freedom, light, loose arrangements and bright colors. That the Winterhaven and Tudor hotels were neither entirely modernist nor decisively modern classical suggests that the term refered to the easy freedom of Swedish design trends. It is possible that the ideological ambivalence of the Swedes was a model for Miami Beach.

Contradictions in the role of the Miami Beach architect are apparent. On the one hand, architects coordinated the murals, etched glass, abstract patterns of terrazzo, ornate stainless steel and tubular steel metalwork, and lighting fixtures; they selected the furnishings, matchbook covers and employee uniforms.[52] On the other hand, the interior decoration of hotels was largely systematized by outside showrooms and designers, like the Maxwell Company and the Moore Furniture Company. These companies, experts in the function and comfort of hotel spaces, were responsible for the outfitting of hundreds of buildings in the latest taste.

previous spread:
Interior view of Hoffman's Cafeteria, Collins Avenue and Española Way, Miami Beach. Henry H. Hohauser, 1939. Courtesy of the Romer Collection, Miami-Dade Public Library.

50   Paul Frankl, *New Dimensions* (New York: Da Capo Press, 1928), 52.

51   Paul Frankl, *Form and Reform,* from *Architecture in Exile*, CD-ROM (Vienna: Science Wonder Productions / Organa, 1995).

52   Lawrence Murray Dixon Jr., 6.

Whereas the Mediterranean Revival spawned industries for the production of period details, the modern architecture of Miami Beach was fed by the dramatic retooling of the American building industry in the 1930s toward the production of modern components. A particularly good example was the changing availability and use of glass, which not only transformed buildings through transparency, but was also used as an ornament. Glass was the most technically advanced material of the 1930s. Its use reflected neither the expressionist fantasy of Bruno Taut, nor the realization of poet Paul Scheerbart's dream of freeing rooms from their enclosed character. Rather its use encompassed many forms.[53] Types of glass used included Vitrolite, plate glass and glass block, mirrors to extend space, obscure glass partitions, decorative etched glass and colored glass. Vitrolite, used in hotel lobbies and even as cladding on building façades, was an integrally colored glass product, designed as a hygienic replacement for marble. Although produced in a variety of colors, mint green, red and especially black were most commonly used. In addition to glass, the modern style was expressed in the use of chrome, stainless steel, aluminum and other alloys that were made available and affordable by industry. These materials were used for purposes such as steel sash windows (originally with bronze insect screens) and metallic nautical railings. Glazed ceramic tiles, mass produced lighting and modern state-of-the-art kitchens were further products and emblems of modernity. Often, buildings evolved into virtual essays on the virtues and possibilities of new materials.

Floridiana and Exotica — Celebrating the Natural, the Ideal and the Picturesque

Miami Beach's 1930s construction boom was the catalyst for an important transformation of ornament into adornment evoking the fantasy of the tropics. Popular motifs reflected Art Deco flamboyance, with its emphasis on themes of abundance and a bright future. Stylized depictions of plant life, sunrays, waves and fountains appeared, complementing the parallel modern tendency toward purely geometric ornament. The congruence between themes that were typically Art Deco and those that celebrated Florida was notable. For example, the sun was a powerful visual symbol of the era, interpreted most famously in the artificial sunrise devised by Roxy

53 A manual entitled *Glass*, published by the Libbey Owns Ford Glass Company and distributed in *Architectural Forum*, illustrated the innovative use of glass at the Home Planning Division of the 1933 Century of Progress Exhibition. New materials often represented advancements in technique, progress that was heralded at the World's Fairs and introduced, not necessarily as style, but as badges of modernity.

for theatrical effect at Radio City Music Hall (1932). Yet in Miami Beach the sun held particular relevance: it was the essence of Florida, the source of its warmth in all seasons, of its flora and the object of its "violet ray" bathers. Florida week at the 1939 World's Fair began symbolically with the "Release of Florida Sun." More explicitly, Florida themes included tropical fish and birds, serpents and reptiles, coconut palms and exotic flora. Natural and organic ornament was printed, sculpted, wrought or cast into the architecture of the city.

The thematic and often episodic use of exotic motifs elevated Florida's Depression-era architecture to a regional expression. It evoked the essence of an environment that was unique enough to be the fundamental reason and defining emblem of the city. Toward this end, Floridiana was employed by architects who considered themselves "modernists." This acceptance of appropriate ornament was supported by American architectural journals of the period, which extensively featured the elaborate iconographic development of buildings in the public realm, whether Rockefeller Center or Bertram Goodhue's Nebraska State Capitol.

Within the framework of modern classical façades, local themes were introduced through the sculptural art of the ornamental frieze, uti-

lizing cut stone, terra-cotta or sculpted plaster. An excellent example was the series of three bas-relief panels placed over the entrance portico of the Miami Beach Public Library in 1937 by sculptor Gustav Bohland. Bohland, who also incised the keystone structure to reveal sculpted seagulls at its corners, created a triptych that represented symbols of nature and progress. The center panel featured a stylized pelican while the other two represented the discovery of America and the wonders of modern transportation and communications: a ship, an airplane, a train and the antenna of Miami Beach's first radio station, WIOD. The *Miami Daily News* characterized Bohland's work as "original creations," free of the influence of any period or style, utilizing "themes he has developed from studies of Florida flora and fauna."[54]

Sculptural elaboration of Floridiana may have been inspired by sculptor Lee Lawrie's stylized depictions of Florida's flora and fauna, created in 1936 at the Bok Singing Tower of the Mountain Lake Sanctuary in central Florida. Designed by Philadelphia architect Milton B. Medary in a garden designed by Frederick Law Olmsted, the site represented a paradise of Florida's native landscape, elaborated by Lawrie in an ornamental frieze in which the interweaving bodies of flamingos, pelicans and swans were composed against a background of stems and leaves.

54 "Art Gallery is Completed at Miami Beach," *Miami Daily News*, 26 December 1937.

Naturalistic ornament was also used, in Sullivanesque fashion, in elaborate and continuous surfaces rising within spandrels, as at Henry Hohauser's Webster Hotel (1936). At Dixon's Pinecrest Apartments (p. 86), the raised tympanum over the front door presented a botanical composition while the recessed spandrels of the Marlin Hotel (1939) depicted tropical fish in aquarium-like scenes. Dixon's aquatic scenes presaged the more modern Albion Hotel, where real aquariums formed screen walls between the main lobby and the ground floor lounge area. At the Surf Hotel (Hohauser, 1937) the recessed spandrel panels developed vertically from a group of flamingos, to a palm tree and finally to a pair of female nudes at the top.[55] Raised from the flat wall surface of Albert Anis's Abbey Hotel (1940), a serpent (an iguana, perhaps) wrapped the stalk of an exotic plant while on either side rose vegetal interpretations of the pinnacles of some world's fair entrance. The life-size cast-stone pelicans that guarded the entrance of the Senator Hotel were used to similar monumental effect, lending the building the dignity of a civic structure.

Important ornamental designs were underway in the hotel interiors as well, particularly in all-important lobby spaces, where painted murals helped establish an exotic character. Mural painting evolved stylistically along with architecture during the 1930s, depicting historical scenes, utopian idealizations and the new reality of American life. And while mural art was increasingly a vehicle for expressing the essence of modern civilization, as witnessed in the scenes of social conflict painted by Diego Rivera at Rockefeller Center (Associated Architects, 1931–33; the mural was famously removed). Another example was Thomas Hart Benton's series "America Today," which decorated the strikingly modern New School of Social Research in Manhattan (Joseph Urban, 1930).

Murals were also used as narrative devices, to illustrate a theme or depict a local connection. As such they were important elements of

Miami Beach's public relations and advertising infrastructure. Little matter that their themes were tied to synthetic visions of the tropics. An example was the flamingo, a celebrated bird that was introduced (largely unsuccessfully) to the resort by developer Carl Fisher for scenographic reasons and in order to promote tourism. The archetypal Miami Beach lobby mural was surely the depiction of flamingos executed by naturalist artist Louis Fuertes in the lobby of the Flamingo Hotel in 1920.

By the 1930s wall murals were practically indispensable in hotels of a certain size. Earl LaPan, a former disciple of New York's Ashcan School of artists and, with Paul Simone and Paul Silverthorne,[56] among the most prolific muralists of the period, noted that "architects were parceling out assignments from their busy offices" on Lincoln Road. LaPan, who in 1939 returned to the North to work on the New York World's Fair under Norman Bel Geddes, found his inspiration and technique in the Miami Beach Public Library, in James Audubon's books on the tropics.[57] Floridiana, combining the typical, the ideal and the fantastic, emerged as a central theme. In the lobby of Henry Hohauser's Essex

56 See John A. Stuart, "Pragmatism Meets Exoticism: An Interview with Paul Silverthorne," *Journal of Decorative and Propaganda Arts* 23 (1998): 360-380.

57 "Earl LaPan," from MDPL Interviews in *Time Present, Time Past: The Art Deco District* (Miami Beach, Florida: Miami Design Preservation League, 1980), unpaginated.

55 Gebhard, 81.

Maps were also illustrated in murals; these evoked Miami Beach's proximity to the Caribbean, and by extension, the romance of that fabled sea just over the local horizon. The maps that decorated the walls of Dixon's Grossinger Beach Hotel (p. 118) and Polevitzky & Russell's Albion Hotel (1939) created an emblematic genre in Miami Beach that persisted into the 1950s with the famous marquee of the Carib Theater on Lincoln Road.

Dixon's Atlantis (1935-36, p. 76-81) was one of a number of hotels that used exotic materials, murals and other ornament to develop its own culture of fantasy around a theme or legend. Through a façade whose lower buttressing masses were encrusted with plant life reminiscent of Auguste Perret's rue Franklin apartment building in Paris (1909), visitors entered an almost Egyptian pillared lobby designed to emulate the "massive marbled halls of lost Atlantis."[58] There, under a twenty-foot-high ceiling covered in shimmering silver leaf (a reminder of Radio City Music Hall), and supported on pillars reflecting the deep blue of the Gulf Stream, the depiction of the lost city by muralist Chester Tingler was but a narrative extension of the architecture. The significance of the theme of Atlantis could not have been lost on patrons aware of Miami Beach's contrasting emergence from the sea. The dining room was similarly lush: wild geese and pink flamingos took flight against a background of azure and ivory and red furnishings. The Atlantis' "American Bar" was more decidedly modern, though similarly eclectic. Surrounded by a double glass-brick wall that provided indirect lighting, it had a blue mirrored ceiling, a chestnut and burnished copper counter, colorful wall seats, and tables and chairs of aluminum with leather upholstering.

The elaboration of thematic environments reached its apex in cinema designs like Thomas W. Lamb's French Casino (1936) and Robert Law Weed and William L. Pereira's Beach Theater (1941). At the Beach Theater, the lobby was alive with artificial plant life, which grew in planters, glass atriums and recessed vitrines and which imbued the detailing of the architecture itself. Guardrails were sinewy like the stems of flowers. Wall murals carried the three-dimensional plant themes to the flat dimensions of the lobby back wall. A theatrical flourish was provided by a grand stairway that ascended to a balcony framed in a stage curtain.

House Hotel, LaPan depicted an Indian poling his dugout canoe through the Florida Everglades. In addition to the subject, LaPan's mural covered an entire wall, expanding the space of the lobby and rendering the stepped fireplace, carved in native Florida keystone, like a freestanding ziggurat. LaPan's mural was juxtaposed, in the compressed space of the Essex House lobby, with etched glass panels (depicting a scene with palm trees), decorative metalwork and geometric terrazzo floors.

While artists like Earl LaPan wrapped Florida in romance, others depicted an imaginary exotic tropical paradise outside of Florida. Escapist themes of life in far-away locales were illustrated in Ramon Chatov's mural at the Plymouth Hotel. There, dancing figures frolicked on a beach against an exotic and idealized landscape. In fact, the bacchanalia of the enchanted dancers, guitar-playing musician, sublime plant life and ravaged life boat brought to mind the Idealist paintings of Claude Lorrain and Nicolas Poussin. At the Colony Hotel, in an overmantel tableau framed in mint green vitrolite, muralist Paul Simone depicted a pastoral scene redolent of the work of American Regionalist painters like Grant Wood, Jerry Bywaters and Alex Hogue. In a far away landscape parched by the sun (in the manner of Depression-era depictions), wild and exotic plants formed the background for the figures that transferred a mysterious liquid between gourds.

above:
Main lobby of the Beach Theatre, 430 Lincoln Road, Miami Beach. Robert Law Weed, with William L. Pereira, 1941. Photograph by Samuel H. Gottscho. Courtesy of the Library of Congress, Prints and Photographs Division, Gottscho-Schleisner Collection. © Doris Schleisner.

opposite:
Night view of the Raleigh Hotel's façade on Collins Avenue, Miami Beach. Photograph by Samuel H. Gottscho. © Doris Schleisner. Collection of the Bass Museum of Art. Gift of Richard B. Dixon.

58 "The Atlantis, Distinctive Miami Beach Hostelry, Open Doors Today — Eight Story Edifice Embodies Advances," *Miami Herald*, 16 January 1936.

Miami Beach's Urban Follies

Here in the Miami Beach of the 1930s, perhaps for the last time to come for many years, America succeeded in evolving an architecture, an entire cityscape, which literally and figuratively opened its doors and communicated its meanings with equal effectiveness not just to the favored few, but to the man in the street as well.[59]

By 1942, the hundreds of new buildings and the countless others remodeled completed the development of large areas of Miami Beach's urban grid and gave the city a new modern look. Of course, it was still an eclectic environment: modern buildings were distributed in the block fabric between Mediterranean palazzos and wood frame houses. The stylistic character of many urban blocks was neutral, and the recurrence of stylistic themes was alternating and unsystematic, not constant.

Yet, the modern layer of the city clearly betrayed the evolution of a unity of thought and purpose, a coordinated message that was the basis for a local civic art. A wide spectrum of Miami Beach's architects, building owners and tourists shared this common culture. The coordination evinced the search for common ideals, the so-called "civic religion" of America.[60] Modern stylistic trends thus played an important role in the construction of a public morality of architecture; architectural activity was the forging of identity, a common language.

The significance of this Depression-era visual culture thus is partly in the way that it chronicled the social and human aspect of the city; that it was the agent capable of defining the city's reason and place. Its buildings expressed optimism, cohesion, authority and glamour. They commented on the era's cultural artifacts, and reflected or parodied its monumental impulses, the attraction of the machine and the wonders of the tropics. In these narrative designs, architecture achieved the pivotal importance described by nineteenth century French novelist Victor Hugo, whose *Notre-Dame de Paris* lamented the decline of architecture as a total art at the hands of literature ("*Le livre tuera l'édifice.*")

This evolution of an architecture expressive of the modern condition was in fact the dream of many modernists. Yet Miami Beach's eclectic, warm and boldly demonstrative architecture had no apparent place in the "cold and abstract Utopias" of modernism. Its architects were not remote to these Utopias, having been educated and having worked in environments where they were sure to have come into close contact with modern ideas. Rather, their designs belonged to the resort Utopias of leisure and pleasure, escape and renewal. The role of the architect was to dress up the hard iconographic relevancy of "industrial-looking" façades of modern housing types.

Architecture was the way and means of transmission of both modern values and popular themes. On the one hand these buildings represented austerity, pragmatic accommodation and common sense. On the other hand, their highly stylized façades exemplified a rhapsodic pole of the spectrum of modern architecture in America. They were the promise of a future with humanistic vibes. The lengthening skyline of the city pushed the expression of leisure and excess wealth to the level of spectacle. It was thus, as noted by *Vanity Fair*, a "mirror of the progress and promise of American life."[61]

Within this utopia, Miami Beach's modern buildings were in fact "follies." Consciously designed as "figures of unreason" and adapted to the needs of pleasure and leisure, they were the furniture of the ideal city. As Anthony Vidler noted, follies were exemplar of industrial progress and culture, they were the realm of the exhibition, the world's fairs and of rhetorical architecture. They were a form of game playing, following plots and themes that were legible though not necessarily logical. This thematic culture of follies, with its implicit criticism of more serious architecture and its rich texture of cultural allusion, underlied a broad spectrum of resort architecture. Outside the mainstream of American design trends, it has seldom received positive acclaim. Nevertheless, this culture led, in the postwar era, directly to the hotel architecture of Morris Lapidus, whose "French" Fontainebleau and "Italianate" Eden Roc hotels reinterpreted the visual culture of the resort for the next generation of tourists.[62]

59 Harris J. Sobin, "Miami Deco Roots and Meanings," ed. Barbara Baer Capitman, Diane Camber, *Time Present, Time Past: The Art Deco District* (Miami Beach, Florida: Miami Design Preservation League, 1980), 11-12.

60 Gelernter, 49.

61 Mark A. Bernheim, "Dos Passos and *Vanity Fair*: The Novel and The Ad," (Ph.D. Dissertation), 8.

62 Anthony Vidler, "History of Follies," in B. J. Archer, *Follies: Architecture for the Late-Twentieth-Century Landscape* (New York: Rizzoli, 1983), 8.

THE HOTELS AND APARTMENT HOUSE
OF LAWRENCE MURRAY DIXON

Detail of the beach façade of the Atlantis Hotel. Photograph by Samuel H. Gottscho.
From *Architectural Record* 80 (July 1936). © Doris Schleisner.

1933 – 34

THE ROYAL ARMS, THE ESTER &
THE OCEAN FRONT APARTMENT HOUSES

top:
The Royal Arms, 1235 Collins Avenue. 1934. Gift of Richard B. Dixon.

opposite top:
The Ester Apartments, 525 Española Way. 1933. Gift of Richard B. Dixon.

opposite bottom:
The Ocean Front Apartments, 1236 Ocean Drive. 1935. Gift of Richard B. Dixon.

THE ATLANTIS HOTEL

2600 Block Collins Avenue. Demolished in 1973.

top:
View of the entrance from Collins Avenue.
Photograph by Samuel H. Gottscho. © Doris Schleisner.
Gift of Lawrence M. Dixon Jr.

right:
Plot plan. From *Architectural Record* 80
(July 1936): 52. © *Architectural Record*.

opposite:
Detail of the entrance portico on Collins Avenue.
Photograph by Samuel H. Gottscho. © Doris Schleisner.
Gift of Lawrence M. Dixon Jr.

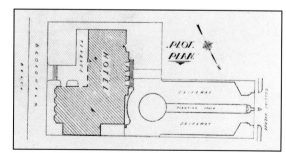

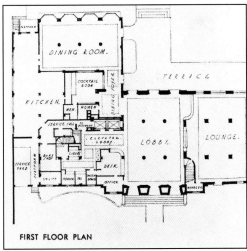

FIRST FLOOR PLAN

opposite:
View of the lobby. Photograph by
Samuel H. Gottscho. © Doris Schleisner.
Gift of Richard B. Dixon.

top:
View of the rear façade from the beach
and the boardwalk. Photograph by
Samuel H. Gottscho. © Doris Schleisner.
Gift of Lawrence M. Dixon Jr.

left:
First floor plan. From *Architectural Record*
80 (July 1936): 52.
© *Architectural Record.*

TYPICAL FLOOR PLAN

THE PINECREST APARTMENTS

24th Street and Pinetree Drive. Demolished.

top:
View of the main façades from Pinetree Drive.
Photograph by Samuel H. Gottscho. © Doris
Schleisner. Gift of Lawrence M. Dixon Jr.

right:
First floor plan and second floor plan. From
American Architect and Architecture (November
1938): 62. © *American Architect and Architecture*

opposite:
Interior of duplex apartment. Photograph by
Samuel H. Gottscho. © Doris Schleisner.
Gift of Richard B. Dixon.

Detail of façade with Roney Plaza Hotel in
the distance. Photograph by Samuel H.

Detail of façade. Photograph by
Samuel H. Gottscho. © Doris Schleisner.

THE FORDE OCEAN APARTMENTS

6690 Collins Avenue. 1935-36.

top:
Entrance to the complex from Collins Avenue.
Photograph by Samuel H. Gottscho. © Doris
Schleisner. Gift of Lawrence M. Dixon Jr.

far right:
View of the inner court toward the entrance.
Photograph by Samuel H. Gottscho. © Doris
Schleisner. Gift of Lawrence M. Dixon Jr.

right:
First floor plan and second floor plan of
the complex. From *American Architect
and Architecture* (November 1938): 63.
© *American Architect and Architecture.*

opposite:
Interior of second floor duplex apartment.
Photograph by Samuel H. Gottscho. © Doris
Schleisner. Gift of Richard B. Dixon.

top:
View of the complex from the beach.
Photograph by Samuel H. Gottscho. © Doris
Schleisner. Gift of Lawrence M. Dixon Jr.

right:
View of the maisonette from the beach.
Photograph by Samuel H. Gottscho. © Doris
Schleisner. Gift of Richard B. Dixon.

1936

THE TIDES HOTEL

1220 Ocean Drive.

TYPICAL FLOOR

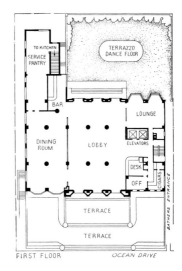

FIRST FLOOR

BASEMENT

top:
View of the lobby from the entrance toward the dining room. Photograph by Samuel H. Gottscho. © Doris Schleisner. Gift of Lawrence M. Dixon Jr.

bottom:
View of the dining room toward Ocean Drive. Photograph by Samuel H. Gottscho. © Doris Schleisner. Gift of Lawrence M. Dixon Jr.

above (from bottom to top):
Basement plan, first floor plan, typical floor plan. From *Architectural Forum* 69 (December 1938): 452. © *Architectural Forum*.

opposite:
Detail of façade on Ocean Drive. Photograph by Samuel H. Gottscho. © Doris Schleisner. Gift of Lawrence M. Dixon Jr.

above:
View of the lobby toward Ocean Drive.
Photograph by Samuel H. Gottscho. © Doris
Schleisner. Gift of Lawrence M. Dixon Jr.

opposite:
Night view of the façade on Ocean Drive.
Photograph by Samuel H. Gottscho.
Gift of Lawrence M. Dixon Jr.
© Doris Schleisner.

THE FAIRMONT HOTEL

1000 Collins Avenue. 1936.

View of façade on Collins Avenue. Photograph by Samuel H. Gottscho.
© Doris Schleisner. Gift of Lawrence M. Dixon Jr.

View of the lobby toward Collins Avenue. Photograph by Samuel H. Gottscho.
© Doris Schleisner. Gift of Lawrence M. Dixon Jr.

THE BEACH PLAZA HOTEL

1401 Collins Avenue. 1936.

View of the lobby along Collins Avenue.
Photograph by Samuel H. Gottscho.
© Doris Schleisner. Gift of Lawrence M. Dixon Jr.

View of façade on Collins Avenue.
Photograph by Samuel H. Gottscho.
© Doris Schleisner. Gift of Lawrence M. Dixon Jr.

1931

THE VICTOR HOTEL

1144 Ocean Drive.

above:
View facing Ocean Drive. Photograph by Samuel H. Gottscho. © Doris Schleisner.
Gift of Lawrence M. Dixon Jr.

opposite:
View of the lobby. Photograph by Samuel H. Gottscho. © Doris Schleisner.
Gift of Richard B. Dixon.

above:
View of the mezzanine above the
lobby toward Ocean Drive. Photograph by
Samuel H. Gottscho. © Doris Schleisner.
Gift of Lawrence M. Dixon Jr.

opposite:
Detail of the lobby with front desk.
Photograph by Samuel H. Gottscho.
© Doris Schleisner. Gift of Lawrence M. Dixon Jr.

THE SEYMOUR BUILDING — GOLDWASSER'S SHOPS

700-712 Lincoln Road, 1630-1646 Euclid Avenue. 1937.

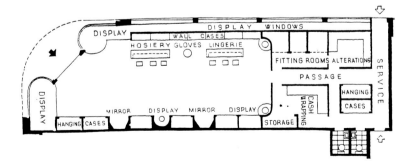

above:
Façades on Lincoln Road and Euclid Avenue. Photograph by Samuel H. Gottscho. © Doris Schleisner. Gift of Richard B. Dixon.

left:
Ground floor plan. From *Architectural Forum* 69(December 1938): 456. © *Architectural Forum*.

opposite:
Detail of street corner with reflections of the Lincoln Theater and Lincoln Building in the glass. Photograph by Samuel H. Gottscho. © Doris Schleisner. Gift of Lawrence M. Dixon Jr.

THE SENATOR

1221 Collins Avenue. 1939. Demolished.

Façades on Collins Avenue and 12th Street with
the Tides in the distance. Photograph by Moser & Son.
Gift of Richard B. Dixon.

THE ADAMS HOTEL

2030 Park Avenue. 1938.

above:

Façades on Park Avenue.
Photograph by Moser & Son.
Gift of Richard B. Dixon.

right:

Detailed elevation of roof tower.
From Jewel Stern, *Jewel Stern/Project Skyline
Modern/Moderne/Modernistic Miami Beach
Hotel Architecture/Circa 1940* (Akron: Akron
Art Institute, 1979).

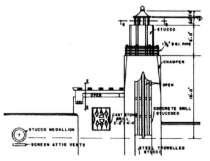

Façade on Collins Avenue. Photograph by
Moser & Son. Gift of Lawrence M. Dixon Jr.

THE MARLIN HOTEL

1200 Collins Avenue. 1939.

Façades on Collins Avenue and 12th Street.
Photograph by Moser & Son.
Gift of Richard B. Dixon.

View of lobby toward Collins Avenue.
Photograph by Moser & Son.
Gift of Richard B. Dixon.

1940

THE RALEIGH HOTEL

1773 Collins Avenue.

above:
View of the lounge. Photograph by
Samuel H. Gottscho. © Doris Schleisner.
Gift of Richard B. Dixon.

right:
View of the dining room toward the beach.
Photograph by Samuel H. Gottscho. © Doris
Schleisner. Gift of Lawrence M. Dixon Jr.

THE CENTRAL APARTMENTS

1608 Drexel Avenue. 1940.

View of entrances wing on Drexel Avenue.
Photograph by Samuel H. Gottscho.
© Doris Schleisner. Gift of Lawrence M. Dixon Jr.

THE ESTILL ARMS APARTMENTS

1341-1345 Meridian Avenue. 1940.

Façade on Meridian Avenue with entrance sideyard. Photograph by Samuel H. Gottscho.
© Doris Schleisner. Gift of Lawrence M. Dixon Jr.

THE NORGATE APARTMENTS

6810 Harding Avenue. c. 1940.

Side façade with entry loggias. Photograph by
Samuel H. Gottscho. © Doris Schleisner.
Gift of Lawrence M. Dixon Jr.

Main façade on Flamingo Drive.
Photograph by Moser & Son.
Gift of Lawrence M. Dixon Jr.

1940

THE GROSSINGER BEACH HOTEL

1701 Collins Avenue

View of the lobby toward the front desk.
Photograph by Samuel H. Gottscho.
© Doris Schleisner. Gift of Lawrence M.
Dixon Jr.

opposite:
View of façade on Collins Avenue and
17th Street. Photograph by Samuel H.
Gottscho. © Doris Schleisner. Gift of
Lawrence M. Dixon Jr.

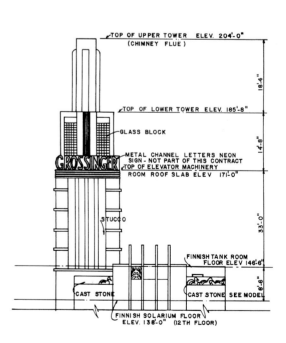

THE McALPIN HOTEL

1424 Ocean Drive. 1940.

above:
View of the lobby. Photograph by Moser & Son. Gift of Lawrence M. Dixon Jr.

opposite:
View of façade on Ocean Drive. Photograph by Moser & Son. Gift of Lawrence M. Dixon Jr.

THE MILJEAN HOTEL

1817 James Avenue. 1940.

View of façade on James Avenue. Photograph by Moser & Son. Gift of Lawrence M. Dixon Jr.

THE CULVER APARTMENTS

1751 James Avenue. 1940.

View of façade on James Avenue. Photograph by Moser & Son. Gift of Richard B. Dixon.

THE LAWRENCE APARTMENTS

1525 Meridian Avenue. 1939-40.

View of façade on Meridian Avenue. Photograph by Moser & Son. Gift of Richard B. Dixon.

APARTMENT BUILDING

Address unknown. c.1940.

View of façade. Photograph by Moser & Son. Gift of Richard B. Dixon.

THE FLETCHER APARTMENTS

1667 Washington Avenue. 1940. Demolished.

View of façade along Washington Avenue. Photograph by Moser & Son. Gift of Richard B. Dixon.

THE HADDON HALL HOTEL

1500 Collins Avenue.

View of façade on Collins Avenue. Photograph by Moser & Son. Gift of Richard B. Dixon.

THE SOUTH SEAS HOTEL

1751 Collins Avenue.

View of façade on Collins Avenue.
Photograph by Moser & Son.
Gift of Richard B. Dixon.

THE RICHMOND HOTEL

1757 Collins Avenue. 1941.

View of façade on Collins Avenue.
Photograph by Moser & Son.
Gift of Richard B. Dixon.

THE CLYDE HOTEL

1300 Ocean Drive. 1941.

View of façade on Ocean Drive.
Photograph by Moser & Son.
Gift of Lawrence M. Dixon Jr.

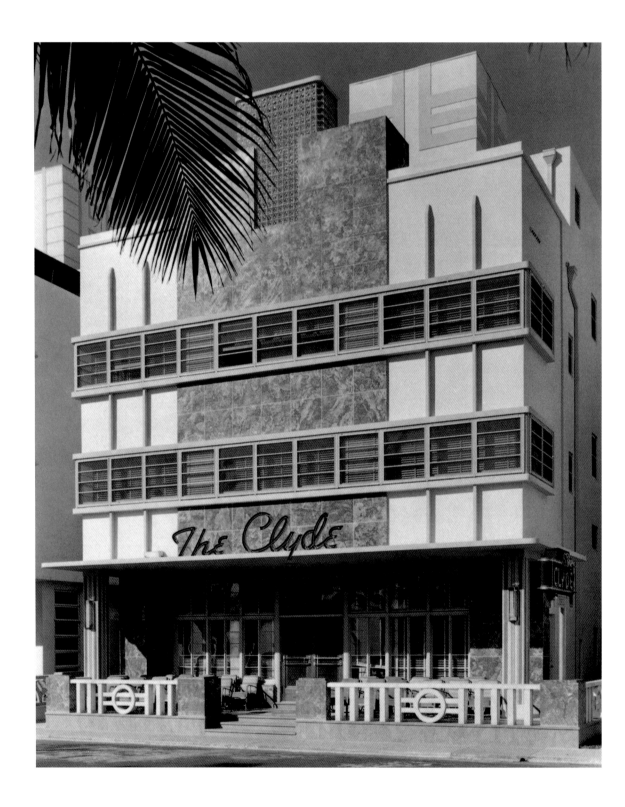

THE GREENBRIER HOTEL

3101 Indian Creek Drive. 1941.

APARTMENT BUILDING

Address unknown. c. 1940-41.

View of façade.
Photograph by Moser & Son.
Gift of Richard B. Dixon.

opposite:
Detail of entrance. Photograph by Samuel H.
Gottscho. Courtesy of the Library of
Congress, Prints and Photographs Division,
Gottscho-Schleisner Collection.
© Doris Schleisner.

1941

THE CARIBBEAN

3700 Collins Avenue.

above:
View of back façade from the pool. Photograph
by Samuel H. Gottscho. © Doris Schleisner.
Gift of Richard B. Dixon.

opposite:
View of façade on Collins Avenue.
Photograph by Samuel H. Gottscho. Courtesy
Library of Congress, Prints and Photographs
Division, Gottscho-Schleisner Collection.
© Doris Schleisner.

Pool and diving board. Photograph by Samuel H. Gottscho. Courtesy of the Library of
Congress, Prints and Photographs Division, Gottscho-Schleisner Collection. © Doris Schleisner.

Staircase, unidentified home. Lawrence Murray Dixon, date unknown. Photograph by Samuel H. Gottscho. © Doris Schleisner. Gift of Lawrence M. Dixon Jr.

LAWRENCE MURRAY DIXON RESIDENCE

above:
Street façade of Lawrence Murray Dixon's family house, 2871 Fairgreen Drive, Miami Beach. Photograph by Samuel H. Gottscho. © Doris Schleisner. Gift of Richard B. Dixon.

right:
First floor plan and second floor plan, Lawrence Murray Dixon's family house, 2871 Fairgreen Drive, Miami Beach. From *American Architect and Architecture* (August 1936): 45.
© *American Architect and Architecture.*

opposite top:
View of the living room, Lawrence Murray Dixon's family house, 2871 Fairgreen Drive, Miami Beach. Photograph by Samuel H. Gottscho. © Doris Schleisner. Gift of Lawrence M. Dixon Jr.

opposite bottom:
View of the entrance with staircase to second floor, Lawrence Murray Dixon's family house, 2871 Fairgreen Drive, Miami Beach. Photograph by Samuel H. Gottscho. © Doris Schleisner. Gift of Lawrence M. Dixon Jr.

above:

Single-family residence, 2065 North Bay Road, Miami Beach. Lawrence Murray Dixon, c.1936. Photograph by Moser & Son. Gift of Richard B. Dixon.

below:

Detail of façade, unidentified residence, Miami Beach. Lawrence Murray Dixon. Date unknown. Photograph by Samuel H. Gottscho. © Doris Schleisner. Gift of Richard B. Dixon.

above:

Single-family residence, 3210 Alton Road, Miami Beach. Lawrence Murray Dixon, 1936. Photograph by Samuel H. Gottscho. © Doris Schleisner. Gift of Lawrence M. Dixon Jr.

below:

Façade, unidentified home. Lawrence Murray Dixon. Date unknown. Photograph by Samuel H. Gottscho. © Doris Schleisner. Gift of Lawrence M. Dixon Jr.

top:
Single-family residence, unidentified, Miami Beach. Lawrence Murray Dixon. Photograph by Samuel H. Gottscho. © Doris Schleisner. Gift of Lawrence M. Dixon Jr.

left:
Single-family residence, unidentified, Miami Beach. Lawrence Murray Dixon. Photograph by Moser & Son. Gift of Richard B. Dixon.

right:
Single-family residence, unidentified, Miami Beach. Lawrence Murray Dixon. Photograph by Moser & Son. Gift of Lawrence M. Dixon Jr.

Single-family residence, 34th Street & Royal Palm Avenue, Miami Beach. Lawrence Murray Dixon, c.1935–36. Photographer unidentified. Gift of Lawrence M. Dixon Jr.

Detail of garden façade, single-family residence, unidentified. Lawrence Murray Dixon, date unknown. Photograph by Moser & Son. Gift of Richard B. Dixon.

Single-family residence, unidentified, Miami Beach. Lawrence Murray Dixon. Photograph by Moser & Son. Gift of Richard B. Dixon.

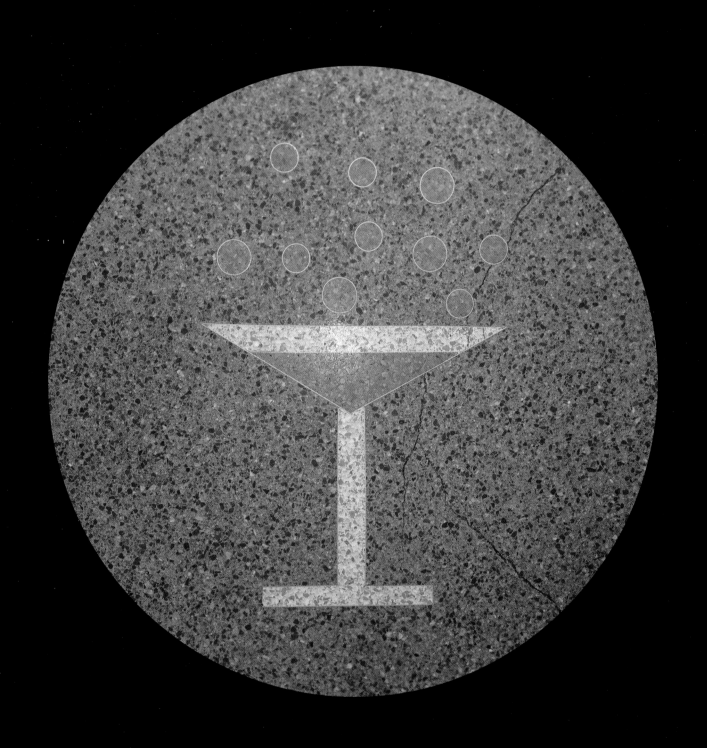

Hotel Waldorf Astoria Hotel, 301 Park Avenue,
New York. Fiftieth Street elevation. Leonard
Schultze & Fullerton Weaver, with Lloyd
Morgan, 1929 – 1931. Pencil, pen and ink wash-
es on colored paper with white ink highlights,
39 x 24". Rendering by Lloyd Morgan. The
Mitchell Wolfson Jr. Collection, The
Wolfsonian-Florida International University.

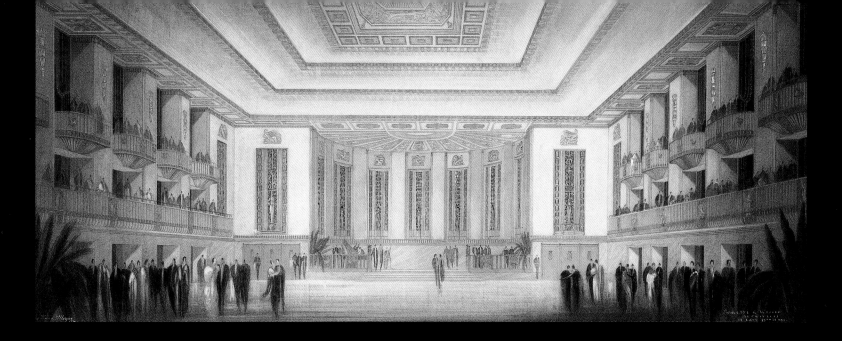

The Waldorf Astoria Hotel, 301 Park Avenue, New York. Perspective of the main ballroom. Leonard Schultze & Fullerton Weaver, with Lloyd Morgan, 1929–1931. Graphite on paper, pencil and eraser, 20 x 49". Rendering by Lloyd Morgan. The Mitchell Wolfson Jr. Collection, The Wolfsonian-Florida International University.

Watercolor from Santorini, Greece. Bernard Rudofsky, 1929. Watercolor on paper,
22 x 30". Getty Research Institute, Research Library. © Mrs. Berta Rudofsky.

Perspective of Phillard Gardens, 2000 Pinetree Drive, Miami Beach. Lawrence Murray Dixon, 1939. Graphite, ink and white pencil on colored paper. Illustrator unidentified. Photograph by Peter Harholdt, 1999. Courtesy of the Museum Walk Apartments, Miami Beach.

FREEDOM

OPPORTUNITY

top:
Mangrove tree, Sunny Isle, Miami Beach. Postcard. Collection Allan T. Shulman.

center:
Dade Canal and Dade Boulevard, Miami Beach. Postcard. Collection Allan T. Shulman.

bottom:
Residence and studio of Henry Salem Hubbell, Miami Beach. Schultze & Weaver, 1925. Postcard. Collection Allan T. Shulman.

top:
Nautilus Hotel, Miami Beach (demolished). Schultze & Weaver, 1924. Postcard. Collection Allan T. Shulman.

center:
Hotel La Flora, Collins Avenue & 12th Street, Miami Beach. Postcard. Collection Allan T. Shulman.

bottom:
Lincoln Road, Miami Beach in the 1920s. Postcard. Collection Allan T. Shulman.

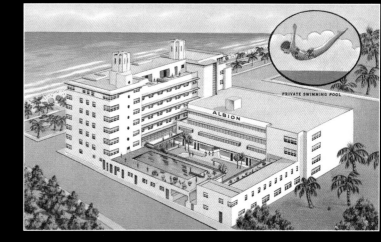

top:
Hotel Cardozo, 1300 Ocean Drive, Miami Beach. Henry Hohauser, 1939. Postcard.
Collection Allan T. Shulman.

center:
The Commodore Hotel, 1360 Collins Avenue, Miami Beach. Henry Hohauser, 1936.
Postcard. Collection Allan T. Shulman.

bottom:
The Essex House, 1001 Collins Avenue, Miami Beach. Henry Hohauser, 1938. Postcard.
Collection Allan T. Shulman.

top:
Helen Mar Apartments, 2421 Lake Pancoast Drive, Miami Beach. Roy F. France, 1937.
Postcard. Collection Allan T. Shulman.

center:
Kenmore Hotel, 1050 Washington Avenue, Miami Beach. Anton Skislewicz, 1936. Postcard.
Collection Allan T. Shulman.

bottom:
The Albion Hotel, 1650 James Avenue. Polevitzky & Russell, 1939. Postcard. Collection
Allan T. Shulman.

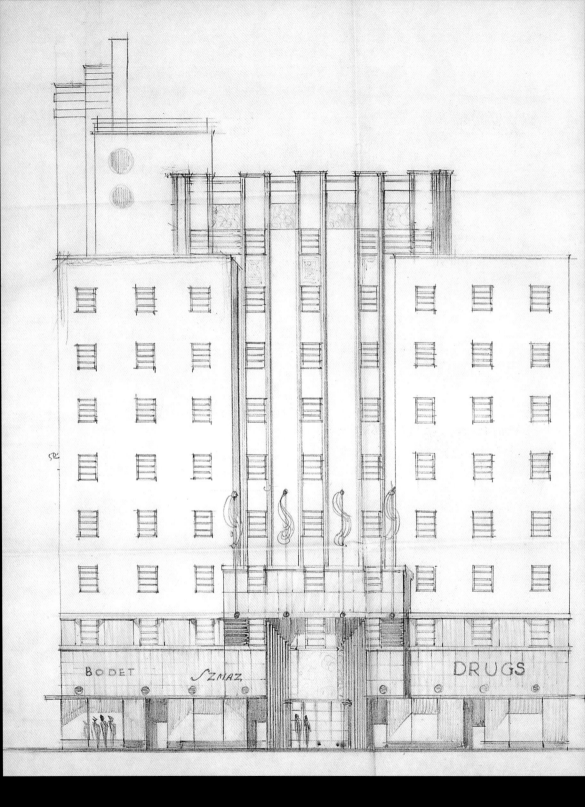

Elevation (location unknown). Lawrence Murray Dixon, date unknown, c. 1936. Graphite and colored pencil on trace paper, 23 x 18". Illustrator unidentified. Gift of Lawrence M. Dixon Jr.

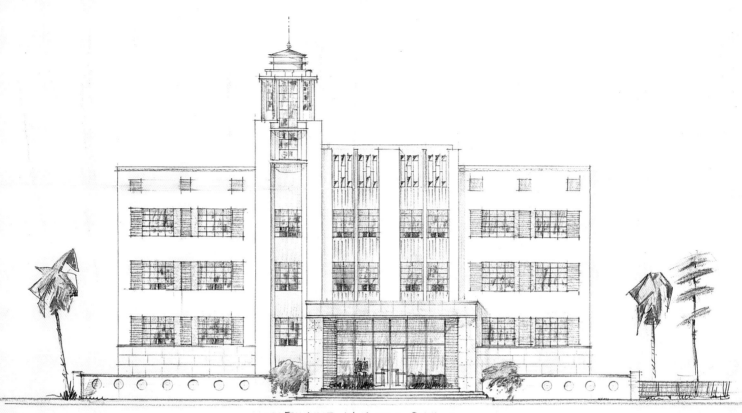

- E L E V A T I O N -
· PRELIMINARY · STUDY · INDIAN CREEK · FAÇADE ·
$\frac{1}{8}" = 1'-0"$

- L · MURRAY · DIXON · ARCHITECT ·
· 1623 · MICHIGAN · AVE · AT · LINCOLN · RD ·

above:
Preliminary study Indian Creek façade, Miami
Beach. Lawrence Murray Dixon, c. 1935.
Graphite and colored pencil on trace paper, 13
1/2 x 22". Illustrated by Ken DeGarmo. Gift of
Richard B. Dixon.

right:
Elevation of the Croydon Hotel, Miami Beach.
Lawrence Murray Dixon, date unknown, c.
1937. Graphite and colored pencil on paper,
17 1/2 x 21". Illustrator unidentified. Gift of
Richard B. Dixon.

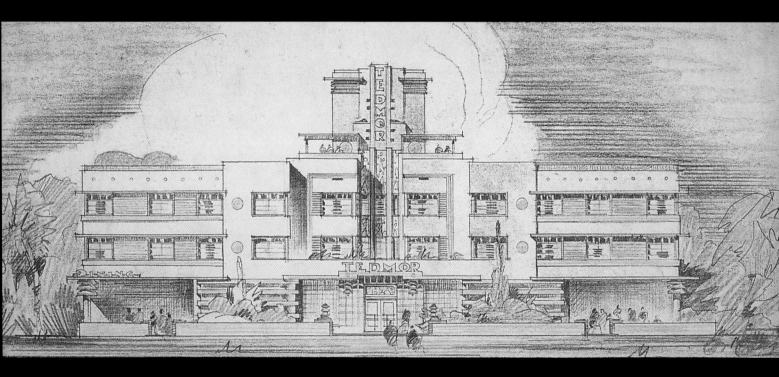

top:
Proposal for Drexel Avenue Apartment Building, Miami Beach. Henry Hohauser, c. 1939. Hand colored lithograph on paper, 7 1/2 x 15 3/4".
Illustrator unidentified. Gift of Malcolm Holzman.

above:
Proposal for Tedmor Hotel, Miami Beach. Henry Hohauser and Frederick A. Gibbs, c. 1939. Hand colored lithograph, 8 1/4 x 19 1/8". Illustrator
unidentified. Gift of Malcolm Holzman.

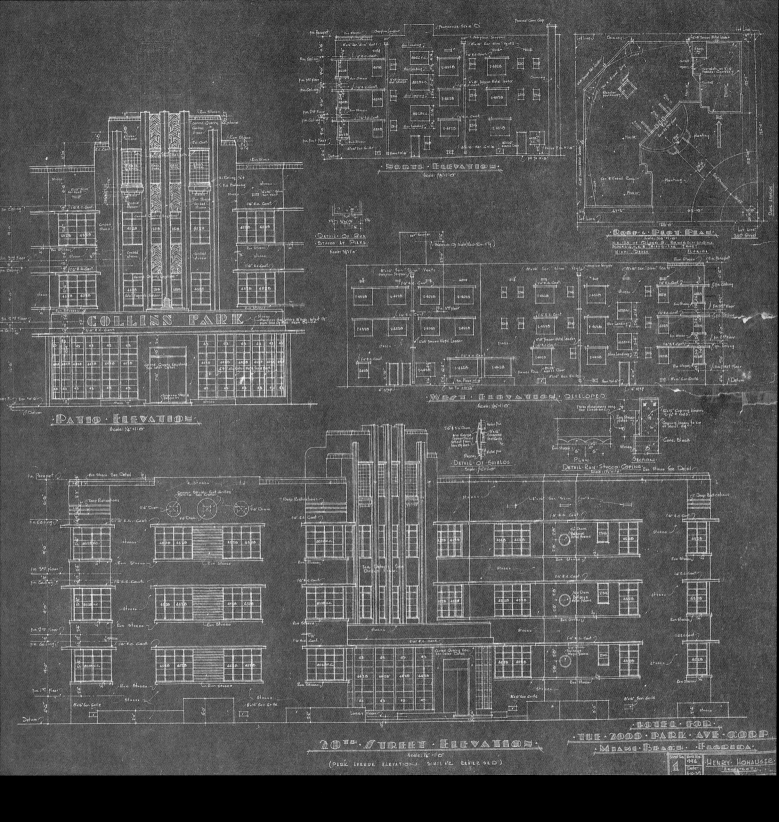

Patio elevation, 20th Street elevation, west elevation, north elevation and plot plan of the Collins Park Hotel, Miami Beach. Henry Hohauser, 1939.
Blueprint, 33 3/8 x 36". The Mitchell Wolfson Jr. Collection, The Wolfsonian–Florida International University.

PRELIMINARY STUDY.
RESIDENCE
for
MR · FRANK LA·CROIX.
MIAMI BEACH

L. MURRAY DIXON ARCHITECT.
REVISED JUNE 17TH 1938.

above:
Preliminary study, residence for Mr. Frank
LaCroix, Miami Beach. Lawrence Murray
Dixon, date unknown. Blueprint, 13 x 19".
Gift of Richard B. Dixon.

right:
First-floor plan, residence for Mr. Frank
LaCroix, Miami Beach. Lawrence Murray
Dixon, date unknown. Blueprint on paper,
20 x 14". Gift of Richard B. Dixon.

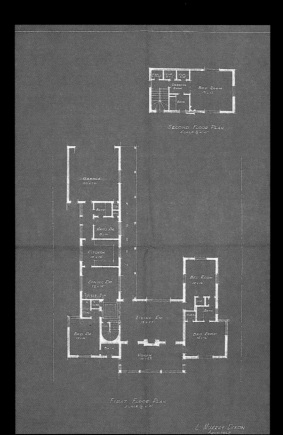

PROPOSED RESIDENCE
FOR
MR. & MRS. JULIUS SIMPSON
SAN MARINO ISLAND
L. MURRAY DIXON
ARCHITECT

"And think of the stars! Driving through space, round and round,

just like the electrons in the atom! But there must be a center

around which all this moves, musn't there? There is in everything else!

And that center must be the Great Mother of Eternal Life,

Electricity, and Dynamo is her Divine Image on earth! Her power

houses are the new churches!"

— Eugene O'Neill, *The Dynamo*, Act III, Scene 1.

LAWRENCE MURRAY DIXON AND HIS COLLEAGUES: COMPETING FOR THE MODERN, 1933–1942

Jean-François Lejeune

At a time when we are striving to re-cycle our architectural heritage, preserve our architectural records, and save our landmarks, it becomes even more necessary to understand what was created, why it was created and how it was accomplished. Our objective is not to deal with the elite, avant-garde architect, but to consider the work of the architectural firms who produced the living architecture and productive buildings demanded by the public of that time, whose concern was to enjoy their newly established status of success and who still experienced a nostalgia for the romantic past and present.[1]

As in New York City, one interesting dimension of the "culture of housing" in Miami Beach between 1933 and 1942 involved the ensemble of architects who worked there and designed the new modern city. Lawrence Murray Dixon (1901–1949) and his colleagues did not build the skyscrapers, grand civic structures or magnificent train stations that would have assured their places in the encyclopedias of architecture. Instead, they produced the modest architecture of the seasonal city's everyday life, its vernacular modern houses, apartment buildings and hotels. These architects had no high-society background; they were middle-class men who partook of the environment that they were building for a predominantly middle-class clientele. Many were Jewish (immigrants or not), in a profession which at that time was dominated by the Anglo-Saxon Protestant male establishment. Most of them did not receive a complete university education. They did not embark on the traditional "Grand Tour" like their prestigious colleagues from the Ivy League.[2]

Of the American-born group, Lawrence Murray Dixon attended two years of study at Georgia Tech in Atlanta; Henry Hohauser (1895–1963) took classes at Pratt Institute; and Roy F. France (1888–1972) and Albert Anis (1889–1964) attended the Armour Institute of Technology in Chicago. However, Robert Law Weed (1897–1961) graduated from the Carnegie and Russell Thorn Pancoast (1898-1972) from Cornell University. An exception was John Llewellyn Skinner (1893–1967), a graduate of Harvard University and recipient of a two-year Nelson Traveling Fellowship.[3] His travel to Europe was a rare privilege, shared by Henry Hohauser and Robert Law Weed, who went to France and England as architects for the army during World War I.[4]

Other Miami Beach architects were immigrants from Central and Eastern Europe. They included Anton Skislewicz (1895–1967), who was born in Dubrovnik and received a bachelor's degree from Columbia University; Robert Swartburg (1895–1975), a native of Bucharest, who studied in Paris and then moved to New York, where he attended the Beaux Arts Institute of Design and spent two years at Columbia University; and Morris Lapidus (born 1902), the postwar leader of Miami Beach architecture, who emigrated from Russia as a boy, moved to New York and graduated from Columbia University. The most educated in that group were German-born Richard Kiehnel (1870–1944), who studied at the University of Breslau and the Ecole Nationale des Beaux Arts in Paris before moving to Pittsburgh, and Igor Polevitzky (1911–1978), who was born in St. Petersburg, Russia, immigrated to New York City in 1922 and graduated in 1934 from the University of Pennsylvania, as a student of Paul Philippe Cret (1876–1945); there he met Thomas Triplett Russell, his partner from 1936 to 1945.

The authors' interviews with Lawrence Murray Dixon Jr. and with Thomas Triplett Russell corroborated that work was so intense between 1933 and 1942 that it left few opportunities for the architects to engage in any communal activities. Yet, even if time had allowed, the absence of an operational school of architecture or of a strong professional association impeded the development of a full-fledged academic culture in the Miami area. Local architects were left without any forum for expressing their ideas.[5] Thus, Miami Beach architects did primarily one thing: build. They did not lecture. They did not write for newspapers and journals. They did not draw visionary sketches. They did not elaborate descriptive *cahiers* of their works. They made simple and attractive renderings of their projects, but produced primarily technical drawings.

opposite:
Interior view of Lawrence Murray Dixon's office in the Seymour Building, 1640 Euclid Avenue, Miami Beach. Lawrence Murray Dixon, 1937. Photograph by Samuel H. Gottscho. © Doris Schleisner. Collection of the Bass Museum of Art. Gift of Richard B. Dixon.

1   This statement is quoted from a short typewritten and unpaginated manuscript conserved within the papers of Schultze & Weaver, Lloyd Morgan Architects in the Mitchell Wolfson Jr. Collection, The Wolfsonian-Florida International University. It was signed by Joseph Caponetto, an architect employee of the firm, who retained the archives in Brooklyn until his death.

2   For a similar discussion of the architects' background, see Richard Plunz, "Reading Bronx Housing, 1890–1940," *Building a Borough: Architecture and Planning in the Bronx, 1890–1940* (New York: The Bronx Museum of the Arts, 1986), 74.

3   All biographical data from: Barbara Capitman, *From Deco Delights: Preserving the Beauty and Joy of Miami Beach Architecture* (New York: E. P. Dutton, 1988); *Miami Beach Art Deco Guide* (Miami Beach: Miami Design Preservation League, 1987).

4   Lawrence Murray Dixon, Jr., interviews by authors at Dixon's home in Melbourne, Florida, June 1997, October 1999. Thomas Triplett Russell, interview by authors at Russell's home in Punta Gorda, Florida, February 1997.

5   In 1925, John Skinner became the first head of the Department of Architecture at the University of Miami in Coral Gables. Following the hurricane of 1926 and the Depression, the department was inactive from 1932 to 1945. The American Institute of Architects had a chapter in Miami, but it cannot be considered an academically active association at that time. The yearly *Florida Architecture and Allied Arts*, whose inaugural issue dates from 1935, was essentially a promotional picture-book, with projects succinctly presented in photographs. Dixon and Hohauser, for instance, were never featured in this publication that focused exclusively on the works of AIA members.

Photograph of Lawrence Murray Dixon. Photographer unknown. Courtesy of the City of Miami Beach.

There was a lack of interest in the architecture of the 1930s that lasted until the 1970s, which took a toll on historical and archival research. Most plans and drawings, either private or municipal, were lost or destroyed, leaving contemporary scholars with a dearth of material to unravel and investigate. Therefore, the weekly real estate columns in the local newspapers The *Miami Herald* and *Miami Daily News* — unsigned but often illustrated with beautiful renderings, now lost — the microfilms conserved at the Miami Beach City Hall, the works published in the national architecture periodicals and some magnificent photographic collections in museums, such as the Bass Museum of Art, constitute the only remaining sources for the history and interpretation of Miami Beach architecture.

This essay aims to present the compressed history of the making of Miami Beach between 1933 and 1942 through the prism of Lawrence Murray Dixon's career. There are three primary reasons for this decision. First, his archives, although incomplete, were the best preserved of all the architects active on Miami Beach before the war.[6] Second, Dixon was the most prolific Miami Beach designer during the 1930s and early 1940s, involved in all types of commercial and residential buildings

from the smallest house to the most lavish oceanfront hotel. In 1947, he wrote that "$11,123,000.00 in building construction has been erected from my architectural services," and officially listed "thirty-eight hotels, eighty-seven apartment buildings, two hundred twenty individual residences, two housing developments, thirty-three store buildings, thirty-one alterations and sixteen miscellaneous."[7]

Third, the works of Lawrence Murray Dixon, along with Henry Hohauser's, stand out "as the most important examples of how avant-garde modernist design was altered for the purpose of low-cost, concrete structures in the Moderne Style on Miami Beach."[8] Miami Beach's first chroniclers and pioneers of the historic preservation movement, the late Barbara Capitman at their helm, emphasized Henry Hohauser as the prime leader of Miami Beach architecture. They credited him with the importation of the "new" styles and viewed him as ascendant over other architects in the area. This unproven thesis has generally influenced other writers, thus unfairly diminishing the importance of Lawrence Murray Dixon. Indeed, like Hohauser, Dixon worked in New York City for some years and possessed first-hand knowledge of its art and architectural circles, a sure influence and advantage for his later career. More significantly, the chronological analysis of the years 1933–1942 through the municipal and press archives revealed that Dixon was in fact the most innovative architect of the period. Not only was he the first to design apartment hotel structures in the Art Deco style, but he also built the first New York-inspired hotel towers in the urban context. He pioneered local interpretation of modernist concepts like the roof terrace, the pilotis on street façades, and the double-height *maisonette* apartment. He introduced major asymmetry in the volumetric composition of his best beachfront hotels and triggered the typological development of the Mediterranean courtyard type.

Finally, Dixon's status as the Beach's leading architect was ascertained by the extensive publication of his works. His buildings were published sixteen times between 1935 and 1942 in leading national periodicals such as *Architectural Record, Architectural Forum, American Architect and Architecture* and *Pencil Points*, a record that no other Florida architect, with the exception of Igor Polevitzky and Thomas T. Russell, was able to match during that time.[9]

6   The biographical sources on Lawrence Murray Dixon are scarce but reliable. The first are the already mentioned interviews with Dixon's son, Lawrence M. Dixon Jr., also an architect. The second is the "Form for Senior Classification—Experience and Record in Professional Practice" filed by Dixon on June 4, 1947, at the National Accreditation Board in Washington. The archives consist of original photographs and about ninety drawings and renderings of unbuilt projects. All other drawings, particularly those documenting the built works, were destroyed in a flood.

7   "Form for Senior Classification (Experience and Record in Professional Practice)", 2.

8   Jennifer Frehling, *Henry Hohauser: Miami Beach Moderne 1935–1948* (master's thesis, University of Virginia, 1994), 47. Maria Lourdes Solera was the first to write about Dixon in her thesis, *Miami Beach During the Streamline Decade and Lawrence Murray Dixon* (master's thesis, University of Virginia, 1991). Both theses were written under the direction of Richard Guy Wilson.

9   Robert Law Weed also had the attention of the national press, whereas Hohauser, Anis and France, to name some of the best architects of the period, were never published nationally during that time.

1923–1933
From New York to Miami with Schultze & Weaver

Lawrence Murray Dixon was born on February 16, 1901 in Live Oak, Florida. His father was a dentist, and his mother was a schoolteacher in the local elementary school in this small town near Orlando. He attended the Technological High School in Atlanta, Georgia, and in 1918 entered the Georgia School of Technology. He left Atlanta in 1920 without completing a degree, and apparently started working in the Miami area shortly thereafter. Among other works, he surveyed the construction of the Country Club in Coral Gables (1922–24) for the architects Hampton and Reimbert. On a train ride headed to Atlanta from Miami, Lawrence Murray Dixon met the New York architect Leonard Schultze, who invited him to work for his firm Schultze & Weaver Architects. He thus moved to New York in 1923.

There, he continued his education with the goal of earning a professional license, a common practice for young architects who worked as apprentices and had not completed their degree. He finished two years of evening study in architectural design at the atelier of Lloyd Morgan. He completed one year of evening study in structural engineering at the office of H. G. Balcom, engineer, another year in mechanical and electrical engineering at the office of C. R. Place and six months in specifications under William Emerson. He became a licensed architect in the state of New York in January 1937 and in the District of Columbia two years later.[10]

The background of Schultze & Weaver was neo-classic and deeply rooted in the traditions established by the parent firm of Warren & Wetmore (1864-1943; 1867-1941), designers of Grand Central Station (1913) in New York. In that firm, Leonard Schultze (1887–1941) was responsible for the urban redevelopment of the station area, before he joined forces with engineer Spencer Fullerton Weaver (1865–1940) in 1921. Together they designed an impressive number of landmark buildings throughout the United States and the Caribbean, and they established themselves as the foremost hotel designers in the country.[11] In 1926 Lloyd Morgan (1892–1970), a graduate of the Ecole des Beaux-Arts in Paris, joined the firm; in 1928 he became a partner. The new chief

designer, a versatile and imaginative artist, planner, decorator and gifted renderer, helped "streamline" Schultze & Weaver's *beaux-arts* classical language, and was responsible for a pioneering change in stylistic expression. This fusion became apparent in the firm's masterpiece in Manhattan, the Waldorf-Astoria Hotel (1930-31), for which Morgan was the lead designer.[12] Its twin bronze-clad towers became landmarks of the Machine Age urban landscape of New York.

"For Schultze and Weaver," Joseph Caponetto wrote, "the preparation of sketches, working drawings and details became a fine art. Architecture was practiced as a comprehensive 'total design' concept, which included siting, engineering, the design of all items of interiors and furnishings in many cases not excluding the design of the tableware."[13] Lawrence Murray Dixon was strongly influenced by this vision of practicing architecture as a "total work of art," for during his entire career he followed the same principle. He and his office designed all elements of every project, particularly the oceanfront hotels, from the architectural and decorative details on the façades to the terrazzo floors, the hotel logos and, in some cases, the employees' uniforms.[14]

Lloyd Morgan's reputation as "maestro" and friend to his many students was also legendary. Although we know that Lawrence Murray Dixon was one of his apprentices, the extent of their relationship has remained unknown. Yet it seems clear that Morgan influenced Dixon and may have taught him the conceptual discipline to progressively detach himself from the picturesque of the Mediterranean style and embark upon the more rational Art Deco language.

During the 1920s boom, Schultze & Weaver built most of South Florida's grandest hotels in an exotic and spectacular Mediterranean style, including the Hotel Nautilus (1924) and the Roney Plaza Hotel in Miami Beach, the Biltmore in Coral Gables (1926), and the Breakers in Palm Beach (1927). In the absence of the office logs, the breadth of Lawrence Murray Dixon's responsibilities remains unknown. The only sure fact is that, between 1925 and 1927, he made frequent trips to Miami Beach in order to supervise the construction of the Roney Plaza Hotel and the Ingraham Building.[15] Dixon left Schultze & Weaver in 1929 and settled permanently in Miami with his wife Elizabeth, neé Golden, and their first son, Lawrence Jr. (1928).

---

10 Balcom was the structural engineer for the Waldorf-Astoria Hotel. The authors found no records of Dixon's activity in Washington DC.

11 On Schultze & Weaver in Miami, see Mark Ormond, *The Biltmore Revisited* (Coral Gables: Metropolitan Museum and Art Center, 1981). Also see Roberto Behar & Maurice Culot, eds., *Coral Gables: An American Garden City* (Paris: Norma, 1997).

12 Isabelle Gournay, "Leonard Schultze and S. Fullerton Weaver," *Dictionnaire de l'architecture du XXè siècle* (Paris: Hazan/Institut français d'architecture, 1996), 802.

13 From Joseph Caponetto, the introduction to *Schultze & Weaver, Lloyd Morgan Papers*. The Mitchell Wolfson Jr. Collection, The Wolfsonian-Florida International University.

14 From the interviews with Lawrence M. Dixon Jr.

15 From the interviews with Lawrence M. Dixon Jr. Schultze & Weaver also built the famous Sevilla-Biltmore Hotel on the Paseo del Prado in Havana (1925).

He went to work with George Fink (1891–1975), one of the architects who, along with developer George Merrick, planned and designed many public and private buildings for the garden city of Coral Gables.[16] Dixon further collaborated with Phineas Paist (1875–1937) and Harold Drake Steward (1896–1987), who were also involved in the construction of Coral Gables. With them he worked on designing and building the United States Post Office in downtown Miami. Occupying an entire block, with a monumental courtyard in its center, the Post Office was a neo-classical structure that presented solemn but conservative façades of oolitic limestone marked by a colossal order; it showed no influence of the Art Deco classical-modern style that was then in great demand to affirm the presence of the Federal Government across the country. Dixon's role in this project was undocumented, but it can be ascertained that Paist and Steward were the leading designers.[17]

At that time, Art Deco architecture had already appeared locally in commercial and public structures, and most of them were concentrated in the heart of downtown Miami. Built on the edge of the Miami River from 1922 to 1924 by Richard Kiehnel and John E. Elliott, the Scottish

top:
Roney Plaza Hotel, Twenty-third street elevation, Miami Beach. Schultze & Weaver Architects, 1925. Pen and ink on linen, 36 x 56." Courtesy of The Mitchell Wolfson Jr. Collection,
The Wolfsonian-Florida International University.

above:
The United States Post Office in downtown Miami, 300 N.E. 1st Avenue. Paist & Steward Architects with Lawrence Murray Dixon, 1928-31. Courtesy of the Romer Collection, Miami-Dade Public Library.

right:
The Scottish Rite Masonic Temple seen from the Miami River, Lummus Park, Downtown Miami. Kiehnel & Elliott Architects, 1922-24. Courtesy of the Romer Collection, Miami-Dade Public Library.

16 They had a second child, Richard. Elizabeth worked in Dixon's office as manager. She was an active participant in Miami Beach's social scene, and the president of the Miami Beach Woman's Club from 1949–1950. On Coral Gables, see note 11.

17 The conservative style of the building relates closely to such classical structures in Coral Gables as the Colonnade Hotel (1925) and the Coral Gables City Hall (1927), both designed by Paist & Steward.

Rite Masonic Temple was actually the first Art Deco building in the area. Topped by a concrete ziggurat-like roof, the Temple was inspired by John Russell Pope's (1874–1937) classical masterpiece, the Scottish Rite Temple in Washington, DC (1910), itself a powerful interpretation of the Mausoleum of Halicarnassus.[18]

Other local Art Deco buildings of note belonged to the period of the early 1930s. The Miami Sears Department Store (1930) was designed by Chicago architects Marsh and Saxelbye at the intersection of Biscayne Boulevard and the approach of the Collins Causeway. Its exterior walls, the prominent polygonal tower and the elegant interior with a grand staircase were adorned with various Art Deco carvings and bas-reliefs. Across the boulevard, Robert Law Weed's Shrine Temple Building (1930) featured bas-reliefs displaying Florida fauna and flora, and flat capitals representing stylized figures of Temple Knights. Nearby, Weed also built the Burdines department store, whose entry doors displayed Viennese-influenced abstract panels. On Miami Beach, Russell T. Pancoast was the architect for the municipal library (1930, now the Bass Museum of Art, see back cover), the first Deco building on the island.

In 1931, Lawrence Murray Dixon became a licensed architect in the State of Florida. That same year, he opened his own office in the Italian-Renaissance style Ingraham Building, another splendid work by Schultze & Weaver completed four years earlier, across from John Eberson's "atmospheric" Olympia Theatre on NE 2nd Avenue.

PART ONE:
HOTELS, APARTMENT HOTELS, AND COMMERCIAL STRUCTURES

1933–1935
The Last Waves of the Mediterranean Style

1933 was a pivotal year in the history of Miami Beach. Construction expenses doubled from the low figures of 1931 and 1932, and from that year on, a new boom took over, which reached its first peak in 1935. As Richard Kiehnel, president of the American Institute of Architects, wrote that year in *Florida Allied Arts and Architecture*, "prosperity is no longer just around the corner, but is actually facing us on all sides."[19] Yet, the new boom started on radical new ground. The indulgent manner of life in the twenties gave way to a more sensible, down-to-earth image in the thirties. The city consciously sought out its clientele from what was termed the "solid" middle class, by replacing land speculation with tourism. Rather than having a handful of grand and elegant hotels such as the Flamingo, the Roney Plaza or the Floridian, Miami Beach offered scores of more modest structures: "an egalitarian image was projected in publicity and official statements to help encourage the broadening of the social status of the Beach."[20] The "reconstruction" of the economy was fueled by the Federal Government, which instituted major programs like the Reconstruction Finance Corporation for low-cost housing and slum clearances, the Federal Housing Administration to stimulate private investment in building operations by insuring mortgages, and the Federal Home Loan Banking System.

Architecturally, 1933 was the year of the Century of Progress Exhibition on the Chicago waterfront. Although the Florida Pavilion was a banal and awkward product of the Mediterranean school, Robert Law Weed's Florida Tropical Home (p. 49) made a strong impression on architectural critics who praised it for its modern and careful adaptation to the Florida environment. "The stagnation of building during the depression years of the early thirties...provided opportunity for some self appraisal as well as a close, analytical look at the area's architectural trends. Money and building materials were scarce. It was clear that some architectural change was necessary."[21]

That year, in the midst of Miami Beach's building resurgence and the country's growing infatuation with the machine aesthetic, Lawrence

18 Steven McLeod Bedford, *John Russell Pope, Architect of Empire* (New York: Rizzoli, 1998). Also see *Miami Herald* 13 March 1924.

19 Richard Kiehnel, "Past, Present & Future Building Conditions of Metropolitan Miami," *Florida Architecture and Allied Arts* (1935), unpaginated.

20 Arlene Olson, "Building to Weather the Depression Decade: Miami Beach 1933–1941," *Southeastern College of Art Conference Review* (1977), 171.

21 Kiehnel.

Murray Dixon moved his office from downtown Miami to Miami Beach at 530 Michigan Avenue. Designed in 1933, the Ester Apartments was his first building of record on the island (p. 75). The Ester was made up of two white "boxes" mirroring each other across a central courtyard, enclosed at the back by a small pedestrian gate. Dixon marked the angles of the buildings with oversized quoins and emphasized the ground-floor windows with slightly protruding frames and small windows protected by iron screens. Projecting balconies over the entrances were simply detailed, and the architect accentuated the horizontality with a continuous water table molding and a horizontal trim on the second level sill. The whole composition, the squarer proportions of the windows and their metallic frames, gave the Ester — and what immediately followed — a hybrid "transitional" appearance. The only genuine remaining stylistic link to the Spanish-Mediterranean of the 1920s was the exposed barrel tiles roof and fascia; a year later Dixon built the first modern structure on Ocean Drive, the Ocean Front Apartments (1934, p. 75). It was typologically and compositionally identical to the Ester with its courtyard and the two symmetrical façades fronting the street. But it displayed a third story, detached from the flat wall with a horizontal trim and designed like an attic with decorated panels between windows. The classical angle quoins and the three medallions on top of the second floor reflected the resilience of traditional decorative elements within the process of increasing abstraction.

With the Royal Arms (1934, p. 74) and particularly the Sadelle Apartments (1935), Dixon went one step further in his process of simplifying the volumes and the ornamentation of his buildings. He eliminated all emphasis on the corners, and reduced the importance of or removed all façade lines and other decorative elements. The Sadelle formed a U-shaped courtyard, with five separate individualized entrances; the center one was trimmed with vitrolite glass and native Florida stone surmounted by a terrace; the others were trimmed in colored tile. Two large projecting corner balconies, Bauhaus-inspired but adorned with Deco metallic guardrails, broke the symmetry of the façade wings for the first time. Although it was still covered with a tiled roof, the central section of the building incorporated the first roof terrace on Miami Beach. Dixon also built the first flat roof on a residential building, the Akers Apartments on 42nd Street.

The rebirth of Miami Beach, or rather its re-making as it "was not quite far enough developed at the time of the boom," was attentively followed by the daily press.[22] On March 17, 1935, a *Miami Herald* advertisement prominently featured a new Miami Beach building.

above:
The Sadelle Apartments, 431 15th Street, Miami Beach. Lawrence Murray Dixon, 1935. Photograph by Moser & Son. Collection of the Bass Museum of Art. Gift of Richard B. Dixon.

right:
The Akers Apartments, 330 42nd Street, Miami Beach. Lawrence Murray Dixon, 1935. Photograph by Moser & Son. Gift of Lawrence M. Dixon Jr.

22 Kiehnel.

Along with it were photographs of the architect, Dixon, the builder and the developer. Under the headline "Thoroughly modern in every respect," the *Miami Herald* summarized the new entrepreneurial and propagandistic spirit that attempted to ignite the developers' market:

"This luxurious apartment house, when completed, will offer the ideal living accommodations in the garden spot of the world. The building is being rushed to completion and in a very short while splendid apartments, beautifully decorated in every detail, will be available. The location is superb, situated between America's finest bathing beach and beautiful Flamingo Park. Here are combined advantages of modern luxury with health and recreation facilities right at its very door, yet only a few minutes from everything worthwhile in Greater Miami. Each unit will be completely and luxuriously furnished, including electric refrigeration, maid's quarters, garages, gas appliances for cooking and cozy fireplaces. Everything you want in a smart, modern, comfortable and desirably located apartment will be soon available at the new Florence Villa."[23]

1935–1936
Dixon's First Series of Art Deco Works

During the years 1935–1936, Lawrence Murray Dixon established himself as the most progressive architect on Miami Beach. His commissions were the most important and the most visible, many of them located on the city's trademark façades, Ocean Drive and Collins Avenue. Soon he became increasingly active in designing larger hotels. One can assume that programmatically this building type allowed him to take bolder steps toward simplification and modernity in design. It is important to note that this evolutionary process must be deducted "in situ," as there is no written or documentary information that substantiates a precise design trajectory or philosophy. Yet, it is undeniable that the greater exposure offered by beachfront hotel projects allowed him to experiment more freely.

During those two productive years, both in built and unbuilt works, Dixon's architecture took a radical turn toward a genuine Art Deco style, marked by flat roofs, the incorporation of large roof terraces, the use of glass bricks and a geometric decoration pattern. He broke away from all Mediterranean ties, but remained conscious of *beaux-arts* principles of balance and symmetry. Moreover, when his buildings were set free from the strict alignment of the city streets, or when he worked with larger structures on L-shaped or corner sites, he started to experiment with volumetrically more elaborate structures, asymmetrical façades and roof-top compositions reminiscent of post-1917 Russian Constructivism.

A series of hotels exemplified this new design attitude: the Empire (1935), the Beach Plaza (1936), the President (1936), the Fairmount (1936) and the Grand Plaza (1936). The smallest, the Empire Hotel at 750 Collins Avenue (1935) was his first abstract Deco structure, with a classically proportioned square façade divided in three sections by thin stucco pilasters. It displayed a powerful trabeated porch and the first example of modernist-inspired pilotis on Miami Beach. Pilotis were one of the "Five Points of Modern Architecture" dictated by Le Corbusier in his manifesto of 1926 and that he employed with great effect in the Villa Savoye (Paris, 1928-31) and other French suburban houses. The modernist concept of lifting the building to liberate the ground-floor plane was fundamentally anti-urban and followed CIAM's objective of "the end of the street" as enclosed space. Yet, as in Tel Aviv, Dixon and other Miami Beach architects adapted the concept to the needs of the urban realm and made it a successful ingredient in the streets' fabric.[24] Theirs was a reinterpretation of the Mediterranean arcade or of the traditional American porch of the South, brought as close to the street as the building code would permit. Whereas the Empire Hotel fronted Collins without attempting to make the corner architectonically special (the same situation could be observed at the President), the Beach Plaza's pilotis wrapped around the corner, creating a free-flowing space that increased the horizontality and the openness of the urban space (p. 96-97). Its façade displayed another strong compositional feature with its four-bay structure developed around the proportions of the Golden Section. The Empire's, the Beach Plaza's and the Fairmont's (p. 94-95) entrance lobbies were elegant rooms with beautiful terrazzo floors, staircases and reception desks, all designed in Dixon's office.

Equally spectacular was the Grand Plaza along the Ocean Creek canal. Its symmetrical entrance façade was quite articulate and plastic. Dixon used thin overlapping planes to create abstract patterns over its surface. Decorated panels of coral stone intersecting a long, triple eyebrow created a dynamic portico over the three entry doors, while a thrusting vertical section defined by four pilasters and honeycomb panels balanced the horizontal lines of the lower section of the façade. The hotel had a contrasting neoclassic lobby, a solarium and roof terrace; according to the architect, the Grand Plaza "was patterned after hotels in Cairo and resorts at the Lido and Biarritz, France."[25]

24   The five points included: the pilotis, the free plan, the free façade, the ribbon windows and the roof terrace. On CIAM and a comparison between Miami Beach and Tel Aviv, see author's essay "The Other Modern: Between the Machine and the Mediterranean."

25   "Grand Plaza, Overlooking Indian Creek and Ocean Beach, is Modern Structure," *Miami Herald*, 29 December 1935.

23   "Thoroughly Modern in Every Respect," *Miami Herald*, 17 March 1935.

The Empire Hotel, 750 Collins Avenue, Miami Beach. Lawrence Murray Dixon, 1935. Photograph by Samuel H. Gottscho. © Doris Schleisner. Collection of the Bass Museum of Art. Gift of Lawrence M. Dixon Jr.

The Grand Plaza Hotel, 3025 Indian Creek Drive, Miami Beach. Lawrence Murray Dixon, 1935. Photograph by Samuel H. Gottscho. © Doris Schleisner. Collection of the Bass Museum of Art. Gift of Lawrence M. Dixon Jr.

In 1935, Dixon completed the private Coburn School, built on a waterfront site in the undeveloped districts to the north of Normandy Isle. The two-story seasonal country day school was "planned according to a European modernistic design."[26] At first, the client intended "to do the building in the usual Mediterranean manner," but by using a flat roof the architect made it possible "to add a great deal of classroom space at no additional cost."[27] The contrast between the published *beaux-arts* plans and the modern, slightly asymmetrical elevations with their long horizontal metallic windows and the simple railing delineating the roof terrace was a striking feature. It can be assumed that the traditional school program dictated the final hybrid solution, perhaps preventing

Dixon from experimenting with a freer plan. The school was given national attention in a special issue of *Architectural Forum* that featured modern schools in Mexico by José V. Garcia and Enrique de la Mora and in California by Richard J. Neutra, along with more traditional projects. William Lescaze, who was represented by his International Style Ansonia project, wrote: "We must decide first what qualities modern education should develop. If they are to be truthfulness, courage, freedom, adaptability, intelligence — then we have automatically decided that what we require is the thinking, planning, functional method of building. We have decided for good modern architecture."[28]

Dixon's presence in the national press continued in 1936, with the publication in the November issue of *American Architect and Architecture* of two apartment complexes, the Pinecrest Apartments and the Forde Ocean Apartments. The projects could not be more different in type and urban conditions, but both displayed similar interior spaces of great volumetric quality. Located outside of the gridded section of Miami Beach, the Pinecrest (p. 84-86) was an urban L-shape type, containing ten apartments, one of which was a duplex. Plans for the Pinecrest were quite elaborate, as the architect abandoned the central corridor, still very

26 "Coburn School Will Erect Structure in Bay Drive, Normandy Isle," *Miami Herald*, 12 May 1935.

27 "Coburn Country Day School, Miami Beach, Florida," *Architectural Record* (June 1936): 469.

28 William Lescaze, "The Functional Approach to School Planning," *Architectural Forum* (June 1936): 481-2.

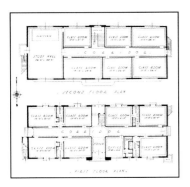

above:
Street façade of the Coburn Country Day School, Rue Versailles, Normandy Isle. Lawrence Murray Dixon, 1935. Photograph by Samuel H. Gottscho. From *Architectural Record* (June 1936): 470.

left:
Plans for the Coburn Country Day School, Rue Versailles, Normandy Isle. Lawrence Murray Dixon, 1935. Photograph by Samuel H. Gottscho. From *Architectural Record* (June 1936): 470.

Interior duplex at the Pinecrest Apartments, 24th Street and Pinetree Drive, Miami Beach. Lawrence Murray Dixon, 1935–36. Photograph by Samuel H. Gottscho. © Doris Schleisner. Collection of the Bass Museum of Art. Gift of Richard B. Dixon.

common in those years, to develop singular apartments with an individual sense of entry and place. The *Miami Herald* took notice, with an article headlined appropriately, "Apartment Building Offers Innovations."[29] The Forde Ocean complex (p. 87-89), on a deep lot facing the ocean on Collins Avenue, appeared like a small village, with its own interior access alley. The *American Architect* praised its "wide variety of layout achieved by the isolated maisonette and the second floor duplex, in addition to the eight other apartments."[30] The maisonette-type apartment used in both buildings was inspired by the Parisian interiors of Robert Mallet-Stevens and Le Corbusier, and had been used to great effect by Robert Law Weed in the Florida Tropical Home in Chicago (1933).[31] Modernist details such as nautical-type railings and staircases abounded, but the architect introduced interesting vernacular elements such as the cypress ceiling that distinguished its spatial atmosphere from European or North American counterparts.

The architectural massing and composition of the Pinecrest Apartments were a major achievement in Dixon's search for a modern tropical image. The double-height windows in the duplex apartment, the two staircase towers leading to the roof terrace with their wide and vertical strips of glass blocks, and the second-floor terrace overlooking the garden court gave specific distinction to the building. Dixon reused some of these elements, mixed with keystone panels, in the Lincoln Apartments at 12th and Pennsylvania, a later work of 1939 (p. 41). On the other hand, the Forde Ocean Apartments was an interesting but somewhat awkward experiment in developing a more abstract language. It is somewhat unfortunate that Dixon did not or could not simplify his language

29 "Two Apartments, Miami Beach, Florida," *American Architect and Architecture* (November 1936): 62-65. "Apartment Building Offers Innovations: New Two-Story Structure Is On Pine Tree Drive, Miami Beach," *Miami Herald,* 19 January 1936.

30 "Two Apartments, Miami Beach, Florida," *American Architect and Architecture,* 65.

31 The Pinecrest Apartments were unfortunately destroyed in the 1970s.

language further: the whole ensemble suffered from an excess of ornamental details that was not consistent with the somewhat Loosian purity
of his volumes. The closer Dixon came to the theses of the International
Style — for instance the maisonette facing the ocean — the more his
ornamental system appeared disconnected and superfluous.

1935–1936
Creating a Skyline on the Ocean

Dixon's grand *oeuvre* of this period, the Atlantis Hotel, was designed in
1935 and completed in March of 1936. Facing the ocean between 26th
and 27th Streets on Collins Avenue, it was the first large-scale Art Deco
hotel in the city (p. 76-83). The Atlantis was deeply set back from the
street and accessed through a long entry court lined with palm trees;
the back façade came up to the paved boardwalk along the beach,
creating an attractive oceanfront environment. Built of steel, concrete
masonry and stucco, the eight-story structure was topped off by a three-
room penthouse tower and a roof garden.[32] Its contrasting façades were
noteworthy and interestingly composed. The street elevation was
slightly asymmetrical and had a square, classical-modern porticoed
entrance. Four hollow piers of quarried keystone, surrounded by vege-
tal-themed Deco panels, created the elegant and deep-shaded entry.
Dixon's compositional skills can be appreciated by the manner in which
he artificially reduced the mass of the two central columns by grooving
them vertically. In contrast to that classical rigor, he defined the façade
above the portico with four colossal pilasters, six stories high and
capped by capitals that looked like electric condensers. The L-shaped
rear façade was just as playful and full of invention. Instead of stone
panels, Dixon used black vitrolite in a pattern that mimicked the plan of
the hotel (p. 73). The whole ensemble, which, unfortunately, was demolished in the 1970s, was somewhat awkward, yet pleasant and witty, as if
the architect intended to demonstrate that the exercise should not be
taken too seriously.

Dixon made good use of the Atlantis' tight L-shaped plan.
Behind the four piers he designed a "transparent" lobby opening onto
the ocean view. Four tall circular pillars, located at its center and reflecting the deep blue of the ocean, supported a twenty-foot-high ceiling finished in silver leaf. They also established a cross axis leading to the
lounge, three steps down and likewise defined by four pillars, square
this time. The visual interaction of these two grand rooms along the

The Atlantis Hotel, 26th Street and Collins Avenue, Miami Beach. Lawrence Murray Dixon,
1935-36. Photograph by Samuel Gottscho. Collection of the Bass Museum of Art. Gift of
Lawrence Murray Dixon Jr.

allée of columns created a powerful and scenographic perspective,
admirably photographed by Samuel H. Gottscho and lyrically praised by
the *Miami Herald*:

"From its massive pillared lobby and lounge, which span the
ground floor from the street entrance to the ocean front, to its spacious
sun lounge on the eighth floor, the structure emulates the massive
beauty of the marble halls which reputedly graced the Atlantis shores
in that long dead age when beauty and culture linked hands in a life
of Elysian leisure."[33]

On the other side of the lobby, the hotel commanded a modern bar,
surrounded by a double glassbrick wall, whose floor was of black terrazzo with inlaid metal designs. Next to the bar was the grand dining
room, opening onto the beach through four diamond-shaped bow windows — a trademark design that Dixon repeated on the front façade of
the Tides Hotel (1936) and on the rear one at the Raleigh Hotel (1941).

A couple of weeks later, construction was completed on the Tides
Hotel, at ten stories high the tallest building on Ocean Drive until the
1980s. *Architectural Forum* described the building as "a good example
of the prevailing style trend in Florida as applied to the numerous establishments of this sort which have been erected for tourists. The night
view shows a simple mass, adequate fenestration, and a characteristically
imposing entrance. It will be noted…that the 'modernistic' touches

32 "Construction Starts on Nine-Story Atlantis Hotel on Ocean Front Plot in Miami
Beach," *Miami Herald*, 19 May 1935.

33 "The Atlantis, Distinctive Miami Beach Hostelry, Opens Doors Today — Eight Story
Edifice Embodies Advances," *Miami Herald*, 19 January 1936.

L. MURRAY DIXON
ARCHITECT

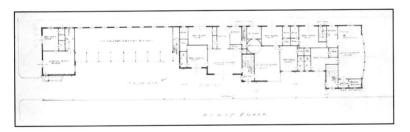

above:
Project for Hotel Evans, Collins Avenue, Miami Beach. Lawrence Murray Dixon, c. 1936. Perspective, pencil and ink on tracing paper, 15 x 28". Collection of the Bass Museum of Art. Gift of Richard B. Dixon.

top left:
Project for Hotel Evans, Collins Avenue, Miami Beach. Lawrence Murray Dixon, 1936. First floor plan, pencil on tracing paper, 18 x 30". Collection of the Bass Museum of Art. Gift of Richard B. Dixon.

bottom left:
Project for a hotel, Collins Avenue, Miami Beach. Lawrence Murray Dixon, c. 1935–36. Perspective, pencil on tracing paper, 18 x 30". Collection of the Bass Museum of Art. Gift of Richard B. Dixon.

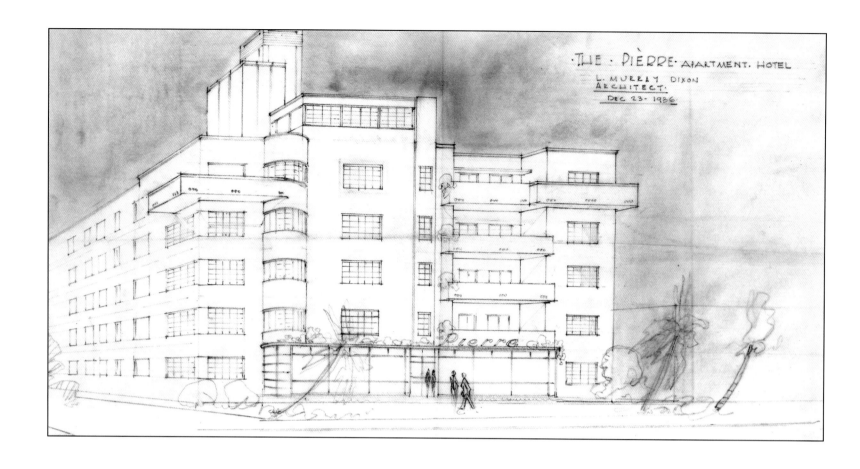

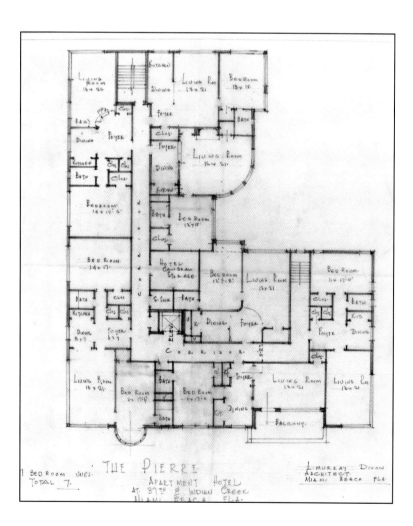

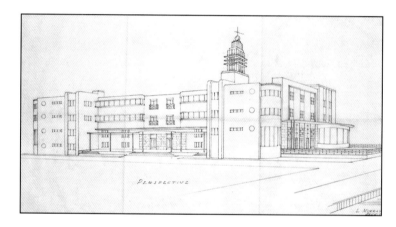

top:
Project for the Pierre Hotel, 3737 Indian Creek Drive, Miami Beach. Lawrence Murray Dixon, c. 1936. Perspective, pen and ink on tracing paper. Collection of the Bass Museum of Art. Gift of Lawrence M. Dixon Jr.

left:
Project for the Pierre Hotel, 3737 Indian Creek Drive, Miami Beach. Lawrence Murray Dixon, c. 1936. Plan, pen and ink on tracing paper. Collection of the Bass Museum of Art. Gift of Lawrence M. Dixon Jr.

above:
Project for a hotel, Collins Avenue, Miami Beach. Lawrence Murray Dixon, c. 1936. Perspective, pencil on tracing paper. Collection of the Bass Museum of Art. Gift of Lawrence M. Dixon Jr.

right page:
Project for an Apartment and Hotel Building, 15th Street and Ocean Drive, Miami Beach. Lawrence Murray Dixon, c. 1936. Pen and ink on tracing paper. Collection of the Bass Museum of Art. Gift of Lawrence M. Dixon Jr.

to be found in most recent Florida work are by no means absent here: they have been definitely subordinated, however, to the well organized general design."[34]

The composition of the façade was at once simplified and more urban than the Atlantis, as if the direct relation to Ocean Drive and the busy sidewalk had enticed Dixon to tame his design. The fifty-foot set-back and the wide staircase facing the street gave the building a public presence and made its height less conspicuous in relation to the adjacent lower structures. Like the Atlantis, the square and deep entrance portico of the Tides was a remarkable example of the classical-modern style, characteristic of what Franco Borsi called "The Monumental Era" and whose spirit fecundated the works of Paul Philippe Cret, John Russell Pope or Gordon B. Kaufmann in California.[35] Particularly interesting was the treatment of the mezzanine floor immediately above the portico, where Dixon projected a wide eyebrow underlining the entrance and its graphic logo. Inside, the lobby and lounge repeated the disposition of the Atlantis, creating a cross-axis made up of modern circular columns. The effect was as spectacular but somewhat less theatrical.

Although most of Dixon's original drawings and plans were lost, a series of sketches survived, documenting unbuilt structures of the years 1935 to 1936. They demonstrate the extent of the architect's ability to experiment outside of the classical composition methods and within an increasingly modern idiom. The perspective of the proposed Pierre Hotel featured a five-story street corner building, with recessed balconies, projecting circular bay windows and boldly cantilevered concrete balconies in the modernist mode. Another sketch (p. 173) showed an unnamed hotel structure, with a powerful front façade topped by an imposing square tower. Both front and side façades were designed with multiple projecting and recessed planes that would have created an unusually dynamic impact on the street corner. A subtle color drawing, not dated but probably of 1936 (p. 154), showed the façade of a ten-story building, somewhat similar to the Tides, but with a recessed central section and a fully commercial ground floor. Also promising were the two long structures — one titled the Evans Hotel (p. 173), the other unnamed — to be built probably between Collins Avenue and the ocean. Finally, Dixon's proposal for a double-tower hotel (on the model of the Tides) would have been the appropriate northern termination of Ocean Drive, bringing a unique focus to the city's blooming skyline.[36]

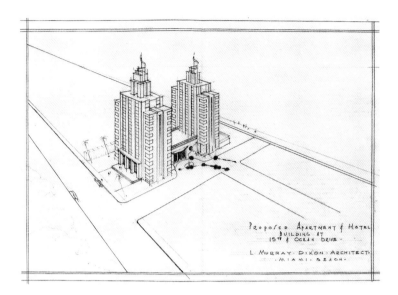

The "Others" in 1935 and 1936

Although Dixon was the local forerunner of modern design in 1935 and 1936, the "competition" was catching up and threatened his stature from 1937 onwards. Other architects were aggressively entering the scene, including Robert E. Collins, Martin L. Hampton, Roy F. France, Anton Skislewicz, Richard Kiehnel and Henry Hohauser. Born and trained in New York, Hohauser worked for a few firms before spending the war in Europe as an architect in the army. Upon his return, he practiced in the office of his cousin, William Hohauser, whose work in New York had been exhibited in a skyscraper exhibition in 1926 and who built two apartment buildings in the Bronx Deco district of the Grand Concourse. Then, in 1932, he moved to Miami, a decision made for health-related reasons.[37]

The commercial album that Hohauser published privately in 1939 revealed that he was a prolific and eclectic architect, "unafraid of experimenting with ornamentation and uninterested in any moral arguments made by modernists."[38] He built about 250 apartment buildings, hotels, stores, synagogues and private homes. Contrary to Dixon, he kept shifting between styles throughout the decade of the 1930s, with the balance tending toward relatively traditional design.

34 "The Tides Hotel, Miami Beach," *Architectural Forum* (December 1938), 452-453.

35 Franco Borsi, *The Monumental Era* (New York: Rizzoli, 1985).

36 Only two drawings have a date, but the style of drawings and the consistency of language suggests that they belong to the same 1935–1936 period.

37 For William Hohauser, see Robert A. M. Stern, Gregory Gilmarting and Thomas Mellin, *New York 1930: Architecture and Urbanism Between the Two World Wars* (New York: Rizzoli, 1987).

38 Frehling, 7. See also Henry Hohauser, *Architecture: Selections from the Works of Henry Hohauser* (Miami: 1939).

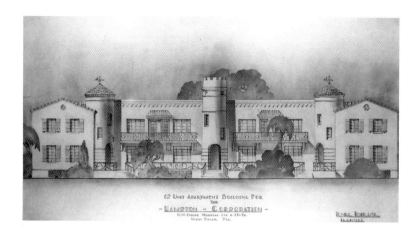

top:
Castle Apartments, Miami Beach. Henry Hohauser, 1935. Rendering. Courtesy of the Romer Collection, Miami-Dade Public Library.

above left:
Beacon Hotel, 720 Ocean Drive, Miami Beach. Harry O. Nelson, 1936. Rendering. From *The Miami Herald*, 19 July 1936.

above right:
Tower Apartments, 6061 Collins Aveune, Miami Beach. Only half of the hotel was built. Martin L. Hampton, 1935. Rendering. From *The Miami Herald*, 27 October 1935.

Evidence of his versatile skills could be admired in the idiosyncratic Mediterranean-modern Edison Hotel (1935, p. 53), the Grandola Apartments along Española Way and the "Old castle on the Rhine," an elegant turreted structure at Meridian and 10th Street.[39] The residential Park Vendôme (1936) had the most genuinely Caribbean courtyard in Miami Beach, a four-sided gallery with wooden balconies and outdoor staircases. Yet, Hohauser's name was quickly associated with some of the most progressive realizations on Ocean Drive and Collins Avenue. The Colony (1934, p. 56) on Ocean Drive can be credited as the first Streamlined design on Miami Beach. The ascending thrust of the vertical central fin supporting the modernistic neon typeface abruptly interrupted by the two bands of windows, whose horizontal effect was reinforced by the projecting eyebrows and the wrapping of the glass surface around the corner with the side alley. The Congress Hotel, built the next year on Ocean Drive, was an interesting variation on the same theme, where Hohauser achieved a similar balance between International Style horizontality and Deco's vertical accents.

Developments along Ocean Drive, Collins Avenue and Washington Avenue were in full swing, with noteworthy buildings like the Astor (T. Hunter Henderson, 1936, p. 178), the Beacon (Harry Nelson, 1936), the Deco Cavalier (Roy F. France, 1936), and the Lafayette (Henry J. Maloney, 1936). Other important works included two mid-rise stripped-down classical structures on Collins Avenue and Ocean Drive, respectively the Alamac Hotel (V. H. Nellenbogen, 1935) and the Netherlands Hotel (E. L. Robertson, 1935–1936). Every week, new buildings were praised for their "advanced," or "modern," design, as the local press clearly understood that the new architecture was becoming a marketing tool for the growing tourist industry. Streets were being built and rebuilt, changing styles and character in a frenzy of "modernization." A record was set by Martin L. Hampton's Tower Hotel. From the beginning of the excavation to occupancy only seventy days elapsed.[40] The hotel was first discussed on October 11; the plot was bought; plans were prepared; and excavation commenced on October 20. In spite of some delay caused by a hurricane, the job was completed two weeks ahead of the scheduled date of January 15. Made of steel and concrete, the building formed the first half of what was to be a 400-room hotel in genuine New York garb. The second half of the project, visible in the beautiful rendering, was unfortunately never built.

From 1935 onward, developer Carl Fisher's dream to see Lincoln Road transformed into the "Fifth Avenue of the South" was well

39   "Old Castle on the Rhine," *Miami Herald*, 23 June 1935.

40   "Apartment Hotel, Miami Beach, Florida," *Architectural Forum* (September 1936): 217.

underway. Lincoln Road was one of the widest thoroughfares in the city and its large sidewalks were planted with royal palms, making it the most attractive in the city. Party-wall buildings with no setbacks made for increased density and active urban life. The first significant change was the construction of the Lincoln Theater (1935–1936) and its mirror image across Drexel Street, the seven-story Lincoln Road Office Building (1936). Robert E. Collins, one of the most talented architects active on Miami Beach, is better known for his Deco masterpiece, the Helen Mar (p. 153), anchored like a ship at the edge of the Indian Creek canal, with its daringly projecting concrete balconies with metallic railings, remotely inspired by Gropius's Bauhaus in Dessau, Germany. The penthouse floor contained one of the most lavish apartments on the entire island, with fifteen-foot high coffered ceilings in the genuine Parisian Art Deco manner. The Lincoln Theatre and Office Building formed a well-conceived ensemble of architecture and urban design. The two curved buildings responded smoothly to each other across the narrow side street in a manner that Erich Mendelsohn had successfully experimented with in Berlin. The Lincoln Theatre itself was designed in collaboration with New Yorker Thomas White Lamb (1870–1942), one of the leaders of American theater architecture. It was an excellent structure, marked by a stretched elliptical lobby and a modern vaulted theater hall, whose painted walls recalled Joseph Urban's pioneering Paramount Theatre in Palm Beach (1927).[41]

Two other important commercial structures opened on Lincoln Road in 1935. The new Burdines department store displayed a simple streamlined façade, curved at the corner to flow with Jefferson Street. Robert Law Weed was the architect, and once again, he innovated by simplifying the esthetic and eliminating almost all external ornamentation. The interior was built on two levels around a large atrium, the first of its kind in the city. Just to the west, Richard Kiehnel designed a multiuse store for the Nunally Company (p. 55). The building was noticeable for its forecourt at the center of the façade on Lincoln Road, which provided space for an outdoor terrace since local ordinances did not permit serving on the sidewalk. The rear section had a large patio with terrazzo floors of modern design, an ornate orchestra shell and a double-deck loggia. The architect commented:

"I feel the owners have shown excellent taste, as well as good business judgment, in selecting this latest type of architecture, which may be said to be strictly functional and ultra-modern, in preference to the so-called modern Spanish type which has been widely used in this area…

Lincoln Theatre, Lincoln Road façade, Miami Beach, with first floor plan and second floor plan. Robert E. Collins, 1935. Photograph by Samuel H. Gottscho. From *American Architect* (July 1936): 47.

41 For a history of theaters in Florida, see Michael D. Kinerk and Dennis W. Wilhelm, "Dream Palaces: The Motion Picture Playhouse in the Sunshine State," *Journal of Decorative and Propaganda Arts* 23 (1998): 208-237. On Joseph Urban, see Randolph Carter and Robert Reed Cole, *Joseph Urban: Architecture-Theatre-Opera-Film* (New York: Abbeville Press, 1992).

The Astor Hotel, Washington Avenue and 10th Street, Miami Beach. T. Hunter Henderson, 1936. Courtesy of the Romer Collection, Miami-Dade Public Library.

Ford Florida Exhibition Building in Bayfront Park downtown Miami. Walter E. Teague, 1937. From *American Architect and Architecture* (March 1937): 83.

Modern business demands modern architecture. In order to make this architecture particularly attractive it was decided to use a number of richly colored marbles and the beautiful Florida quarried keystone on the exterior."[42]

1937–1939
The Streamlined Years

In 1937, the spirit of the 1933-34 Chicago World's Fair and its accompanying commercial hoopla could be seen in Miami's Bayfront Park. Designed by industrial designer Walter Dorwin Teague, the Ford Florida Exhibition Building formed a temporary U-shaped hall, laid out around a tropical patio. This "merchandising medium" had to "look permanent" and "express the dignity of industry and at the same time appear festive."[43] The Exhibition marked the entry of the new industrial design and the associated streamlined products and shapes in South Florida. Concurrently, the more traditional Art Deco forms started to subside and the streamlined image imposed itself.

Lawrence Murray Dixon's first attempt at the Streamlined Modern style was a "coup de maître" and one of the most spectacular on Miami

Beach. The setting was Lincoln Road, where he designed the Seymour Building, a one-story corner structure also known as Goldwasser's Shops (p. 102-3). Its flat and undecorated white walls recalled Weed's Burdines department store two blocks down the road, but its curved corner, in the form of a half cloverleaf, was built entirely out of large curved panes of glass. This modernist corner was the first of its type in Miami, and brought to mind Jan Pieter Oud's works in the Kiefhoek district of Rotterdam (1924). Along the Euclid Avenue façade, Dixon built a twenty-five-foot-wide symmetrical storefront, where he moved his offices in 1937 (p. 237).

The Victor (1937, p. 98-101), one block south of the Tides on Ocean Drive, was radically different from its predecessor. Its street corner site induced the architect to design a thin asymmetrical slab, fifty-feet wide and rising eight floors. The massing echoed International Style architecture, but here Dixon was not as successful at articulating the two façades. Instead of connecting them with wrap-around windows — as Hohauser had successfully done at the Colony and later at the Greystone — he dissociated them, thus creating a strong, yet hybrid-looking building. The two-story-high lobby was, on the other hand, one of his best interior spaces, with elegant railings and exquisite frescoes. The Adams Hotel, built in 1938 (p. 105), was another large Deco-style building that integrated streamlined elements. It was the first multi-story

42 "Plans are Completed by Nunally Company for $200,000 Store Building: Construction Will Start At Once," *Miami Herald*, 2 June 1935.

43 "Ford Florida Exhibition Building," *American Architect and Architecture* (March 1937): 83-84.

Lake Drive Apartments, Flamingo Drive, Miami Beach. Lawrence Murray Dixon, 1937. Photograph by Samuel H. Gottscho. From *Architectural Record* (October 1937): 132. © *Architectural Record*.

Courtyard of the Lincoln Center on Lincoln Road, Miami Beach. Polevitzky & Russell Architects, 1937. Photograph by Samuel H. Gottscho. Courtesy of the Historical Museum of Southern Florida.

structure, along with Hohauser's Essex Hotel (1938, p. 181), to feature a curved façade as compositional center symmetrically composed about the diagonal. The main element of asymmetry was created by a powerful elevator tower giving access to the roof terrace and topped by a fluted lantern. The Lake Drive Apartments (1937), published in *Architectural Record*, was a relatively banal example of Dixon's vernacular of those years, but it displayed particular details of construction that adapted well to the issues of local climate and regional character, and anticipated the postwar era. In particular, it featured cornice soffits open to admit air under the roof and thus lessen the intensity of the summer heat.[44]

The increasing versatility of South Florida's architects and the range of their commissions in the making of Miami Beach was reflected widely in the national architectural press. The September 1937 issue of the architectural magazine *Pencil Points* contained an interesting essay by the Boston architect Maurice Feather. He praised the modern construction techniques, well adapted to resist hurricanes due to the extensive use of concrete, and made important comments on the vernacular-modern architecture of the period:

"In Florida one is not sensible of the struggle between the traditional and the modern method of design. Examples of each style seem to exist side by side, if not in complete harmony, at least without the jarring dissonance, which such juxtaposition would produce in the

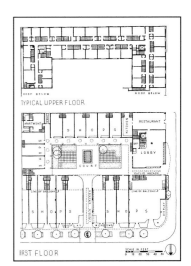

Ground floor plan and upper floor plan, Lincoln Center, Miami Beach. Polevitzky & Russell Architects, 1937. From *Architectural Forum* (December 1938): 451.

North. After a time, whether stylist or modernist, one acquires an impartial attitude in the matter, explainable perhaps from the fact that whatever the form of style of the exterior covering, the structural core is substantially the same and receives its outer skin in the modern or traditional manner with equal propriety."[45]

Periodicals ran numerous advertising pages highlighting the modernity of construction techniques in Miami Beach, like architectural concrete, flat roof sealing materials, and the burgeoning industry of year-long

44   "Lake Drive Apartments, Miami Beach, Florida," *Architectural Record* (March 1938): 486.

45   Maurice Feather, "Some Observations on Building in Florida," *Pencil Points* 18 (July-December 1937): 618.

Advertisement with Seymour Building and Tides Hotel as illustrations. From *Architectural Record* (July 1939): 17.

Advertisement for freon in air conditioners, with Lincoln Theater as illustration. From *Architectural Forum* (November 1939): 19.

airconditioning. In December 1938, *Architectural Forum* devoted a sixteen-page portfolio to the new architecture of Miami Beach. The article was ambiguous at best, yet the selection of projects clearly outlined how the forces of the market were at work adopting the modern concepts. It also alluded to the growing regional trend at work in the state: "In the growing understanding of the nature of modern planning, however, there is the basis for an architecture in Florida that is both local in character and contemporary."[46] Among the published works were the Tides Hotel and Goldwasser's Shops by Lawrence Murray Dixon and several houses and buildings by the future leader of the "regional" movement in Florida, Igor Polevitzky.[47] Polevitzky and his partner, Thomas Triplett Russell, built relatively few structures on Miami Beach before the war, but each of their early projects was given ample coverage in leading professional journals. From the start, Polevitzky & Russell's architecture was the most modern in the city, and their uncompromising design orientation — a symbiosis between International Style, highly abstracted ornamentation, and regional tendencies — quickly spurred their national recognition. In 1937, Polevitzky built his first mixed-use complex, the Lincoln Center Hotel on Lincoln Road. Behind the long, unadorned façade of the shops, he designed a modernist, yet Caribbean-inspired, courtyard overlooked by the three-story hotel and the shops' mezzanines. The flatness of the walls, the abrupt transition between the masses and the horizontality of the complex

dialogued directly with Dixon's new Seymour Building across the street. Such acts of esthetic integration on Miami Beach were not rare, given the collaborative spirit that reigned among the architects in spite of their being asked to titillate the clients. The simple urban code and the architects' willingness to respect the rules of the game often generated a richer level of urban design than what the anonymous grid would normally permit. One example was the close encounter between Hohauser's Cardozo (1939) and Kiehnel & Elliott's Carlyle (1941) hotels on Ocean Drive. Another display of urban and architectural virtuosity was visible at the intersection of Jefferson and 13th Street, where Dixon designed both corner buildings in an open L-shape form, almost establishing the contours of an indented plaza (see plan p. 36-37).

For Dixon, 1939 was a golden year. His most spectacular works were concentrated on Collins Avenue, which he literally transformed into an "urban stage." There he designed a spectacular sequence of hotels, succeeding each other along four city blocks. Henry Hohauser had in fact initiated the concept with the Essex Hotel whose vertical corner spire marked an important street intersection. Topped by their heraldic spires and signposts, the Senator (1939, p. 104), the Marlin (1939, p. 107), the Tudor (1939), the modern and asymmetrical Kent (1939), the Palmer House (1939, p. 106), the Tiffany (1939) and the Essex (1938) formed a unique and genuine urban composition. It exalted the neutrality of the grid and the pleasure of walking and driving on its streets.

47 See Allan Shulman, "Igor Polevitzky's Architectural Vision for a Modern Miami," *The Journal of Decorative and Propaganda Arts* 23 (1998 Theme issue: Florida): 335-359. In 1934, Polevitzky established his first firm in Miami with Thomas T. Russell.

46 *Architectural Forum* (December 1938): 3.

left page:
Tiffany Hotel, 801 Collins Avenue, Miami Beach. 1939. Rendering. From the *The Miami Herald*, 30 April 1939. © *The Miami Herald*.

top:
Tudor Hotel, 1111 Collins Avenue, Miami Beach. Lawrence Murray Dixon, 1939. Photograph by Moser & Son. Collection of the Bass Museum of Art. Gift of Richard B. Dixon.

above left:
Kent Hotel, 1131 Collins Avenue, Miami Beach. Lawrence Murray Dixon, 1939. Photograph by Moser & Son. Collection of the Bass Museum of Art. Gift of Lawrence M. Dixon Jr.

above right:
Essex House, 1001 Collins Avenue, Miami Beach. Henry Hohauser, 1938. Courtesy of the Romer Collection, Miami-Dade Public Library.

top:
Crescent Hotel, Ocean Drive, Miami Beach. Henry Hohauser, 1938. Rendering.
Courtesy of the Romer Collection, Miami-Dade Public Library.

above:
Governor Hotel, 435 21st Street, Miami Beach. Henry Hohauser, 1940. Rendering.
Courtesy of the Romer Collection, Miami-Dade Public Library.

opposite top:
Greystone Hotel, 1920 Collins Avenue, Miami Beach. Henry Hohauser, 1939. Rendering.
Courtesy of the Romer Collection, Miami-Dade Public Library.

opposite:
Winterhaven Hotel, 1300 Ocean Drive, Miami Beach. Albert A. Anis, 1939.
Courtesy of the Romer Collection, Miami-Dade Public Library.

Noteworthy as well, in their blending the influence of modernist ideas with urban traditions, were the many porches on pilotis that appeared on Ocean Drive and at major intersections along Collins Avenue.

Driven by this friendly competition between architects and clients, the average quality of architectural design at the end of the 1930s was remarkably high. Henry Hohauser designed a series of interesting, fifty-foot-wide apartment hotels. It is fascinating to study the evolution of his façades, from the flatness of the Webster (1936) to the richly layered 1211 Pennsylvania Avenue (1939, p. 62). There the architect abandoned the flat surface for a symmetrical composition with a strong tri-dimensional character. With its setback terraces and wrap-around windows, the building seems to be made up of two cubes — the front one grounded by gravity, the rear one seemingly expanding toward the sides in "anti-gravity" fashion.[48] With some notable exceptions like the musical façade of the Crescent on Ocean Drive (1938) and the powerful, streamlined Greystone on a corner facing Collins (1939), Hohauser's best works remained essentially symmetrical and flat compositions. Most evident was the Park Central (1939) on Ocean Drive, Hohauser's elegant response to Dixon's Tides. Its beautiful lobby ascended in separate platforms toward the alley and culminated in an elevated dining room attached as a glazed box to the side of the hotel and providing superb views of the ocean. The horizontal streamlined Governor with its stainless steel applied panels was another outstanding example of balanced composition and care for details. The most spectacular of all was the Collins Park Hotel (1939, p. 157), a symmetrical L-shaped building whose entrance was located on the diagonal at the very center of the front courtyard. Yet, for most Beach denizens of the period, Henry Hohauser's name was associated with Hoffman's Cafeteria at the corner of Española Way and Collins Avenue, with its Doric-inspired tower and "Viennese" interior of steel, concrete, glass block, chromium hardware and stainless steel windows (p. 58; 64-65).

Other important buildings of 1939 included the Clevelander, the Winterhaven and the Bancroft hotels, all by Albert Anis. Both Robert Law Weed's Miami Beach Fire Station and Anton Skislewicz's Breakwater Hotel displayed a soaring tower inspired by the 1939 World's Fair. The Albion Hotel, completed that same year by Polevitzky & Russell, marked another step in the development of their tropical modernism. Its roof fins and towers seemed to echo the Soviet Constructivist era, whereas the four-story-high projecting loggia appeared like a modernist interpretation of a vernacular Caribbean wood loggia. With its 120-foot-long zigzag

48 See the analysis by Françoise Astorg Bollack in *Everyday Masterpieces: Memory and Modernity* (Modena: Edizioni Panini, 1988), 17-18.

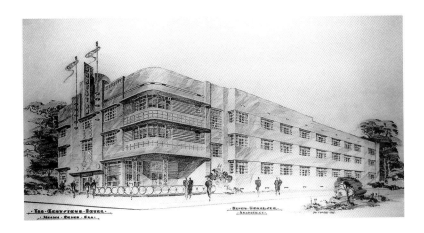

window along Lincoln Road, its projecting flat roof that recalled Philip Goodwin's Museum of Modern Art in New York (1939), and the Hollywoodian portholes that dotted the side of its elevated swimming pool, the Albion became the most modern and the most cosmopolitan structure of the city, a prime subject for photographers.[49]

1940–1941
The Last Masterworks

"Boom Over Miami" was the title of an article in the December 1940 issue of *Architectural Forum*. Forty-one hotels with 2,789 rooms and 166 apartment buildings containing 1,683 apartment units accounted for the major portion of Miami Beach's building activity in 1940, higher than any other year on record.[50] Work at Dixon's office was frenetic and more than twenty buildings were built or started construction that year. The most important, the Raleigh Hotel and the Grossinger Beach Hotel, completed the parade of large oceanfront hotels designed by the firm on Ocean Drive and Collins Avenue, which included the Atlantis, the Tides and the Victor. With this sequence of buildings, Dixon magisterially demonstrated his capacity to work with various formal syntaxes and to interact with the specific urban context. Situated at both ends of the 1700 block of Collins Avenue, the Raleigh and the Grossinger shared the same street corner condition and were deeply set back in order to provide for a forecourt and a garden. Any resemblance stopped there as Dixon used two radically different design strategies. At the Raleigh (p. 108-112), the entrance façade was symmetrically composed, but Dixon distorted it by framing the farther left vertical series of windows with a tall protruding portico and by adding a sixth floor in line with the elevator tower. To the left of it, an elegant curved façade with five stories of horizontal windows connected the front and the side of the L-shaped building around the corner.

Dixon designed the Grossinger Beach Hotel as a classical Art Deco skyscraper (p. 118-121). He exhibited the building mass in an urban, New York-like manner, and made no attempt at emphasizing the street corner. The ground level of the front elevation was particularly striking. A long and narrow elevated terrace wrapped the whole length of the building. At its center was a revolving entry door projecting out as a curved bay window made of glass and stainless steel. A group of three tall windows framed by Egyptian-like pylons flanked the entrance on

following spread:
Lincoln Road with Albion Hotel at night. Polevitzky and Russell, 1939. Photograph by Samuel H. Gottscho. Courtesy of the Library of Congress, Prints and Photographs Division, Gottscho-Schleisner Collection. © Doris Schleisner.

49   It is interesting to point out that Philip Goodwin worked in New York in Schultze & Weaver's office. According to Barbara Capitman in *Deco Delights*, he and Dixon may have shared a desk for some time.

50   "Boom Over Miami," *Architectural Forum* (December 1940): 6.

Oceanfront view of the Grossinger Beach Hotel, 1701 Collins Avenue, Miami Beach. Lawrence Murray Dixon, 1940. Photograph by Samuel H. Gottscho. © Doris Schleisner. Collection of the Bass Museum of Art. Gift of Richard B. Dixon.

either side; above it was a long horizontal strip of windows within one single continuous frame (p. 121). The beach façade was equally well designed, with a semi-circular dining room opening onto the pool area through a series of nicely proportioned vertical openings. Dixon was a master of this type of tall opening, made up of a modern and dynamic arrangement of windows, visible for instance at the Raleigh and the Caribbean hotels. Also to be admired was the Raleigh's amoeba-shaped three-level pool and bar pavilion, a little jewel of modernist design.

Like on the Tides and the Victor, Dixon gave each roof a strong image and identity. The single-letter "R" signage on top of the Raleigh commanded the façade, whereas the Grossinger's spire was designed to majestically terminate the vista down 17th Street toward the beach. Over the next year, Roy F. France's National Hotel and Igor Polevitzky's Shelborne completed the unique and extravagant skyline. The sight of these mini-skyscrapers, more or less isolated, generated an interesting commentary in the press:

"Good luck rather than municipal planning has spaced these hotels in fairly regular intervals along the Beach — falling into a pattern of which Le Corbusier would approve. Eleven to fifteen stories each, braced against hurricane, using steel and reenforced [sic] concrete, each holds aloft its distinctive bid for attention — name, tower, pinnacle or what have you."[51]

The urban importance of the Grossinger Beach and the Raleigh hotels should not obscure the quality of Dixon's other works during the early 1940s. Among the most interesting were the Norgate and the Flamingo Drive apartments, featuring large "nautical" terraces (p. 116-7); the Miljean and the Greenbrier hotels with their prominent curved façades and their heraldic posts (p. 124; 133); and the Howard Court and its streamlined, covered entryway to the courtyard (p. 26). Dixon's last buildings were among his best. The two-dimensionality of his first Deco buildings — with the flat façade as architectural billboard — gave way to more plastic volumes, as a sort of Baroque extravaganza to end almost a decade of design. The Richmond and South Seas (p. 130-1) bear witness to this evolution, but the most eloquent example was Haddon Hall (p. 129). Not only did Dixon achieve his purest streamlined image, but he also proved once again that he was a talented contextual architect. The large site prompted him to open the courtyard on Collins Avenue, yet he understood that in this very urban section of the street, continuity of the urban space was as critical as the respect of the traditional dimension of street fronts. The fluidity of surface and volume achieved

The Sea Isles Hotel, 3025 Collins Avenue, Miami Beach. Roy F. France, 1940. Photograph by Peter Harholdt. Courtesy of the Miami Beach Ocean Resort.

by the connecting curves of the design and the absence of setbacks recalled the urban design methods of Erich Mendelsohn.

Dixon's colleagues were equally productive during these last two years of the boom. The most notable buildings were Roy F. France's mid-rise towers of elegant simplicity, the already mentioned National (1940) and the Sea Isles (1940), Anton Skislewicz's Plymouth Hotel, whose angle tower was like an architectural transcription of Margaret Bourke-White's famous photograph of the tail of a DC3 for *Life* magazine (p. 50), the "Baroque" Abbey by Albert Anis, the streamlined new façade designed by Victor Nellenbogen for the Patio building on Lincoln Road and the Nero Hotel (1940, demolished) by Henry Hohauser. With the New Yorker (1940, demolished) and the Dempsey-Vanderbilt (1940), Hohauser was finally given the opportunity to compete with Dixon's

---

51 "Boom Over Miami," *Architectural Forum* (December 1940): 6. This commentary made reference to Le Corbusier's criticism of New York in *Quand les cathédrales étaient blanches, voyage au pays des timides* (Paris: Plon, 1937) and his alternative, which was to place skyscrapers in an isolated manner.

top left:
Driveway and entrance of the Shelborne Hotel, 1810 Collins Avenue, Miami Beach. Polevitzky & Russell Architects, 1940–41. Photograph by Samuel H. Gottscho. Courtesy of the Historical Museum of Southern Florida.

top right:
Lobby of the Shelborne Hotel toward Collins Avenue, 1810 Collins Avenue, Miami Beach. Polevitzky & Russell Architects, 1940–41. Photograph by Samuel H. Gottscho. Courtesy of the Historical Museum of Southern Florida.

right:
Dempsey-Vanderbilt Hotel, 3100 Collins Avenue, Miami Beach. Henry H. Hohauser, 1940. Rendering. Courtesy of the Romer Collection, Miami-Dade Public Library.

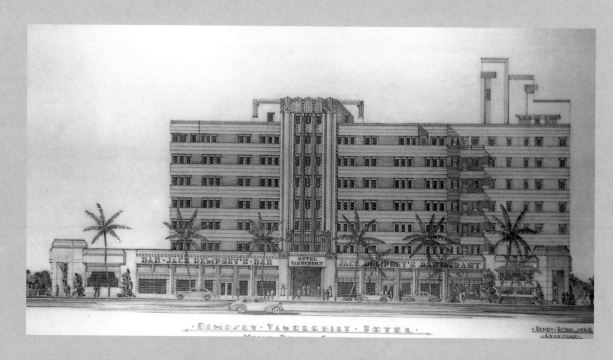

The Betsy Ross Hotel on Ocean Drive, Miami Beach. Lawrence Murray Dixon, 1941. Photograph by Samuel H. Gottscho. © Doris Schleisner. Collection of the Bass Museum of Art. Gift of Richard B. Dixon.

Interior of the Betsy Ross Hotel on Ocean Drive, Miami Beach. Lawrence Murray Dixon, 1941. Photograph by Samuel H. Gottscho. © Doris Schleisner. Collection of the Bass Museum of Art. Gift of Richard B. Dixon.

large-scale structures. The New Yorker, facing the beach on Collins, was a flamboyant streamlined version of the Grossinger Beach (p. 60). The Dempsey — which received the rare honor of being selected by the Royal Institute of British Architects (RIBA) to be part of their London collection — showed an interesting façade whose unusual length was reinforced by the horizontal bands mixing windows and stucco panels; for the first time on the Beach, the ground floor footprint was partially independent of the upper stories.

Then came, at the end of 1941, the neo-colonial Betsy Ross on Ocean Drive, notable for its traditional porch and wood columns, its gables, shutters and wood cladding, as well as its frescoes featuring scenes of colonial history. It is difficult to speculate on Dixon's intentions for this hotel, a stylistic "oddball" located at the end of Ocean Drive. Lourdes Solera's explanation of the "patriotic approach" of the Betsy Ross's style in a time of war effort and the style's propagandistic values is reasonable and believable, but it probably reflected the clients' requests more than the architect's change of direction.[52] In contrast, one can't help but juxtapose the deliberate jump into the future that Polevitzky achieved with the Shelborne, built that same year on Collins Avenue across from the Raleigh. Polevitzky and Russell later described the Shelborne as a radical advance in Miami architecture: "Running counter to the currently prevailing design trend, which was Art-Deco, with its mediocre planning and its meretricious decoration,

the building was designed in the simple Bauhaus manner, devoid of useless ornament and planned to take maximum advantage of its fine site."[53]

Indeed, the building was rich with innovations, yet the above description was self-promoting and exaggerated, as most of the details — projecting windows, wrap-around windows — were similar to previous works by Dixon and Hohauser. As for its spectacular interior, only the white spiral staircase marked a modernist International Style departure from the Art Deco grandeur of the Raleigh or the Grossinger. The real change was in the ground floor plan, which floated, not unlike the Dempsey, independent of the contours of the tower that jutted above it. Polevitzky and Russell designed it as an asymmetrical Oscar Niemeyer-inspired series of interconnecting spaces that would later influence the works of Morris Lapidus. The street façade also displayed an audacious entrance piece, a thin wood and glass loggia that stuck out of the building as an inviting finger. It is in that single detail that the architects captured the essence of what modern tropical architecture would be in the 1950s and 1960s in South Florida.

In conclusion, it is interesting to contrast the Shelborne with Dixon's Caribbean Hotel, his last completed building before the war. His vision of the Caribbean remained essentially decorative, even if it was beautifully crafted, like in the airy bar and dining room with its columns clad in reflective metal, its straw chairs and its elegant wallpapers and fabrics displaying the palms and flora of the region.

52 Solera, 36.

53 *The Work of Polevitzky and Russell 1936–1941*, typewritten, from the collection of Thomas Triplett Russell (compilation date unknown), 346-7.

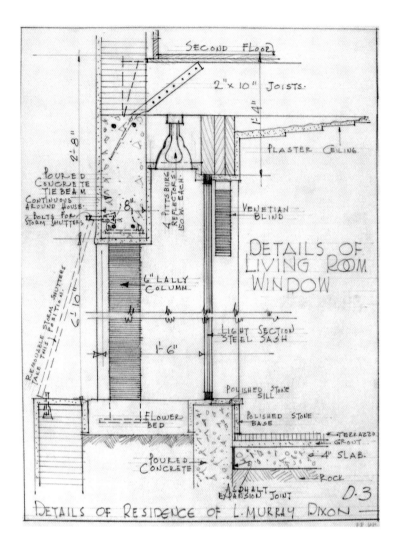

Detail of living room window, Dixon residence, 2871 Fairgreen Drive, Miami Beach. Lawrence Murray Dixon, 1935–36. Ink drawing in sketchbook. Collection of the Bass Museum of Art. Gift of Lawrence M. Dixon Jr.

PART TWO
HOUSES BETWEEN THE SOUTHERN TRADITION
AND MODERNITY

All over the country we are feeling our way toward a new style of architecture, a style that is more expressive of the way we live today. I believe that South Florida is taking a large part in showing us how to design homes, modern without elaborate details, plain and yet beautiful, and withal appropriate to a semi-tropical climate and a free out-of-door life... I hope that South Florida will continue to build with wide, plain surfaces, wide, open porches, terraces, and tile roofs. Appropriateness is South Florida's contribution to the architecture of this country.[54]

According to his own notes, Lawrence Murray Dixon built two hundred and twenty residences between 1931 and 1947.[55] Most of them were in Miami Beach, but newspapers and photographic records show some structures in neighboring Coral Gables and at least one in Miami Shores. Dixon, like all residential architects practicing on Miami Beach in the 1930s until the war, did not follow any idiosyncratic personal language or any strict stylistic direction. Rather, their production could be characterized as "modern eclecticism." Yet, in spite of their stylistic differences, the residences that made up the Miami Beach neighborhoods north of the Dade Canal were quite vernacular in character. They followed a limited number of typical plans and thus formed a relatively homogeneous esthetic environment. William Orr Ludlow, chairman of public information for the American Institute of Architects in Washington, stressed this phenomenon in an article of 1939:

"Instead of a jumble of houses, colonial, English, Monterey and Cape Cod, which sort of hodgepodge irreparably mars the appearance of most towns and cities of this country, South Florida can sincerely boast of an architecture that is a harmony of color, form and style."[56]

The national architectural press had already taken note of this trend at the outset of the Depression. The March 1935 issue of *American Architect* contained an essay titled "Miami Beach Today…" It featured "five recent houses, typical of 'Florida Architecture' — the result of adopting traditional design to the service of modern, comfortable living

---

54 William Orr Ludlow, "Florida Architecture Praised," *Miami Herald*, 5 March 1939. Ludlow was the chairman of the committee on public information for the American Institute of Architects.

55 Lawrence Murray Dixon, "Form for Senior Classification — Experience and Record in Professional Practice" (June 4, 1947), 2. It is important to state that this part of the essay does not attempt to provide a comprehensive survey of Dixon's production in the residential field.

56 Ludlow.

top:
Mediterranean-style residence, Miami Beach. Lawrence Murray Dixon, date unknown.
Photograph by Moser & Son. Collection of the Bass Museum of Art. Gift of Richard B. Dixon.

right:
Mediterranean-style residence, Miami Beach. Lawrence Murray Dixon, date unknown.
Photograph by Moser & Son. Collection of the Bass Museum of Art. Gift of Richard B. Dixon.

Exterior of the Eastman residence with entrance door, 5959 La Gorce Drive, Miami Beach. Robert Law Weed, 1935. From *Robert Law Weed, Architect* (New York: Architectural Catalog Co., 1937).

in almost-tropical America."[57] The selection of houses was astutely made as all were, in some way, a compromise between tradition and modernity. None of them was truly traditional or truly modern, as might have occurred in California or New York, for instance. The essay featured a sprawling one-story hacienda-like brick and stucco house (Shoeppl & Southwell), a Mediterranean-type mansion with Deco details (Russell T. Pancoast), a modern-pioneer house by August Geiger with walls of keystone and wood balconies, a modern Southern colonial home with a second-floor balcony wrapping around three façades (Robert Law Weed) and an elegant Art Deco classical two-story house by J. & C. Skinner, displaying a bold circular concrete stairway cantilevered over the living room. All five houses were cross-ventilated and had patios, loggias and porches for "outdoor living."

The "Deco-Mediterranean" Houses

In a text published in 1991, Andres Duany and Elizabeth Plater-Zyberk defined the "Three Traditions" of Miami. They argued that in the city's first decades, "the traditions emerged sequentially, but they did not entirely replace each other." They were the "simple wooden vernacular" of the first forty years, the "sophisticated and abused Mediterranean Revival" of the 1920s, and "that peculiar brand of frivolous Modernism" that began in Miami Beach in the 1930s.[58] These traditions have continued to co-exist and to interact throughout the twentieth century, but in fact, by the mid-1930s, the blending of the three traditions into a regional form of the modern movement was well underway. Dixon's residential production was a good example of this crisscrossing of influences and it can be divided into three main areas, whose development was simultaneous: the "Deco-Mediterranean," the "Deco-Modern" and the "Vernacular-Modern."

Dixon's training in *beaux-arts* architecture and his apprenticeship in Coral Gables provided him with the tools to excel in the use of the "Deco-Mediterranean." One of his first commissions was a group of ten small and simple middle-class residences, known as the Española Villas, that he built in 1934 and 1935 in a quiet and remote section of Española Way. Dixon's own version of Mediterranean Revival architecture was a hybrid of Spanish and Caribbean Mediterranean, as can be found in the early years of Coral Gables, mixed with subtle doses of Art Deco,

57   "Miami Beach Today...," *American Architect* (March 1935): 15-30. Dixon was not featured in this essay.

58   Andres Duany and Elizabeth Plater-Zyberk, "The Three Traditions of Miami," in Jean-François Lejeune and Maurice Culot, eds., *Miami Architecture of the Tropics* (New York: Princeton Architectural Press, 1991), 79.

particularly around the entrance doors. His Mediterranean style was not aristocratic like Addison Mizner's in Palm Beach or August Geiger's in 1920s Miami Beach. As in many of his works, his architectural vocabulary was vast, eclectic, witty and at times humorous, particularly in his treatment of large-scale arched windows and openings, some divided vertically or screened with masonry in a vernacular Caribbean way.

The "Deco-Modern" Houses

Miami Beach's earliest "Deco-modern" home was the Eastman residence at 5959 La Gorce Drive, designed by Robert Law Weed and also known as the General Electric Model Home. It was a direct spin-off of the Tropical Home of 1933 and helped establish the parameters of the "Deco-Modern" in the local residential market. The "electric" house was in fact a demonstration home of sorts, replete with traditional and new materials. Large roof terraces with metallic tube railings covered the house; glass block was used extensively; the flora- and fauna-carved stone panels surrounding the entry door contrasted sharply with the formica panel that covered the latter. The house featured many technical innovations, among them an automatic garage door and a curtain wall that could be converted into a movie screen.[59]

Dixon was equally able to master this language, as demonstrated in the series of modern houses he designed, complete with flat roofs, terraces, and many Deco or modernist details such as keystone panels, circular windows and chimneys with a three-fin motif (p. 143, bottom). Most houses were two stories high and fronted the streets in a quite urban way. One of the most successful (p. 143, top) appeared like a cubist assemblage in which Dixon explored the esthetic effect of thin metallic columns and cantilevering floors that seemed to be suspended from above. The most curious design was at the intersection of 34th Street and Royal Palm Avenue (p.144, top). Not only did the house feature nautical details such as the ship-like railings and the hexagonal porthole-like windows, but its very massing, made up of a long and flat base from which protruded a second floor, was clearly reminiscent of a submarine. The horizontal band of first-floor windows underscored the horizontality of the deck, whereas the strips of windows at the top accentuated the verticality of the shaft-like second floor.

Interior of the Eastman residence with entrance door, 5959 La Gorce Drive, Miami Beach. Robert Law Weed, 1935. From *Robert Law Weed, Architect* (New York: Architectural Catalog Co., 1937).

59   Robert Law Weed, *Robert Law Weed, Architect* (New York, Architectural Catalog Co., 1937). Also see *Miami Herald*, 16 June 1935.

The "Vernacular-Modern" Houses
"Modern is Regional"

The last category, the "Vernacular-Modern," included Dixon's own house and some notable works in the Miami Beach districts north of Lincoln Road. The house that Dixon built for his family in 1935–36 was a small, compact, and very urban home, with a two-story façade on a quiet residential street (p. 140-1). It was one of the "Fourteen Examples of The Better House of Concrete" published by *American Architect* in August 1936. The house had overhanging eaves to offer sun protection, a simple shingle roof, concrete block construction painted with stucco finish and an artificial chimney used as a water storage tank. The interior was modest but elegantly laid out, with a beautiful staircase landing and glassblock windows. The most significant detail was the modernist treatment of the house corner: Dixon pushed the wrap-around window to the inside in order to reveal the circular concrete column (p. 190). This detail may have been a discreet commentary on the issue of modernity and construction, as it does not seem to have appeared anywhere else. To some extent the house could also be read like a manifesto for middle-class housing. Dixon had investigated that theme in 1935 when he had "prepared a series of twenty residences, which included plans and renderings together with a description of construction and decoration." These were run weekly in local newspapers "to encourage people of moderate income to build."[60]

top:
Elevation of waterfront residence, Miami Beach. Lawrence Murray Dixon, date unknown. Graphite on tracing paper, 10 1/4" x 18." Illustrator unidentified. Collection of the Bass Museum of Art. Gift of Richard B. Dixon.

center:
Mason residence, 923 Catalonia Avenue, Coral Gables. Lawrence Murray Dixon, 1940. Photograph by Moser & Son. Collection of the Bass Museum of Art. Gift of Richard B. Dixon.

bottom:
Plan of Mrs. Ruth Norton Natelson's house, Miami Beach. From *Architectural Forum* (March 1938): 252.

60   Lawrence Murray Dixon, "Senior Form for Classification.", 2.

At 3210 Alton Road, Dixon built a similar type of residence (p. 142, top right), a simple and compact rectangle, well proportioned with an open terrace cut into the volume on its garden site. The 2065 North Bay Road residence was smaller and more Caribbean in appearance (p. 142, top left), with a projecting street balcony contrasting with the resolutely modern windows surrounding the ground floor. All of these houses were equally urban and urbane; their two-story volumes stood high and resolutely fronted the streets.

Dixon displayed the same inventiveness in his residential architecture as he did in his larger hotel and apartment projects. Entry porches, for instance, were often moments of idiosyncratic composition (p. 142), revealing a mix of influences that probably reflected conflicting requests from the owners. Yet, the most outstanding details were to be found in the fenestration patterns where he revealed masterful compositional skills that gave these elements identity and made them contemporary. One of the most elegant houses was at 923 Catalonia Avenue in Coral Gables. It appeared like an Anglo-Caribbean version of Weed's Tropical Home in Chicago. The combination of roofs and volumes was quite successful, as was the design of the dramatically high window lighting the double-height living room and making a powerful transition with the L-shaped one-story extensions on both sides. Dixon attached a loggia along the garage wing and opened it toward the front yard, and an elaborate gateway structure appeared like a pavilion toward the street. This typology was a Dixon trademark, and had several variations depending on the size of the lot, the orientation and its relation to the water (p. 193, top; p. 196, middle & bottom). It was particularly appropriate to deep lots, such as the Lacroix residence on North Bay Road (p. 158) or the Julius Simpson residence on San Marino Island (p. 159). Dixon adapted it also to more modern flat structures like the Waterson residence on one of the Sunset Islands (p. 196, center).

The latter type of house was a more suburban one, and Dixon experimented further in that direction with some sprawling one-story volumes whose composition could not be discerned anymore as a whole. One unidentified waterfront residence (p. 196, top), with its flat and seemingly detached glass wall defining the family room, and the Natelson house were the best examples. In the Natelson residence (p. 194, plan), Dixon abandoned the street-fronting high volume for a loose arrangement of low-pitched volumes, garden and terrace walls, as if the house had grown organically, by accretion of its parts, around a central court or patio. This house was praised by *Architectural Forum*:

"In addition to illustrating the trend of South Florida residential work towards less stylistic modes of expression, this house has a number of features of unusual interest. Sleeping accommodations while concentrated in one compact unit, have been designed to give privacy to parents, children, and guests. The sharp overhangs, necessitated by the climate, serve to further accentuate the horizontality of the one-story design. The L-shaped plan gives full scope to the possibilities of year-round outdoor living."[61]

This emphasis on environmental control and on adaptation to climate and region had functionalist overtones that made this type of house compatible with the dominant discourse on modernism in the United States. The same argument had already been made in 1933 with regard to the Florida Tropical Home, featured at the Century of Progress Exhibition in Chicago. As a modern house it was praised as uniquely conditioned to the landscape and climate of Florida: "Nowhere in America has architecture been so thoroly [sic] adapted to local conditions as it has in Florida, and the Florida Tropical Home is the last word in the small home architecture of Florida."[62]

Most critics of the prewar era recognized that the International Style design was not very popular in general, and even less so within the private residential market. Thus modernity's survival was predicated upon the designers' ability to propose less threatening options for the middle-income family. Designers had to express themselves differently, in a more informal and organic manner, a trend definitely influenced by Frank Lloyd Wright. As a result, the environment, the climate, the orientation and all functional elements related to a site-specific house were stressed accordingly. Katherine Murrow Ford pointedly summarized this new trend in the March 1941 issue of the popular magazine *House and Garden*, in which Florida was represented by a Philip Goodwin house in Winter Park:

"Native essentials characteristic of our best regional folk architecture are gradually being fused with the vitality of freed design. Contrary to some popular impressions, modern architecture cannot be reduced to a precise formula. Nor is it regimented into the universal placing of a standard mold indiscriminately in the north, the south, the east or the west. Lack of studied uniformity is one of its virtues. Environmental influences are enormously important. Concessions made to climate alone result in modifications in orientation, construction and external forms. Sensitiveness to materials — new and old — and their appropriate use is another of the many facets of the new architecture."[63]

62 Earl W. Brown, "Florida—Where Summer spends the Winter," *The Florida Tropical Home at the Century of Progress 1933* (New York: Kuhne Galleries, 1933). Quoted in Shulman "Igor Polevitzky": 337.

63 Katherine Murrow Ford, "Modern is Regional," *House and Garden* (March 1941): 35, quoted in Mitchell Schwarzer, "Modern Architecture Ideology in Cold War America," *The Education of an Architect* (Cambridge: The MIT Press, 1997), 100.

61 "House for Mrs. Ruth Norton Natelson, Miami Beach," *Architectural Forum* (March 1938): 252.

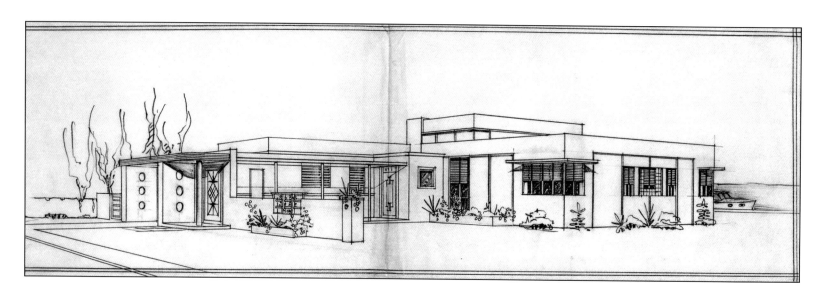

The extent of the new spirit in residential architecture was made resolutely clear in the Federal Housing Administration's recommendations to homeowners, published at the outset of the war:

"Do the elevations express frankly the plan contained therein, or is the design of a freakish nature aimed at the picturesque? In whatever style the building has been designed, does it express to a reasonable degree refinement and proper interpretation of that style, or does the design indulge in the use of superfluous ornament or an improper use of materials as they relate to each other? Are the windows and door openings arranged to result in a pleasing effect? Are room proportions pleasing? Are interior details so designed as to be appropriate and attractive? Is the entire ensemble, including the arrangement of buildings and the plot plan attractive? Do the accessory buildings tie in the composition of the entire project? Has the entire project a pleasing appeal to the typical potential purchaser?"[64]

Lawrence Murray Dixon, like his colleagues Robert Law Weed, Hunter Henderson, Theodore Virrick, Henry Hohauser, Robert Little, and the most innovative of all, Igor Polevitzky, integrated the changes in architectural attitudes that shocked Europe and America in the 1920s and 1930s, and made them acceptable to a large segment of South Florida society. Their architecture became increasingly regional, but also suburban, as the new organic forms and flatter volumes were not really able to respond to the street in the manner of the Mediterranean or the Deco-Modern style.[65]

CONCLUSION
1945–1949: The Postwar Years

Pearl Harbor signaled the end of residential and leisure construction on Miami Beach. The war effort reoriented architectural production toward more patriotic objects, such as armament factories and prefabricated houses for workers and residents. Dixon joined the army in 1942. According to his own notes, "during the war, as Major, Corps of Engineers, I designed and executed a wide variety of unusual buildings for the military establishment."[66]

When he got back from the war, he reopened his office at 605 Lincoln Road, Miami Beach. Dixon and his colleagues continued to build hotels and apartment houses, but they were often undistinguishable from the prewar era and with little spark of inspiration — a good example was the Helen Marie built in 1947 on 11th Street. The world of architecture was in flux and it was not until the 1950s that specific new trends would appear. Yet, a more open-minded attitude was developing toward forms, natural materials and types of roofs, thus reflecting the growing trend in regionalist interest that had, before the war, already influenced the residential market. In the apartment districts of Miami Beach, the mood started to timidly shift to a simplified modern Anglo-Caribbean vernacular. Gently sloped roofs, overhanging eaves and louvers came into view along its eclectic but urban streets. Again, history repeated itself and the typological persistence absorbed another layer of stylistic diversity.

From this period of transition, two buildings of note emerged along the Miami Beach oceanfront: Robert Swartburg's Delano Hotel and Henry Hohauser's Sherry Frontenac Hotel, both completed on Collins Avenue in 1947. The Delano's top spire recalled the science-fiction world of Buck Rogers, whereas the "folded planes" and projecting window frames that defined the façades made a direct reference to Brazilian and postwar Italian modernism, in particular to Oscar Niemeyer's and Gio Ponti's works. The Sherry Frontenac Hotel also featured similar architectural features, and in some way announced the architecture of the postwar leaders in Miami Beach, Norman Giller and Morris Lapidus.[67]

64 "Seven Questions that the Prospective Homeowner Must Ask: Design Hints by Federal Housing Administration," *Miami Herald*, 27 May 1940.

65 The many houses published in the *Miami Herald* and *Miami News* were often the most traditional, sometimes in strange languages such as Georgian or Monterey-style. None of Dixon's most modern houses were published, which contrasts with the coverage received by Igor Polevitzky for his modern production.

66 Lawrence Murray Dixon, "Form for Senior Classification." His works for the army were located in Pasco, WA, in Savannah and in California.

67 In this perspective, see the influencial exhibition and catalogue *Brazil Builds* (New York: The Museum of Modern Art, 1944).

and Morris Lapidus.[67]

Lawrence Murray Dixon's abrupt death, at the age forty-eight in Long Island, New York, interrupted a brilliant career, which was on the brink of a new direction. In 1946–47, Dixon designed the addition to the Hollywood Beach Hotel, north of Miami Beach. The ornament-free horizontality of the long cabana wings and of the outdoor bar surrounding the swimming pool, the use of brick on some large vertical walls and the more abstract conception of volumes and details revealed that Dixon's architectural vocabulary was evolving. The success of the hotel project prompted the owner to invite the architect to collaborate on some new ventures in Manhattan and the New York area. Dixon applied for a transfer of architectural license with the intention of opening a second office in New York City. It was at the end of a business meeting with his new clients that he collapsed, victim of a fatal stroke.[68]

Dixon's legacy on Miami Beach belongs to all the citizens of and visitors to the city. A few of his works have unfortunately disappeared, due to indifference, speculation and greed: the Atlantis is long gone and very few remember its monumental columns and silver leaf ceilings; the Senator was destroyed in spite of a long battle led by Barbara Capitman; and the Pinecrest Apartments were also lost. But most of his works remain. In particular, his large oceanfront hotels have endured, and the elegance of their lobbies can still be admired by the tens of thousands of guests who visit them each year. Most apartment hotels have been renovated and often converted into condominiums.

In all his buildings, from the more modest to the most glamorous, Dixon demonstrated his innate sense of balance and proportion. Symmetrical or not, most of the façades used the square or the golden section rectangle as basic elements of composition. His well-noted sense of rhythm — Dixon was a talented musician all his life — was reflected in his architecture, as evidenced in his many musical, "score-like" façades such as the McAlpin (p. 122-3) and the Clyde on Ocean Drive (p. 132), and in his masterful designs of the large window openings at the Grossinger Beach and the Raleigh.[69] The same sense of rhythm, mixed with a good dose of humor and unpretentiousness, was obvious in the idiosyncratic series of small apartment buildings built in the Flamingo Park area. The Culver, the Catherine, the Lawrence and the Fletcher Apartments (p. 125-8), among others, were nothing less

Addition and renovation of the Hollywood Beach Hotel, Hollywood. Lawrence Murray Dixon, 1947-48. Photograph by Joseph B. Brignolo. © Doris Schleisner. Gift of Lawrence M. Dixon Jr.

than witty exercises, variations on a theme, inventive improvisations in the manner of the Jazz era. One of the few sketches conserved at the Bass Museum shows the elegant square façade of an unbuilt project, with musical keys as ornaments on top of the entry portico. Dixon selected construction and decoration materials carefully, and made them an integral part of his compositional system. The sparkling martini glass inscribed in the terrazzo floor of the Raleigh's bar still accompanies late-night encounters (p. 145), while the metallic spire of the Tiffany continues to welcome passersby on their way to the beach.

Lawrence Murray Dixon loved the city and respected its often tacit rules and conventions. His unpretentious, clever and whimsical architecture was first and foremost an urban one. It showed confidence in the city and in city life. It was, to use Morris Lapidus' words, a genuine "architecture of joy."[70] Dixon, Hohauser, Anis, France, Skislewicz, Kiehnel & Elliott, Polevitzky & Russell, and so many others, formed an ensemble cast of actors, at work designing and building a new city. As in a theater, they exchanged roles and tirades, and they tried to outshine each other, but they shared and read the same text: the language and the "architecture of the city."[71]

68 Lawrence Murray Dixon designed the Varadero Beach Hotel in Cuba's famous resort of Varadero, east of Havana. Information on this hotel, the date of construction and the names of the collaborating local architects have not been found at this time.

69 In his youth, Lawrence Murray Dixon imagined a career as jazz musician. In Atlanta, he played for awhile with the Jan Garber Jazz Orchestra. Instead of moving with them to New York and Los Angeles, where they became famous, Dixon went to college and enrolled in the architecture department of Georgia Tech University.

70 Morris Lapidus. *An Architecture of Joy* (Miami: E.A. Seemann, 1979). Interestingly, Lapidus's postwar assessement of the Art Deco period was far from positive, yet it is undeniable that he was himself a "child" of the 1930s.

71 Aldo Rossi, *The Architecture of the City* (Cambridge: The MIT Press, 1981).

Detail of the addition and renovation of the Hollywood Beach Hotel, Hollywood, Florida. Lawrence Murray Dixon, 1947-48. Photograph by Joseph B. Brignolo. Gift of Lawrence M. Dixon Jr.

THE OTHER MODERN:
BETWEEN THE MACHINE AND THE MEDITERRANEAN

Jean-François Lejeune

Miami Beach, the Grand Concourse in the Bronx, the colonial "quartiers" of Rabat or Cairo may not be up to the Greek islands (are we so sure they are not architecturally)... But they are worlds made by ordinary men with ordinary talents and if what we want is a better world, they merit our attention! Of course, for those who love these buildings, they are sufficient, like any true art work, but in order to see them one must jettison the art history progression dominant in criticism today.[1]

Until the late 1960s, most architectural historians equated the term "modern" with the modernist movement and its ideology of technological determinism. Modernist mythology implied that it was in the natural order of things that the "truer" forms of modern architecture should replace revivalist eclecticism, regionalism, and more generally what Henry-Russell Hitchcock defined as "New Traditionalism" in an important essay of 1928.[2] In the 1930s and the following decades, the biased slant of influential writers like Nikolaus Pevsner (1902–1983) and Siegfried Giedion (1893–1968) caused buildings that did not ally themselves to the dictates of the International Style promoters, and to the theses defended by the *Congrès Internationaux d'Architecture Moderne* (CIAM), to be considered "inferior," or unworthy of consideration.[3] The pivotal moment occurred at the château of La Sarraz, in 1928, when French, German, Swiss and Dutch modernist architects gathered with the mission of ending their marginal status within the profession. At this first meeting of CIAM, its founding members staked a proprietary claim on the architectural expression of "the modern," a claim that set the groundwork for Alfred Barr (1902–1981), Henry-Russell Hitchcock (1903–1987) and Lewis Mumford's (1895–1989) International Style Exhibition of 1932. In this perspective, the exclusive relegation of the machine and of machine aesthetics to the International Style and its progeny was one of the most impressive victories and sales pitches of the twentieth century.[4] The Museum of Modern Art has always insisted that it, rather than the nascent profession of industrial design, shaped the modern visual culture of the United States and set its standards. The 1932 Exhibition was the keystone of this thesis, which contrasted the "purity" of the Internationalist architects as artists to the "streamline-type" architects and industrial designers, who were seen as producers of contemptible kitsch.[5] Yet, in spite of this high-level discourse, MoMA's strategy was conceived on business lines in terms of "production" and "distribution." For director Alfred Barr, the museum was selling a product called Modern Art:

"Basically, the Museum 'produces' art knowledge, criticism, scholarship, understanding, taste…. Once a product is made, the next job is distribution. An exhibition in the galleries is distribution. Circulation of exhibition catalogues, memberships, publicity, radio, are all distribution."[6]

The insidious aspect of the International Style Exhibition was the systematic treatment of buildings as isolated objects. Most of the selected buildings were isolated from the city, either in the countryside or in new suburban neighborhoods. Even when they were integrated within the urban fabric, buildings were de-contextualized, and misrepresentation was prevalent. Photography was often articulated in such a way as to detach them from their surroundings.[7] The exhibition's stance on the city and urban space was thus a direct reflection of CIAM's conception of the urban structure of the modern city. Its members emphasized principles such as the death of the street-corridor, the functional zoning of traditionally mixed urban functions, the destruction of vernacular urban fabric and its replacement with isolated buildings in the new urban landscape. These theses culminated in the Charter of Athens of 1942, which became the source of inspiration for the most destructive urban renewal operations in Europe and America. Moreover, following the totalitarian reaction against the avant-garde, particularly in Nazi Germany and Mussolini's Italy after 1938, all uses of traditional urban forms were later seen as "monumental," "regressive" and "reactionary."

opposite:

Detail from *View of Town, No. 2, Positano, Italy.* Louis I. Kahn, 1929. Watercolor on paper. 10 1/2" x 8 3/4." Private collection.

1   Tom Killian, "A Decent Table," in Joselita Raspi Serra, François Astorg Bollack, and Tom Killian, *Everyday Masterpieces: Memory and Modernity — A Study of an International Vernacular Architecture Between the Two Wars* (Modena: Edizioni Panini, 1988), 14.

2   Henry-Russell Hitchcock, "The New Traditionalists," *Architectural Record* (February 1928): 336-351.

3   William J. R. Curtis, *Modern Architecture Since 1900* (London: Phaidon, 1997), 141.

4   David Gebhard, *Kem Weber: The Moderne in Southern California* (Santa Barbara: The Art Galleries, University of California, Santa Barbara, 1964), 6.

5   Terry Smith, *Making the Modern: Industry, Art, and Design in America* (Chicago and London: The University of Chicago Press, 1993), 395, 399. See Clement Greenberg's 1939 essay, "Avant-Garde and Kitsch" in *Art and Culture* (Boston: Beacon, 1961).

6   Alfred Barr, *Present Status and Future Direction of the Museum of Modern Art*, 2. MoMA Archives: 1933, AHB Papers (AAA: 3266; 122). Quoted by James Putnam, *The New Millennium of Modern Art Museums* (Roma: La Repubblica of the Arts, 1999): http://www.repubblicarts.kataweb.it.

7   The case of the Bauhaus in Dessau is such an example of photographic manipulation. See Jean-François Lejeune, "From Hellerau to the Bauhaus: Memory and Modernity of the German Garden City," *The New City* 3 (New York: Princeton Architectural Press, 1996): 35.

In recent years, CIAM's self-awarded patent on "modern" architecture and "modern" urbanism has been challenged by scholars bearing a host of new contenders for consideration. Current explorations of cultural modernity share a consensus on one point in particular: there is no single normative twentieth century standard, a premise that had been the central tenet of the first CIAM sessions. On the architectural end, Art Deco/ Moderne, Czech and German expressionism, neoclassicism, Soviet "realism," classical modernism and a variety of twentieth century regionalisms have resurfaced as genuine streams of modernity. On the urban planning side, the theories of Camillo Sitte (1843–1903), the legacy of the garden city, the grid-based urban expansions of the first decades, or the traditionally based postwar reconstruction plans of Munich or Florence, have been rehabilitated and are slowly entering the realm of twentieth century scholarship in urbanism. Surprisingly, it was Henry-Russell Hitchcock who opened the Pandora's box when he acknowledged in 1961 that diverse strands of modern architecture had retained their independence and continued with varying degrees of vitality alongside the International Style. Thirty-five years later, Hitchcock rediscovered those architects he had labeled "The New Traditionalists," in 1928 — Sullivan, Wright, Perret, Piacentini, Ostberg, Goodhue, and Dudok:

"They are also modern in that they feel free to use and combine without regard for archeological properties the elements thus borrowed. The essential principle which governs both their retrospection and their modernity is the belief that not any one period of the past but the works of the past as a whole offer the surest guide."[8]

He recalled "forgotten heroes" such as Hendrik Berlage (1856–1934), Adolf Loos (1870–1933) and Otto Wagner (1841–1918), and emphasized trends like the "organic architecture" of Wright and the expressionism of the Amsterdam School: "Now that a younger generation of critics and historians is turning the light of scholarly research on the 1920s, legends are being corrected; De Klerk, Mendelsohn, Häring, Böhm, and other individualists are being reassessed; and at least statistical recognition is given to the immense volume of architectural production of the 1920s that was untouched by the rising International Style."[9]

In the last two decades, Jean-Louis Cohen, Richard Guy Wilson, David Gebhard, John Zukowsky, Hartmut Frank, Vittorio Magnago Lampugnani, Maurice Culot, Robert Stern, William Curtis and Winfried

"Il faut tuer la rue-corridor." Le Corbusier, 1929. From *Précisions sur un état présent de l'urbanisme* (Paris: 1930). © Fondation Le Corbusier, Paris.

Nerdinger — to name only a few of the "new historians" — have not only responded to Hitchcock's expectations, but they have also "dug out" archives and periodicals to reveal the quantitative and qualitative extent of "The Other Modern" of the twentieth century. This generic label, launched in Bologna in 2000, was coined to denominate the hundreds of architects and urbanists whose vision of modernity and progress did not partake in the determinist ideology of the machine and technology, but anchored itself on the continuity of the classical and vernacular traditions, while at the same time renewing them through the prism of modernist theses and advances.[10] Jean-Louis Cohen's question can summarize this new historical construct:

"Can we continue to reserve the label of 'modern' only to those architects who have simultaneously worked on the renovation of forms, on the transformation of uses and the development of techniques, while embracing radical political points of view?"[11]

Paralleling Alan Colqhoun's argument that, by focusing on the vernacular hut, Laugier was seeking to return to the pure sources of classicism and thus "re-vernacularize" it, the first section of this essay explores how a similar reaction took place in the late 1920s–early 1930s within the modernist discourse. At that time, Le Corbusier (1887–1965) and other modernist architects like Josep Lluis Sert (1902–1983) embarked on a quest for the vernacular roots of the modern movement as a way to substantiate the myth of the origin beyond the machine and other technological analogies. In doing so, they unwillingly

8   Hitchcock, "The New Traditionalists," 340. For this discussion of modernity, the author is indebted to Greg Castillo's essay "Modernità, modernismo e la ricerca di una posizione egemonica," *L'altra modernità* (Savona: Dogma, 2000), 145-149.

9   Henry-Russell Hitchcock, postscript to the 1966 edition of Henry-Russell Hitchcock and Philip Johnson, *The International Style: Architecture Since 1922* (New York: W.W. Norton, 1932; 1966), xi-xii.

10   See Gabriele Tagliaventi, ed., *L'altra modernità 1900-2000* (Savona: Dogma, 2000) and the related exhibition curated by Jean-François Lejeune, Michael Lykoudis and Gabriele Tagliaventi. The term was used previously in two German books: *O. R. Salvisberg: die andere Moderne* (Zürich: GTA, 1995) and Wolfgang Pehnt, *Rudolf Schwarz 1897-1961: Architekt einer anderen Moderne* (Ostfildern-Ruit: G. Hatje, 1997).

11   Jean-Louis Cohen, "Mouvement moderne," *Dictionnaire de l'architecture du XXè siècle* (Paris: Hazan/Institut français d'architecture, 1996), 630.

joined the ranks of the "other modern" architects who have unceasingly searched for a modern "architecture of the everyday" — from the pioneers Schinkel, Loos and Hoffmann, to Dixon, Hohauser and, more recently, Aldo Rossi. In this "fin-de-siècle", after "the collapse of the referent in morality, history, nature, religion, cities, space… the everyday, established and consolidated — philosopher Henri Lefebvre wrote in 1972 — remains a sole surviving common sense referent and point of reference."[12]

At the urban scale, Gunnar Asplund (1885–1940), Paul Philippe Cret (1876–1945), Marcello Piacentini (1881–1960), Josef Plecnik (1872–1957), Paul Schmitthenner (1884–1972), Bruno Taut (1880–1938) and all the "other modern" architects aimed and generally succeeded at integrating their works within the traditional parameters of an urbanism of streets and squares. Similarly, architect-urbanists like Theodor Fischer (1862–1938), Henri Prost (1874–1959), Donat Alfred Agache (1875–1959), Patrick Geddes (1854–1932), Fritz Schumacher (1869–1947), Tony Garnier (1869–1948) or Eliel Saarinen (1873–1950) planned, designed and built modern cities, neighborhoods and new towns of the twentieth century that adapted the traditional city and its typologies to the current conditions of life. Others were in fact planned by engineers, at times with strong shortcomings and less artistic interest, but in all of them, the street pattern was maintained as the fundamental organizing principle of urban space.

Miami Beach will be discussed here as one of those unrecognized "other modern" cities. As in Tel Aviv, Casablanca, Copacabana, the Spanish *ensanches*, or the Parioli in Rome, the deep anchoring of traditional urban culture and the pragmatic realities of a small, incremented, lot-based real estate prevailed in Miami Beach and enticed the modern-oriented architects to mediate between urban scale and individual expression. As Gabriele Tagliaventi wrote:

"We know now that the twentieth century generated another culture of modernity, a culture which refuted the modernist dogmas, the myth of progress, and the blind confidence in technology; a culture which nevertheless confronted the problems of mass society, of mass transportation and communication. With no desire to break with the past, it considered the confrontation with the world as a necessary challenge, and assumed tradition as a cultural bridge that allowed the society to grow, change, and move forward without losing the good heritage generated earlier."[13]

Cover of the catalogue published for the sixtieth anniversary of the International Style Exhibition of 1932. Terence Riley, *The International Style: Exhibition 15 and the Museum of Modern Art* (New York: Rizzoli/Columbia Books of Architecture, 1992).
Right: Glass skyscraper. Mies Van der Rohe, 1922; top: Hotel Nord-Sud. André Lurçat, 1931; bottom: "Rush City Reformed." Richard Neutra (with Air, Dovell and Wordlar), 1928–1931.

Aerial photograph of the Bauhausplatz in Dessau, with the Bauhaus building in the background and the housing bars built in the late 1920s / early 1930s. Photograph by Barthold, 1992. Courtesy of Stiftung Bauhaus Dessau.

12 Alan Colquhoun, "Vernacular Classicism," *Modernity and the Classical Tradition—Architectural Essays 1980-1987* (Cambridge-London: The MIT Press, 1989), 21-31. Henri Lefebvre, "The Everyday and Everydayness," in Harris, Steven & Deborah Berke, *Architecture of the Everyday* (New York/New Haven: Princeton Architectural Press/Yale Publications on Architecture, 1997), 35.

13 Gabriele Tagliaventi, "Nel secolo delle ideologie e dell'innovazione tecnologica. Guida alla scoperta dell'architettura politicamente scorretta del Novecento," *L'altra modernità 1900-2000*, 30.

PART ONE:
IN SEARCH OF A MODERN VERNACULAR

All nationalist architecture is bad, but all good architecture is national.[14]

In its traditional sense vernacular architecture can be seen "as the repository of a timeless way of building, marrying practicality and economy with unselfconscious artistic effect, using local materials and responsive to local needs and climate."[15] Etymologically, the word "vernacular" is derived from the Latin *verna*, meaning a slave born in the house of his or her master. By extension, the adjective vernacular in classical times came to mean association with the place of birth, or as a noun, a native, usually a peasant or dependent. The word was identified with a local or village society and implied a way of life devoted to work — usually farm work — and to family.

The opposition between high art — from the Renaissance to the Revival styles of the nineteenth century — and the simple truths of vernacular architecture was a constant theme even through the first four decades of the twentieth century. Renewed interest in the vernacular originated in England during the nineteenth century. The Industrial Revolution had a traumatic impact on the development and quality of life of cities and on the conditions of workers' housing, thus engaging architects, social scientists and artists in attempting a return to the sources. In England, and later in France, the medieval Gothic vernacular and the structural principles of Gothic construction became the sources of inspiration for a new architecture that defined itself in opposition to the neo-Palladian principles that dominated the eighteenth and the first decades of the nineteenth centuries. Values of Christian life and faith, adequation of form and construction, as well as the nationalistic over-tones of the Gothic style sustained the development of the new school of English theory initiated by Augustus Pugin (1812–1852). His followers John Ruskin (1819–1900) and William Morris (1834–1896) were the progenitors of the Arts and Crafts and the spiritual inspiration for the Garden City, two deeply interconnected movements which were to spread across Europe and the United States at the turn of the century. In Germany, Herman Muthesius's (1861–1927) book *Das englische Haus* of 1904

left:
Woodcut for the *Manifesto and Program of the Staatlichen Bauhaus Weimar.* Lyonel Feininger. Print, 12 5/8 x 7 5/8" Photograph by Atelier Schneider. Courtesy of Bauhaus-Archiv Berlin.

pioneered the new spirit. Talking about the English house and its functionalist design inspired by farmhouses and other English vernacular elements, he wrote that "these houses are foundation stones of a new architecture…they are modern in the best sense of the word, because they are built reasonably and built for the middle class."[16] From the Arts and Crafts movement he opened the way to the Deutsche Werkbund (founded in 1907) but also to the vernacular-inspired works of Paul Schmitthenner, Paul Mebes (1872–1938), Theodor Fischer, Paul Schultze-Naumburg (1869–1949) and Bruno Taut. Mebes' book *Um 1800* (1908) and Schultze-Naumburg's *Kulturarbeiten* (1901–17) made the vernacular references accessible to architects and the public alike.

The program of the Staatliche Bauhaus that opened in Weimar in 1919 under the direction of Walter Gropius (1883–1969) relied on two apparently contradictory tenets, the pre-1914 Werkbund doctrine and the Expressionist medievalism of Taut and Poelzig (1869–1936). Yet, both movements were partially related to the concept of vernacular. Within the Werkbund, Fritz Schumacher and Peter Behrens attempted to bridge the gap between craft and industry by advocating full-fledged artistic cooperation. In the debate of July 1914, Muthesius strongly defended the idea of "standard" or "type," against Henri Van de Velde, (1863–1957)

14 Bruno Taut, *Architekturlehre* (Hamburg: Verlag für der Studium der Arbeiterbewegung, 1977), 333. Quoted in Sibel Bozdogan, "Against Style: Bruno Taut's Pedagogical Program in Turkey, 1936-1938," *The Education of an Architect: Historiography, Urbanism, and the Growth of Architectural Knowledge — Essays Presented to Stanford Anderson* (Cambridge: The MIT Press, 1997), 163-192.

15 For this section on the vernacular and its influence on modern architecture the author is indebted to Richard A. Etlin's "A Modern Vernacular Architecture," *Modernism in Italian Architecture, 1890–1940* (Cambridge-London: The MIT Press, 1991), 129-161. The definition is on page 129. Also J. B. Jackson, "Vernacular," *American Architecture: Tradition and Innovation* (New York: Rizzoli, 1986), 144.

16 Herman Muthesius, *Das englische Haus: Entwicklung, Bedingungen, Anlage, Aufbau, Einrichtung und Innenraum* (Berlin: E. Wasmuth, 1904). Quoted in Julius Posener, *From Schinkel to the Bauhaus* (New York: George Wittenborn, Inc.), 18.

for whom the individuality of the artist had to prevail. In contrast, the Expressionists condemned utility and function, and dreamt of a realm of pure beauty with the medieval cathedral as the main symbol and reference. Gropius' debt to Expressionist medievalism was unequivocally suggested in the program for the Bauhaus: "Architects, sculptors, painters, we must all return to handicraft."[17] During Gropius', Hannes Meyer's (1898–1954) and Mies Van der Rohe's (1889–1969) tenures at the helm of the Bauhaus in Dessau, the postwar craft-oriented theories increasingly led to a machine-based sophisticated aesthetic and to the apology of industrialization as the ultimate form of vernacular.

The Mediterranean Roots of Modern Architecture

And it is exactly as a myth, as a fantasy of building simply and harmoniously, as simulacrum of the absence of decoration and of pure Euclidean volumes, as symbolic form of the arithmetic canons of the "divine proportion," as shadow of the Apollonian beauty, and as echo of the sirens transmitted by the waves of the sea, that the "mediterraneità" will be evaluated, beyond its own objective ascertaining.[18]

From the eighteenth century the "Mediterranean" exercised a major influence on western European architecture and arts. The "Grand Tour" became a necessary rite of passage for well-to-do French, English or German artists, architects and writers. At first, they limited their travels to the northern regions of Italy and Rome. In time, they progressively traveled down south, attracted by the publication of the antiquities of Pompeii and Hercolanum, and the surveys of the Doric temples of Paestum. The progenitor was Wolfgang von Goethe (1749–1832), who in his *Italienische Reise* exported to Germany the cult of the "Apollonian serenity of the Mediterranean culture."[19] He was followed by Karl Friedrich Schinkel (1781–1841), who at the age of twenty-two expanded the horizon of his Italian travels, interests and sketches. Schinkel was not content to study the ruins and monuments of antique and modern Rome, but studied both the logic and the constructive

systems of the southern vernacular of the Roman countryside and the Neapolitan coast as well. His study of the houses of Capri, their constructive details, their relation to the landscape and their pure volumetric composition with their outdoor stairs, terraces and pergolas, announced Schinkel's later reinterpretation of Naples' Casino Reale del Chiatamone in the summer pavilion built in the gardens of Schloß Charlottenburg in Berlin (1826–1825). Schinkel introduced the white walls, balconies, louvers and the Mediterranean flat roof, all architectonic elements that were to resurface later as necessary conditions of modernity.[20]

At the end of a century dominated by neo-classicism but also by an increasingly pompous revivalist eclecticism, Muthesius' embrace of the English movement was a return to the simplicity of Schinkel's organic designs; the pioneers of the Austrian modern movement reinvented his Mediterranean allegiances. Two years before the launching of the Secession movement and on the invitation of Josef Olbrich, the young Austrian Josef Hoffmann (1870–1956) went on the Grand Tour. Like Schinkel, he was captivated by the southern vernacular and brought back more than two hundred sketches of Capri, Pozzuoli and other coastal villages. His sketches focused on the simple white walls, their small and low openings, the cupolas and barrel vaulted roofs, as well as the wide

---

17 Posener, 47. The very name Bauhaus was medieval, evoking the *Bauhütte* of the cathedrals.

18 Benedetto Gravagnuolo, *Il mito mediterraneo nell'architettura contemporanea* (Napoli: Electa Napoli, 1994), 8. Also see Gaetana Cantone and Italo Prozzillo, "La casa di capri e il novirento rodenno," *Case de Capri, Palazzi, Grandi Dinore* (Napoli: Electa Napoli/Edizioni la Conchiglia, 1994), 147-173.

19 Wolfgang von Goethe, *Italienische Reise* (Italian journey) (1786-88; reprint, Princeton: Princeton University Press, 1989).

above:
"Rural House in Capri." Karl Friedrich Schinkel, 1803–4, From *Reisen nach Italien. Tagebücher, Briefe, Zeichnungen, Aquarelle* (Berlin: Rütten & Loening, 1979 & 1982).

20 Karl Friedrich Schinkel, *Reisen nach Italien. Tagebücher, Briefe, Zeichnungen, Aquarelle* (Berlin: Rütten & Loenig, 1979).

exterior staircases that gave a highly plastic quality to the vernacular architecture of the islands. Undoubtedly, his sketches provided the inspiration for his increasingly minimalist tendencies in design. In a short essay he published in 1897 in *Der Architekt*, he wrote:

"The island of Capri remains in the memory of all those who have embarked on the Italian journey…. The perennial architectonic image expresses itself harmoniously in its absolute simplicity, free from artificial superstructures and bad taste decoration. Such simplicity, within the stifling landscape, brings relief to the soul, and speaks a clear language, understandable to all."[22]

Like Hoffmann, Adolf Loos (1870–1933) did integrate the elements of a genuine Mediterranean culture of dwelling. Loos' polemical writings always tended to conceal the reality of his architecture and of his clearly avowed debt to Schinkel and classicism, as expressed in one of his most important essays, "Architektur," published in 1910, the same year the Looshaus was completed on Michaelerplatz in Vienna. In his series of houses as well as his apartment projects, Loos carried the experiment further. He played with all aspects of the vernacular, from the chalet-type of Landhaus Khuner (1929–30) to the unbuilt Mediterranean project for the Villa Alexander Moissi (1923) on the Lido of Venice, itself loosely based on Schinkel's own project in the Postdam area (Lusthaus, 1823). In so doing and in opposition to the radical interpretation of his works based upon his essay, "Ornament and Crime,"[23] Loos foreshadowed the amalgam of modernity with classical and vernacular traditions that characterized most of the "other modern" of the twentieth century. Along with Muthesius and Loos, Peter Behrens (1868–1940)

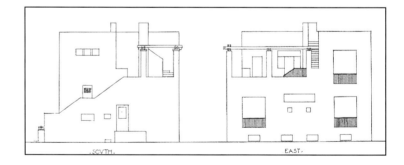

top left:
Development of exterior staircases for a house in Amalfi. Virgilio Marchi, 1922. From *Architettura e Arte Decorativi*, 1922.

top right:
House in Capri. Josef Hoffmann, 1896. From *Der Architekt* (Vienna, 1897).

bottom:
Project for the Villa Alexander Moissi (south and east façade), Lido of Venice, Italy. Adolf Loos, 1923. Courtesy of the Adolf Loos Archives, Graphische Sammlung Albertina, Vienna.

22 Author's translation from Josef Hoffman, "Architektonisches von der Insel Capri," *Der Architekt III* (1897): 13.

23 Benedetto Gravagnuolo, *Adolf Loos, Theory and Works* (New York: Rizzoli, 1982). *Ornament and Crime* was published in 1905.

also saw in Schinkel's simplified and quasi-vernacular classicism "a combination of nationalist and idealistic associations suitable to his own task of formulating an imagery for the industrial elite."[24] Not only did the Berlin architect establish the classical vernacular of metropolitan industry, but he also radically influenced the development of a modern version of classicism, where the abstracted form of the Doric temples in Paestum "entered the twentieth century, once more as absolute image and primary essentiality."[25] Heinrich Tessenow (1876–1950) continued in Behrens' footsteps, but focused on the small house and the small town in connection with the post-World War I Garden City movement. It is in his delicately drawn and solidly built works in Hellerau and Berlin that the synthesis between both twentieth century vernaculars — the classical and the picturesque — was fully realized.[26]

In northern Europe, the National Romantic Movement that accompanied the new political landscape in the first decades of the century had brought a renewed eclecticism, blending together medieval and modern inspirations with vernacular forms and traditions. Eliel Saarinen (1873–1950), Ivar Tengbom (1878–1968), Lars Sonck (1870–1956) and Ragnar Ostberg (1866–1945) epitomized northern modernity between 1900 and 1920, the latter spending fourteen years to complete one of the masterpieces of the "other modern," the Stockholm City Hall (1909–1923). The youngest of the group, Gunnar Asplund, traveled to the Mediterranean during the first months of 1914, an "unorthodox journey" that led him to Sicily and Tunisia, and whose implication on the understanding of his architecture and modern classicism in Europe has been amply extolled. From Tunisia, Asplund wrote:

24 Curtis, 101.

25 Joselita Raspi Serra, *Everyday Masterpieces*, exhibition catalogue, 138. It is Karl Friedrich Schinkel who introduced the Doric in Berlin. Also refer to *La fortuna di Paestum e la memoria moderna del dorico 1750–1830* (Firenze: 1986).

26 Marco de Michelis, *Heinrich Tessenow, 1876–1950* (Milano: Electa, 1991).

top:
Competition entry for the Royal Chancellery in Stockholm, façade on the water.
Gunnar Asplund with Ture Ryberg, 1921. Courtesy of the Swedish Architecture Museum.

bottom:
First version of the project for the Institute Jaques-Dalcroze, Hellerau, Germany.
Heinrich Tessenow, 1910. Courtesy Institut für Denkmalpflege, Dresden.

Aerial view of the new town of Sabaudia. c. 1934. Gruppo Urbanisti Romani, 1933-34. From "Sabaudia," *Architettura* XIII (June 1934).

"…Tunis, this is the most amusing I have come across in the twenty-eight years of my existence!…Above our heads a sky clear and deep the like of which I have never seen, such a tone in the color that I am constantly imagining the sky as a vast blue-painted dome."[27]

The sky as a "vault" was the inspiration for the Skandia Cinema's starred ceiling (1924) and for the spatial layout of the Woodland Cemetery (1915 to 1940, with Sigurd Lewerentz); the Woodland Chapel appeared like a Nordic vernacular transformation of the Pantheon in Rome (1918); and the Venetian typologies and the façades of the Grand Canal influenced the unbuilt project of the Royal Chancellery, also in Stockholm (1929).

In Italy itself, the importance of vernacular architecture as a stimulus for a modern idiom cannot be overemphasized.[28] The movement started in Rome under the guidance of Gustavo Giovannoni (1873–1947) and Marcello Piacentini (1881–1960), both members of the Roman Associazione Artistica fra i Cultori di Architettura and founders of the first architectural magazine, *Architettura e Arti Decorative,* in 1921. In its columns, Piacentini praised the new "rustic" architecture developing in Europe and in the United States, as one of the three principal schools of modern architecture with an avant-garde and modern classicism.[29]

In the north, Giovanni Muzio (1893–1982) and Gio Ponti (1891–1979) defined the parameters of the Novecento style, which modernized the classical vernacular of the Milanese region and impregnated it with the metaphysical spirit of Giorgio De Chirico's urban visions. In the 1930s, Ponti increasingly developed the concept of *mediterraneità*, which embodied two seemingly disparate ideals, the classical and the vernacular. Yet, the most surprising embrace of the vernacular and Capri as a mythical mirage came from the Italian Futurists. Led by Filippo Marinetti (1876–1944), the Futurists had embarked during the 1910s on a violent campaign against all traditions and academic pursuits, with slogans like, "Speed is our God, the new canon of beauty; a roaring motorcar, which runs like a machine gun."[30] After the disaster of World War I, Futurists like Virgilio Marchi (1895–1960) relinquished their ardent embrace of the machine and sheltered themselves in the architecture of the Neapolitan coast, conveying their newly found conviction in sketches, paintings and poems.[31] At the same time, Gruppo 7's Rationalist manifestos also advocated an architecture that combined international values and national identity. This "contextual avant-garde," with Giuseppe Terragni (1904-1943) and Adalberto Libera (1903-1963) at its head, looked for an Italian way of being modern, and saw in Giotto the symbolic figure connecting "architetture antiche e moderne."[32] Their search for modern vernacular types, echoed by the Fascist regime's emphasis on rural values, found its best expression in the new towns of Sabaudia (1934) and Guidonia (1936-38), and other iconic works like Libera and Curzio Malaparte's (1898-1957) Villa Malaparte in Capri (1939-1942).

The North-South Debate

In the early 1930s, at the time that MoMA was initiating its brilliant campaign of propaganda on the American continent, the tenets of the Bauhaus and the International Style came under heavy scrutiny by modernist European architects. On the one hand, in Germany itself, Hugo Häring (1882–1958) became a sharp critic of Gropius and

27 Quoted from Asplund's diary by Elias Cornell in "The Sky as a Vault…," Claes Oldenby and Olof Hultin, *Asplund* (New York: Rizzoli, 1986). Also see Luca Ortelli "Heading South: Asplund's Impressions," *Lotus International* 68 (1991): 23-33.

28 Richard A. Etlin, *Modernism in Italian Architecture, 1890–1940* (Cambridge: The MIT Press, 1991), 139.

29 Piacentini shifted in the 1930s to an increasingly abstract "classical modern" style, which became through his followers a recognizable vernacular of 1930s Rome.

30 Filippo Marinetti, "Manifeste futuriste," *Le Figaro,* February 20, 1909.

31 See for instance the sketches of Virgilio Marchi, *Architettura Futurista* (Roma: 1924) and Marinetti's discourse of 1923 advocating the protection of Capri in *Il convegno del paesaggio (1923),* reprinted in 1993 by Edizioni La Conchiglia (Capri).

32 From Giovanni Michelucci, "Contacts between Ancient and Modern Architectures," *Domus* (March 1932). Il Gruppo 7, "Architettura," *Rassegna Italiana* 18 (December 1926), translated in *Oppositions* 6 (1976), 86-102. The term "contextual avant-garde" is quoted from Etlin, 255.

Le Corbusier, whom he accused of working too much as "architects" and not enough as "builders," thus criticizing their classical influences and the anti-vernacular quality of their architecture. Instead he advocated a search for a modern organic design that would be anchored in the regional realities of Germany.[33] On the other hand, some members of CIAM like Josep Lluis Sert and Le Corbusier initiated a retreat from the "machine" and its "international" symbolic value, and reoriented their strategy toward the Mediterranean as a source of inspiration for their architecture. In effect, it was the politically and socially polarized climate of Europe that resulted in the establishment of two distinct and antagonistic fronts that could be labeled as "Northern modernism" and "Southern modernism." As editor of the magazine *A.C.*, Sert published special issues on Mediterranean vernacular architecture, and the island of Ibiza became as important a symbol as Capri for Piacentini and his Italian colleagues.

"If, having examined several examples of Mediterranean vernacular constructions, we compare them to the best creations of modern architecture," Sert wrote, "we cannot help but notice characteristics in common, not in details but in those 'constants' that endow the architectural work with its spirit. Why, therefore, has modern architecture been called Germanic?… Technically speaking, modern architecture is largely the discovery of the Nordic countries, but spiritually it is Mediterranean architecture without style that influences this new architecture. Modern architecture is a return to the pure, traditional forms of the Mediterranean. It is one more triumph of the Latin Sea!"[34]

In 1931, Le Corbusier traveled to Barcelona to meet Sert and other members of GATCPAC, hoping that they might support him and collaborate in the mythicization of the Mediterranean as the indispensable basis for a new architecture, far removed from the mists of the North and its obsessions with objectivity. "Being in possession of the Mediterranean," Josep Rovira wrote in reference to this encounter, "meant being in possession of the new architecture."[35] The North-South debate officially started during the famous CIAM IV held on the *Patris II*, that sailed from Marseilles to Athens from July 29 to August 13, 1933. It was accentuated by the political turmoil of the 1930s when its ideological framework became increasingly linked to issues of national purity and identity. It is in the French right-wing magazine *Préludes* that Le Corbusier issued some of his statements on the matter.[36]

top:
Nazi caricature with Arabs in the Weissenhofsiedlung in Stuttgart, 1938. Postcard. © Schwäbing Kunstverlag, H. Boettcher, Stuttgart.

right:
View of Esquivel during construction, Spain. Alejandro de la Sota, 1948-52. From Pedro de Llano, Alejandro de la Sota: O nacemento dunha arquitectura (Pontevedra: Deputación Provincial,1994)

In Nazi Germany, the propagandistic and populist attack against modernist architecture was equally ideological. On the one hand, the nationalist argument was used "a contrario" to stigmatize the "degenerated" and "Mediterranean" architecture of the Bauhaus, and forcefully promote a return to the Germanic vernacular of mythical medieval times. The photomontage of Arab men riding camels around the Weissenhofsiedlung became a legendary image for this very reason. On the other hand, as historians John Zukowsky, Winfried Nerdinger and Hartmut Frank demonstrated, Hitler's military-industrial complex adopted modernist architecture and was in opposition to the official discourse.

From his exile in Turkey, Bruno Taut — who achieved an effective symbiosis between German vernacular types and modernist ideals in his

33 Posener, 33.

34 Josep Lluis Sert, "Arquitectura sense 'estil' i sense 'arquitecte,'" *D'Ací i d'Allà* 179 (December 1934). Reprinted in Antonio Pizza, ed., *J. LL. Sert and Mediterranean Culture* (Barcelona: Col-legi d'Arquitectes de Catalunya, 1997), 210.

35 Josep Rovira, "The Mediterranean Is His Cradle," in Pizza, 65. The GATCPAC's (Grupo de artistas y tecnicos por el progreso de arquitectura contemporánea) magazine *A.C.* emphasized the relationship between modernist architecture and the Mediterranean vernacular. In issue 1, Oud's townhouses at the Weissenhofsiedlung in Stuttgart (1927) were compared to fishermen's houses on the Catalan coast.

36 See Jean-Claude Vigato, *Le jeu des modéles — Les modéles en jeu* (Nancy: C.E.R.P.A., 1980) and Antonio Pizza, "The Mediterranean: Creation and Development of a Myth," in J. L. Sert, 12-45. The journal *Prelude*, published from 1933 to 1936, occupied an ambiguous position between fascism and collectivism. Le Corbusier was a member of its editorial board.

housing estates in Berlin — summed up the prevailing mood a decade after the opening of the Bauhaus and on the brink of World War II:

"Those looking for a particular 'party line' in architecture have never been able to go beyond formal issues. Even those who set out to abandon historical styles have ended up selecting a few rational aspects of architecture and declaring them 'the style of the age' and labeling them with various *isms*...."[37]

In 1935, three years before his exile to America following General Franco's victory, Josep Lluis Sert sounded equally nationalistic and shattered the so-called monolithic image of the avant-garde:

"Every country has a timeless architecture which is generally termed vernacular, not in the sense as understood in architecture schools, which means regional, but rather vernacular of the lowest class, classified according to the economic means at their disposal.... The pure functionalism of the 'machine à habiter' is dead. Architects and theorists, above all Germanic, carried functionalist experiments to absurd extremes."[38]

The devastation of the Spanish Civil War renewed the debate about the place and virtue of the vernacular in the process of reconstruction. The Department of Devastated Regions embarked on a successful ten-year program of reconstruction of devastated cities and towns, as well as construction of new towns to replace destroyed settlements. As in Warsaw or Munich, the prevailing return to tradition and to the vernacular forms of building was not only an ideological but also a pragmatic solution imposed by the economic and technical difficulties in the country. Yet, it is in the new towns of Gimenells (1943) and Esquivel (1948-52), developed for the Instituto Nacional de Colonización (I. N. C.) and designed by Alejandro de la Sota (1913–1997) that a genuine vernacular modern was implemented. In one essay about Spanish architecture of the post-Civil War decades, William Curtis wrote:

"Let us look at the plan for Esquivel. It is without doubt a project of urbanization, whose roots lie in the quality of local vernacular architecture. We find in Esquivel the traditional manner of designing urban spaces, but they have been abstracted in order to adapt them to a new order and a new landscape. The forms of the buildings in the plan of the town do not differ from other attempts to reach a regional expression. Yet, it is also clear that we are not in the presence of another vernacular imitation, it is the touch of surrealism that permeates its reality."[39]

top:
Duplex house, Lenox Avenue and 6th Street, Miami Beach. Henry Hohauser, 1936. Rendering. From the *Miami Herald*, 1 November 1936.

bottom:
Henkel Observatory, Miami Beach. Architect, date and location unknown. Courtesy of the Romer Collection, Miami-Dade Public Library.

37   Taut, *Architekturlehre*, 334. Quoted in Bozdogan, 188.

38   Josep Lluis Sert, "Raices mediterráneas de la arquitectura moderna," *A.C.* 18 (1935). Reprinted in Pizza, 217-18.

39   Author's translation of William Curtis, "Dúas obras," *Grial* 109 (Vigo 1991): 17. Quoted by Pedro de Llano in *Alejandro de la Sota: O nacemento dunha arquitectura* (Pontevedra: Deputación Provincial de Pontevedra, 1994), 41.

The American Urban Vernacular

The vernacular in its traditional sense has always been a feature of the American city. With its fabric of freestanding single-family homes and the importance of wood as primary residential construction material, the American city has maintained a solid connection with the early vernacular of the country, and particularly the colonial-based typologies. Yet at the turn of the century, following the English example, the search for an American style in opposition to the growing influence of the *beaux-arts* American Renaissance accelerated. On the East Coast, Marianne Van Rensselaer extolled the creation of a new American "vernacular" house, known as the Shingle Style, whose modernity was brilliantly revealed in Vincent Scully's seminal work of 1955.[40] Its correspondent on the West Coast was found in the "craftsman" ideals of Bernard Maybeck (1862–1957) and Greene & Greene (1868–1957; 1870–1954), as well as in the stripped and abstracted language of Irving Gill (1870–1936).

In the Midwest, Frank Lloyd Wright (1869–1959) developed his sophisticated elaboration of a Prairie vernacular, which would in turn, through the publication of the Wasmuth Portfolio in Germany in 1909, stimulate the European milieu, and particularly the young Dutch school. In Southern California, Florida and other Southern states like Texas, the Spanish-Mediterranean idiom and its variants, Mission Style and Mediterranean Revival, became the style of choice to provide a regional identity to the new towns and cities that sprung up, almost overnight, during the 1910s and 1920s. Indeed, upon the advent of World War I, the traditional architects' Italian Grand Tour was interrupted and displaced to a war-free Spain; Andalusia was discovered by young and ambitious architects who spent many months drawing, photographing and writing about the examples of untouched classical and vernacular architecture that they encountered.[41] Bertram Goodhue, George Washington Smith (1876–1930), Carrère & Hastings (1858–1911; 1860–1929), Gordon B. Kaufmann (1888-1949), Schultze & Weaver (1860–1951; 1865–1940), Addison Mizner (1872–1933) and many others fashioned an intensely innovative and genuinely modern architecture for California and the developing southern regions: "the conscious or unconscious task which these men set for themselves was to strip off the specific historic details, and then to think in terms of elemental shapes and forms — the cube, the rectangle, and the arch."[42]

top:
Big Mama Court, detail of arched openings into garages and stairways, Los Angeles. George Washington Smith, 1932. Photograph by Julius Shulman. From Stefanos Polyzoides, Roger Sherwood and James Tice, *Courtyard Housing in Los Angeles: A Typological Analysis* (Berkeley: University of California Press, 1982).
bottom:
El Cadiz Apartments, Hollywood. Milton J. Black, 1936. Photograph by Julius Shulman. From Stefanos Polyzoides, Roger Sherwood and James Tice, *Courtyard Housing in Los Angeles: A Typological Analysis* (Berkeley: University of California Press, 1982).

40 Vincent Scully, *The Shingle Style: Architectural Theory and Design from Richardson to the Origins of Wright* (New Haven: Yale University Press, 1955). Also see Esther McCoy, *Five California Architects* (New York: Reinhold Pub., 1960).

41 Bertram Goodhue, preface to Austin Whittlesey, *The Minor Ecclesiastical, Domestic, and Garden Architecture of Southern Spain* (New York: Architectural Book Publishing, 1923), v-viii.

42 David Gebhard, "The Spanish Colonial Revival in Southern California (1895–1930)," *Journal of the Society of Architectural Historians* 37 (May 1967):140.

Yet, the most important urban innovation of the first decades of the twentieth century was a specifically American response to the issue of urban identity in the Garden City movement, and it was built upon the urban potential of Mediterranean culture. Contrary to the Shingle Style or the Prairie School, the "Mediterranean vernacular" had a considerable impact on American urbanism, and it led to the creation, ex novo, of a new urban morphology. What the White City of Chicago of 1893 did for the revival of classical planning in the City Beautiful movement, the Panama California International Exposition of San Diego in 1915 (planned by Bertram Grosvenor Goodhue in Balboa Park) did for the new morphology and its emphasis on rational but picturesque planning. Clarence Stein wrote: "… the San Diego Fair is the apotheosis of all those elements of charm and variety that we associate with the cities of Italy and Spain. It has the varied symmetry and underlying order of the Latin cities without the squalor of the crowded quarters."[43]

The most impressive spin-offs of the Fair were the new towns and garden cities built in the Mediterranean Revival style and its variations, and their central public spaces, genuine Spanish-inspired plazas and paseos. They included the industrial new town of Tyrone in New Mexico (Bertram Goodhue, 1917, demolished), the reconstruction of Santa Barbara after the earthquake of 1925 and its theatrical system of alleys and courtyards initiated by Charles Cheney in 1922, John Gaw Meem's (1894–1987) reconstruction of the center of Santa Fe (1930s) in neo-Pueblo style, as well as a series of plaza-like shopping districts, Malaga Cove in Palos Verdes (Olmsted, 1922–1923), Highland Park Shopping Village in Dallas (1931), Westwood in Los Angeles (from 1926) and Country Club Plaza in Kansas City (from 1922). It is during the same period that architects and developers built hundreds of courtyard apartment buildings along the streets of Los Angeles and Hollywood, inventing a new "culture of housing" around the traditional Spanish-colonial patio for the hectic, car-oriented life of California.

In Florida, new "cities of leisure" rose out of the flatlands and marshes. They were seen as "ideal cities" imbued with the upper- and middle-class search for an urban utopia, pregnant with Mediterranean romanticism, far from the industrial world, and as socially homogeneous

A group of courtyard buildings in West Hollywood, Los Angeles, south of Sunset Boulevard between Harper and Havenhurst. From Stefanos Polyzoides, Roger Sherwood and James Tice, op. cit. Photograph by Julius Shulman.

environments that pretended to be free of class conflicts. At the higher end of the social spectrum, Addison Mizner designed and built the scenographic town center of Palm Beach (1919–1926), whereas George Merrick and his architects developed Coral Gables (founded in 1921) as "the city in the garden" for the middle class. Palm Beach's Via Parigi and Via Mizner, the Douglas Entrance and the Biltmore Hotel became outstanding, yet too rare, "moments" of urbanity.[44] In the 1930s, Florida found itself involved in the classic battle between a desire for regionalism and an equally strong urge to become part of the national and international scene. On the regional side, the Spanish Mediterranean went into a transformation process that brought it closer to the Caribbean and in particular to the vernacular of the Anglo-colonial islands. On the national/international side, the late Art Deco and its follower the Streamlined were the modern responses; yet, with their traditional elevations, plans and stucco surfaces, they suggested "that their modernity grew out of the earlier Hispanic-Mediterranean tradition."[45]

43   Carleton M. Winslow (introduction by Bertram Grosvenor Goodhue; with an essay by Clarence Stein), *The Architecture and the Gardens of the San Diego Exposition: A Pictorial Survey of the Aesthetic Features of the Panama California International Exposition* (San Francisco: P. Elder and Co., 1916), 11.

44   See Jean-François Lejeune, "Searching for Paradise / Garden Cities in Florida: The Grid, the Park, and the Model-T," *Garden City / A Century of Theories, Models, and Experiences* (Roma: Gangemi, 1994), 221-266.

45   David Gebhard, *The Elusive Image: Regionalism in Twentieth Century Architecture* (Christchurch, New Zealand: School of Fine Arts University of Canterbury, 1993), 20.

Original proposal for the Douglas Entrance (Puerta del Sol), Coral Gables. Walter De Garmo, Phineas E. Paist and Denman Fink, 1924. Courtesy of the Otto G. Richter Library, University of Miami.

revolution," he wrote in *Architectural Forum*," has forcefully focused our attention on some principles of composition, not new to be sure, but somewhat neglected during the past hundred years, such as the value of restraint, the value of designing volumes instead of merely decorating surfaces and the value of empty surfaces as elements of composition."[47]

International Style Versus Vernacular Modern

Art Deco was urban, proteiform and contextual. It expressed best the modernity of an enterprising bourgeoisie, young, and free from moral prejudices. It seduced because it made reference to an art of living, it spoke to the imagination, brought to mind visions of an ideal modern life….In the growing multicultural metropolis of the pre-war era, it integrated, in the manner of a musician who composes an oriental march, all the cultures: thus, Art Deco was the absolute opposite of the International Style and the functionalist movement which rejected them all to impose their own and only values.[48]

As Terry Smith wrote in *Making the Modern: Industry, Art, and Design in America*, "modernity became normal"[49] in the second half of the 1930s. The reality of the post-Depression economy forced the nation into evolving new ways of living and more economical forms and materials. The aesthetic message was to declare the hope in the future and the innate capacity of modern design to improve man's daily life. The American industrial designer became "the twentieth century answer to William Morris' lament of the separation of the machine and the artist. It perfectly fulfilled the dream that all 'progressive' Europeans and Americans had pursued from the nineteenth century on. Here was the Bauhaus ideal realized."[50]

The battle for modernity in the United States during the inter-war period was not only a conflict between the proponents of historicist architecture and the modernist one, but between two modern styles, and even more so between two visions of the city. It revolved in fact around

While the Spanish Mediterranean was established as the primary style of the post-World War I real estate boom, by the early 1930s Art Deco and its simplified forms and volumes became the accepted norm in the American metropolis. In New York — like in Chicago and Los Angeles — most commercially successful architects embraced it and established it as the modern metropolitan vernacular for public buildings, for the mid-rise fabric of the Upper West and East Side, and the new "monuments" like the Chrysler Building. Vincent Scully wrote enthusiastically of the "skyscraper vernacular" of New York, loved by the public but usually disregarded by modernist historians on the basis of Le Corbusier's and CIAM's criticism. Its lower floors respected the street in the model of the palazzo, while the upper stories "leaped and pointed upward with all a spire's fantasy of a colonial church."[46]

In his article "Ten Years of Modern Architecture," Paul Philippe Cret (1876–1945), the leader of the classical-modern movement in the United States and one of the figureheads of the University of Pennsylvania, summarized the architectural trend of the decade: "The modernist

46   Vincent Scully, "American Architecture: the Real and the Ideal," *American Architecture: Innovation and Tradition* (New York: Rizzoli, 1986), 19-20. Also see Francesco Mujica, *History of the Skyscraper* (Paris-New York: Archaeology & Architecture Press, 1929).

47   Paul Philippe Cret, "Ten Years of Modernism," *Architectural Forum* (August 1933): 94.

48   Author's translation of Maurice Culot, *Bruxelles Art Déco* (Brussels: Archives d'Architecture Moderne, 1997), 10, 13.

49   Smith, 425.

50   Gebhard, *Kem Weber*, 26.

Plates II, "Evolution of the Skyscraper." Francisco Mujica, 1929. From Francisco Mujica, *History of the Skyscraper* (Paris-New York: Archaeology & Architecture Press,1929).

two concepts of abstraction: one abstracting the elements of decoration, which was the thesis defended by the proponents and builders of the urban Art Deco-Moderne; the other one abolishing decoration entirely, thus making the edifice itself the focus of the abstraction process.

The first trend, emulated by the "other modern" architects, fertilized the city, as it encouraged new building design to maintain the solidarity with the urban realm, providing modern identity and character to the buildings, while simultaneously subordinating them to an urban order. The second trend implied that the edifice would become less and less connected to the city, as the architects' effort to express individuality obliged them to abuse volumes. Thus "the characterization of buildings by means of their volumetry signified the destruction of the figurative urban space of the pre-war periods" as well as the end of the urban vernacular.[51] Architectural and urban design projects that questioned or refused the hegemony of the street as the fundamental organizing principle of urban space were systematically assimilated to a progressive development of architectural and urban history. This concept formed the basis of the modernist housing tradition defended by the CIAM. Exemplified in projects such as the Siedlung Rothenburg by Otto Haesler

in Kassel (1930) and Richard Neutra's (1892–1970) vision for Rush City Reformed (1928–31), it was based on typological discontinuity, and expressed the pursuit of egalitarian symbolism based on uniformity and repetition, as well as the emphasis on economic formulas and machine-based production. Such a doctrine was bound to hit the housing residents' desires frontally. In an astonishing display of cynicism, the authors of the International Style catalogue of 1932 wrote that the architect was allowed to disregard all local conditions and traditions: "His aim…is to approach an ideal standard. But houses should not be functionally so advanced that they are lived in under protest."[52]

The stand-off between the International Style's planners and the "other moderns" in fact reflected two radically opposed visions of the modern city: the small-scale, typically capitalist vision of speculation on land traditionally divided into small lots, and the rise of "Corporate State modernity" based on public-private lot assemblage. Thus it can be said that the urban, plot-based "other modern" was fundamentally an urban middle-class architecture that respected the rules and codes of its urban context, and architectonically exploited them to their fullest extent. It is not a surprise that MoMA's director, Alfred Barr, wrote in the International Style catalogue:

"We are asked to take seriously the architectural taste of real-estate speculators, renting agents, and mortgage brokers. It is not surprising that the modern critic should feel more sympathy with the sound academic achievements of conservative contemporaries than with these modernistic impresarios."[53]

Mumford's criticism may have been significant in this matter. It reflected the prevalent ideology among twentieth-century intellectuals for whom progress in housing was more often than not equated with an ideological vision of social housing. Such an attitude did in effect disburden the private sector of its responsibility, thus favoring lot assemblage and large-scale operations, and the *de facto* devaluation of the small investor's critical role in the shaping of the urban fabric.

The International Style Exhibition was expectedly attacked in the press by the most important architects of the time including Frank Lloyd Wright; yet, some of its own promoters did not shy away from serious criticism, as testified to in the correspondence between Lewis Mumford and Douglas Haskell, future editor of *Architectural Forum*:

51 This argument is made by Fernando Diez in "Abstraçaõ e urbanismo: sobre a relaçaõ entre urbanismo e decoraçaõ," *Art Deco na América Latina (1º Seminario Internacional, Centro de Arquitectura e Urbanismo do Rio de Janeiro, April 14-16, 1996)* (Rio de Janeiro: Prefeitura da Cidade do Rio de Janeiro, 1997), 111.

52 *The International Style*, 94.

53 Alfred Barr, *The International Style*, 14.

"Much of the architecture which Johnson and Hitchcock...have been so loud in praise of seemed a little seedy, or at least, incompletely thought out.... Now that you and I have both seen the work, we can at least challenge them on the ground where they have hitherto been pre-eminent, for lack of rivalry....."[54]

Both critics wondered whether the exhibited works truly represented everything that could or should have been included under the label of modern architecture and whether they formed a school that superseded everything else contemporary to them. Yet, it seems that no criticism was addressed to the urban tenets of the show, a gap that was to widen after the war.

With the advent of World War II, the "international" started to give way to the "national" or the "regional." The search for a new vernacular, more human and closer to the public's desires, was on the way, and the interpretation of "modern" became increasingly regional. In 1944 Elizabeth Mock (born 1911) curated the show *Built in the USA — Since 1932* at the Museum of Modern Art in New York. The exhibition documented the ideological shift occurring within the previously puritanical modernist camp. The displayed projects were wide-ranging both in type and in the diversity of materials used for construction, an astonishing sight in regard to the International Style Exhibition. White abstract walls and "glass boxes" were no longer the exclusive images of modernity. Brick, stone and wood could be modern also, along with sloped roofs that had been ostracized just a few years earlier.[55] Intense debates took place where critics discussed the ills and virtues of regionalist experiments like William Wurster's (1895–1973) Bay Area Style. Prototype houses such as the Case Study Houses, built between 1945 and 1961, helped define the paradigm of suburban modern living in California.[55]

Nevertheless, it must be emphasized that this reevaluation of the concept of modern architecture had no positive impact on the tenets governing the design of cities. The story of the machine's acceptance by American architectural culture was far from uncomplicated and the postwar era would reflect the increasing contradictions, particularly between the vision of the central city and its residential suburban districts. In America, suburbs had started to dominate the scene, and there, the modern could and had to be tempered: "regional" architecture became

Zoning Envelopes: Third and Fourth Stage. Hugh Ferriss, 1922. From William Corbett, "Zoning and the Envelope of the Building," *Pencil Points* (April 1923): 15-18. Courtesy Cooper-Hewitt Museum of Design.

the "garb" that made acceptable the mass-produced tract houses of the postwar baby boom. In contrast, within the city, the International Style remained uncontested and the CIAM's principles were advocated more than ever. The belief in a new world and its formal translation was so strong that, in the midst of the war, Mumford argued "to continue to do, in a more deliberate and rational fashion, what the bombs have done by brutal hit-or-miss, if we have space enough to live and produce the proper means of living."[56]

Thus, as late as 1944, Art Deco and the Streamlined Moderne remained dangerous, not only because of their decorative content, but also because they were, in fact, the last urban styles of the metropolis. Philip Goodwin (1885–1958) summarized the issue brutally in his preface to Built in the USA: "Why continue the crusade after it has been won? But, with the trend away from the old styles has come a new type of streamlined 'modernistic' that needs to be combated as vigorously as ever. The fight must go on against superficiality or sensationalism by the encouragement of sound, sincere building, as well as for wider acceptance of and interest in town and city planning."[57]

54   Robert Benson, "Douglas Haskell and the Criticism of International Modernism," in *Modern Architecture in America: Visions and Revisions*, ed. Richard Guy Wilson and Sidney K. Robinson (Ames: Iowa State University Press, 1991), 180-181. The letter from Lewis Mumford to Douglas Haskell was dated 4 July 1932.

54   Elizabeth Mock, *Built in USA — Since 1932* (New York: The Museum of Modern Art, 1944). On the discussion of regionalism, the author is indebted to Mitchell Schwarzer, "Modern Architecture Ideology in Cold War America," *The Education of an Architect* (Cambridge: The MIT Press, 1997), 87-109.

55   Marc Treib, *An Everyday Modernism: The Houses of William Wurster* (San Francisco: San Francisco Museum of Art, 1995); *Blueprints for Modern Living: History and Legacy of the Case Study Houses* (Los Angeles: Museum of Contemporary Art, 1989).

56   Lewis Mumford, "The Social Foundations of Post-War Building," *City Development— Studies in Disintegration and Renewal* (New York: Harcourt, Brace and Company, 1945. The essay was first written in 1942.

57   Philip Goodwin, preface to Mock, 8.

Typology or the Return to the City

I feel the role of prima donna culture hero even in its modern form as prima donna anticulture anti-hero is a late Romantic theme as obsolete for the architect and for the complex interdependencies of architectural practice today as is the "heroic and original" building for architecture.[58]

In 1964 the Museum of Modern Art in New York hosted the exhibition *Architecture without Architects — An Introduction to Non-Pedigreed Architecture*. Curated by Austrian-born architect Bernard Rudofsky (1905–1988), the show consisted of a sequence of photographs ranging from barrel-vaulted villages of the Mediterranean to medieval squares of Poland and streets of India. This architecture was "so little known that we don't even have a name for it. For want of a generic label, we shall call it vernacular, anonymous, spontaneous, indigenous or rural, as the case may be."[59] In this exhibition and book, Rudofsky returned to his adopted intellectual roots: the Mediterranean islands, Capri, Procida and the Gulf of Naples. Like Schinkel, Hoffmann and Loos before him, Rudofsky produced superb sketches of the Mediterranean vernacular, such as those of Santorini in 1929 (p. 148). He used them for his doctoral thesis *A Primitive Use of Concrete in Architecture*, which he presented at the Technische Universität Wien in 1931. His first built work, the Villa Oro (1934–37), was distinguished by its white cubic forms cantilevering over the Gulf of Naples. Designed in collaboration with Luigi Cosenza (1905–1984), it was a literal manifesto for the integration of modernism with the traditional forms of the Mediterranean.

Throughout his career, Rudofsky labeled himself a modernist, yet he contrasted the dogma of the styles with his research on other ways of life, sometimes forgotten ones. He wanted to liberate the modern movement from its formalism, bringing it back to the basic questions of human scale and comfortable life. Rudofsky's biggest criticism targeted the "historical establishment" that remained entrenched within the high end of architecture: "Architectural history, as written and taught in the Western world, has never been concerned with more than a few select cultures…. It amounts to a little more than a who's who of architects who commemorated power and wealth; an anthology of buildings of, by, and for the privileged — the houses of true and false gods, of merchant princes and princes of the blood — with never a word about the houses of lesser people. Such preoccupation with noble architecture and architectural nobility to the exclusion of all other kinds may have been understandable as late as a generation ago… but today, when the copying of historical forms is on the wane, when banking houses or railroad stations do not necessarily have to resemble prayers in stone to inspire confidence, such self-imposed limitations appear absurd."[60]

Rudofsky's approach to the vernacular was essentially urban, and marked a radical departure from the modernist vision of Le Corbusier or Josep Lluis Sert. The urban spaces created by the assemblage of buildings, and the urban life and relationships that they generated, interested him more than the very architectural forms. In 1969, Rudofsky extended his research by producing his most important book, *Streets for People: A Primer for Americans*. Dedicated to the "unknown pedestrian," it was a broad-scoped treatise on the urban environment, and a direct attack on the automobile-oriented urban renewal policies of the modern movement. Whereas *Architecture without Architects* emphasized "the other cultures," *Streets for People*, whose cover featured Mengoni's Galleria in Milan, focused on European and North American cities.[61]

Rudofsky was not the only scholar to rediscover the polemical nature of "everyday" buildings, particularly those in the context of the traditional city, its streets, blocks and squares. In 1961, Jane Jacobs, then an associate editor of *Architectural Forum*, published her first book, *The Death and Life of Great American Cities*. In the midst of Robert Moses' plans for destructive highway construction in New York, Jacobs launched her defense of the traditional city along with a blistering attack on the "anti-urban" forces that threatened it. Her advocacy of the dense mixed-use city, of its streets and sidewalks, influenced the post-1968 "return to the city" movements and induced the revitalization of deteriorating districts like Haight-Ashbury in San Francisco, Greenwich Village in New York and the southern districts of Miami Beach itself.

Winds of change also came from Northern Europe with the works of Alvar Aalto (1898–1976). His civic centers at Säynätsalo (1950–1952) and Seinäjoki (1960s) created a poetic symbiosis between Northern building vernacular and Italian vernacular urbanism, thus reconnecting Northern and Southern modernism. In America, it was Louis I. Kahn (1901–1974) who became the leader of the postwar modernism.

58 Robert Venturi, Denise Scott Brown and Steve Izenour, *Learning from Las Vegas* (Cambridge: The MIT Press, 1972), xii.

59 Bernard Rudofsky, *Architecture without Architects* (New York: Wittenborg, 1964), unpaginated.

60 Rudofsky, "Acknowledgments," unpaginated. Rudofsky wrote about the study grants "that might never have been given without the enthusiastic recommendations of the architects Walter Gropius, Pietro Belluschi, José Lluis Sert, Richard Neutra, Gio Ponti, Kenzo Tange, and the Museum's Director René d'Harnoncourt, all of whom hail from countries rich in vernacular architecture."

61 Bernard Rudofsky, *Streets For People: A Primer for Americans* (Garden City, NY: Doubleday, 1969).

Interestingly, Kahn, a student of Paul Philippe Cret is at the University of Pennsylvania, had also traveled to southern Europe in the late 1920s and produced a series of masterful sketches of the Amalfitan Coast. Vincent Scully explained their importance: "Kahn broke the hold of the International Style on modern architecture and opened the way for the revival of the vernacular and classical traditions of architecture which has been going on during the past generation and was initiated by Robert Venturi, along with Charles Moore and Aldo Rossi, each indebted to Kahn in fundamental ways."[62]

The year 1966 saw the publication, on both sides of the Atlantic ocean, of two seminal works of the second half of the twentieth century, Aldo Rossi's (1931–1997) original edition of *L'architettura della città* and Robert Venturi's (born 1925) *Complexity and Contradiction in Architecture*. In Peter Eisenman's words, *The Architecture of the City* was seen as "an attempt to build a different kind of castle from that of the moderns. It is an elaborate scaffold erected for and by someone who can no longer climb its steps to die a hero's death." Rossi proposed "an *other* architecture, an *other* architect, and most importantly, an *other* process for their understanding…."[63] Based upon a new "reading of the city," the book established the basis of a post-modernist rational reconstruction of architecture and the tenets of the movement *La Tendenza*. They included the return to the city as locus of history, its description in terms of relationship between morphology and typology, and the rediscovered link between city plan, monuments and Maurice Halbwachs' thesis of the "Collective Memory."[64]

Published under the patronage of the Museum of Modern Art in New York, Robert Venturi's *Complexity and Contradiction in Architecture* became, in Vincent Scully's analysis, the indispensable complement to Le Corbusier's *Toward a New Architecture* of 1923: "the older book demanded a noble purism in architecture, in single buildings and in the city as a whole; the new book welcomes the contradictions and complexities of urban experience at all scales." Venturi's inspiration did not come from Le Corbusier's Greek temple, but from its opposite, "the urban façades of Italy, with their endless adjustments to the counter-requirements of inside-outside and their inflection with all the business of everyday life."[65] *Learning from Las Vegas* by Robert Venturi and Denise Scott Brown was published six years later. The folio-size book

brought forward the concept of the "decorated shed," and stressed the reference to the "market" and the commercial reality of architecture in the contemporary American city and suburb. The authors provocatively criticized the "elitist approach" of the International Style followers, who had taken a genuine iconoclastic delight in propounding points of view that ridiculed traditional bourgeois and vernacular values and images.

A decade later, Colin Rowe's (1935–99) and Fred Koetter's (born 1946) *Collage City* introduced the concept of "figure-ground," a graphic tool that emphasized the formal quality of urban public spaces and their graphic representation using the abstract method of Gianbattista Nolli (1701–56) in his *Pianta Grande di Roma* of 1748. Rowe's urban design studios at Cornell University, contemporary with Maurice Culot's (born 1939) projects for "The Reconstruction of the European City" in Brussels, as well as Rob Krier (born 1938) and Leon Krier's (born 1946) proposals for Berlin, Luxemburg and Washington D.C., completed the process of rehabilitation of the traditional city and its urban form.[66]

These seminal works broadened the definition of the term "vernacular." For modern historians, the traditional rural- and climate-oriented definition had become inadequate to explain the developments in the nineteenth and twentieth centuries as it omitted the dwellings of the urban worker, the craftsman and the small merchant. In response, J. B. Jackson defined the vernacular in a new, open and dynamic way that recognized a historical continuum: "The average working-class vernacular dwelling is a minimal dwelling, with little space for storage, and dependent on the community for many services and amenities…. It is often the product of new techniques and new and unorthodox materials, built with some haste in order to be of immediate use as an implement in the business of making a living or the providing of shelter."[67]

In this context, it is interesting to look back at the Werkbund's theories and particularly Peter Behrens' manifesto of 1914. In this important text he alluded to the typological nature of the modern city by connecting it to the concept of type developed by Muthesius: "An artist's best designs will always constitute types…We see the proof of this in the standardized ground plans and elevations which the domestic architecture It is that relationship between vernacular type and city that was destroyed by CIAM's attacks against the street and the traditional city. Josep Lluis Sert and Aldo Van Eyck (1918–1999), leader of

62   Vincent Scully, introduction to Jan Hochstim, *The Paintings and Sketches of Louis I. Kahn* (New York: Rizzoli, 1991), 16.

63   Peter Eisenman, "The Houses of Memory: The Texts of Analogy," preface to *The Architecture of the City* (Cambridge: The MIT Press, 1982), 4.

64   Maurice Halbwachs, *La mémoire collective* (Paris: PUF, 1950).

65   Vincent Scully, introduction to Robert Venturi, *Complexity and Contradiction in Architecture* (New York: The Museum of Modern Art, 1966), 10.

66   Colin Rowe and Fred Koetter, *Collage City* (Cambridge: The MIT Press, 1978). See also *Rational Architecture: The Reconstruction of the European City* (Brussels: Editions des archives d'architecture moderne, 1978).

67   Jackson, "Vernacular," *American Architecture: Innovation and Tradition* (New York: Rizzoli, 1996), 147, 150.

68   Dennis Sharp, preface to Posener, 7. It is also important to mention Taut's theory of the type and its relationship to "locality," thus to climate, region, etc. (from Bozdogan, 183).

View of Ben Yehuda Street, Tel Aviv c. 1936. Photograph by Eric Matson. Courtesy Library of Congress, Eric Matson Collection.

Avmenikend Boulevard, Bakou, 1929. Alexandre Ivanitski, urbanist. From *Dictionnaire de l'architecture du XXième siècle* (Paris: Hazan, 1996), 435.

CIAM's dissident group Team X, were the first to break the rigidity of those modernist principles and propose a less mechanical vision of the city, where the square and the street were allowed a "timid" return.[69] At the same time, Italian architects and theorists Saverio Muratori (1910–73), Ernesto Rogers (1909–69), Gianfranco Caniggia (1933–87) and their disciple Aldo Rossi initiated scientific studies of the urban fabric, in search of its typological components and rules of assemblage. They laid out the concept that the term vernacular should be extended from the singular architectural object to the urban realm and its typologies. Cities were made incrementally, lot by lot, and built with various types defined by culture, space and uses. The type could evolve and take new historical forms in relation to history and the evolution of the society. Types could survive or change, but the urban lots and the street system were primary elements whose persistence across history was almost a natural law. Typology became the conceptual tool that, for the first time since the beginning of the search for a new vernacular, linked the architectural object and its urban context. of so many cities evinces."[68] For Behrens, the type was clearly defined in relation to its urban context.

PART TWO
THE "OTHER MODERN" CITIES

The trust of a city street is formed over time from many little public sidewalk contacts. It grows out of people stopping by the bar for a beer, getting advice from the grocer and giving advice to the newsstand man, comparing opinions with other customers at the bakery and nodding hello to the two boys drinking pop on the stoop, eying the girls while waiting to be called for dinner, admonishing the children, hearing about a job from the hardware man and borrowing a dollar from the druggist, admiring new babies and sympathizing over the way a coat faded.[70]

On par with the history of architecture and housing, the history of the modern city has been biased by "modernist propaganda." In their ideological attempt to link the search for the "brave New World" to the "new architecture of the modern age," historians of twentieth-century urbanism have continuously focused on and praised ambiguous experiments such as Radburn or Brasilia, while discussing endlessly theoretical anti-urban projects including Ludwig Hilberseimer's Vertical City (1924) and Frank Lloyd Wright's Broadacre City (1932). In contrast they have

69 Sert was a primaryfigure in CIAM VIII's "The Core of the City" at Hoddesdon (1951). The creation of Team X followed CIAM IX at Aix-en-Provence in 1953. Other founders of Team X included Jaap Bakema, Georges Candilis, and Peter and Allison Smithson.

70 Jane Jacobs, *The Death and Life of Great American Cities* (New York: Random House, 1961), 56.

Apartment Building, avenue du Général d'Amade, Casablanca. Xavier Rendu & Roger Ponsard, 1930-31. Photograph by Jean-Louis Cohen.

Assayag Building, boulevard de la Marine, Casablanca. Marius Boyer, 1930.

tragically overlooked the legacy of the "other modern" cities and of their creators, architects, urbanists and more often than not, engineers.

Far from being a mere period of intellectual stagnation and "inhuman" urban speculation, the decades encompassing the 1890s to the 1940s were an extraordinary period for the theory and history of urbanism. Indeed, it is during those years that Camillo Sitte, Werner Hegemann (1881–1936), Jean-Claude Nicolas Forestier (1861–1930), and John Nolen (1869–1937) — to name only a few — wrote their theories of modern urbanism. Perhaps even more important were the manuals published by engineers like Josef Stübben (1845–1936) and Reinhard Baumeister (1833–1917), who with their predecessors Baron Georges-Eugène Haussman (1809–1891) and Ildefons Cerdà (1816–1876) were in fact responsible for most of the plans of urban modernization and expansion in Europe.[71]

The "other modern" city of the engineer — and its most representative models, Cerdà's Ensanche of Barcelona or James Hobrecht's Plan for Berlin (1864–79) — was remarkably well set up to handle the enormous technological, social and economic changes that traversed the late nineteenth- and early twentieth-century society and economy. It consisted of the expansion of an existing urban center, or at times of a new

foundation, and was generally laid out as a "vernacular" grid, complete with generous sidewalks and well-aligned trees along the avenues. In spite of its "artistic flaws" — in the criticism of Camillo Sitte — the grid was usually the most rational system to provide developable lots and absorb the increasing number of vehicles. Blocks were large in order to handle density and mixed-use functions such as artisanal and industrial activities. In fact, it was often this very condition of "adaptability" that made the city too fragile and sensible to unbridled speculation. Yet, for decades, that urban design strategy was able to withstand "the interminable parade of vanities of the architects and their clients, and assured that the 'maniac' city formed a whole, efficiently connecting what existed before and was to come later, offering a track for the automobile movement, ground floors to the new consumerism of commerce, cafés, cinemas."[72] Thus, the history of the construction of those districts "goes much beyond the succession of its 'décors,' or beyond the syndrome of the Potemkin City."[73]

During the first decades of the twentieth century, the "traditional" city was a place of intense urban innovation, the apex of the metropolis. After 1890 and under the prime influence of Camillo Sitte, Ebenezer Howard (1850–1928) and various reformist movements, new concepts

71 Among those: Camillo Sitte, *Der Städtebau nach seinen künstlerischen Grundsätzen* (Wien: C. Graeser, 1889); Werner Hegemann and Elbert Peets, *The American Vitruvius: An Architect's Handbook of Civic Art* (1922, reprint, New York: Princeton Architectural Press, 1988); John Nolen, *City Planning: A Series of Papers Presenting the Essential Elements of a City Plan* (New York: D. Appleton & Co., 1917); Ildefons Cerdà, *Teoría general de la Urbanización y aplicación de sus principios y doctrinas a lareforma del ensanche de Barcelona* (Barcelona: 1867); Reinhard Baumeister, *Stadterweiterungen in technischer baupolizeilicher und wirtschaflicher Beziehung* (Berlin: Ernst & Korn, 1876); Josef Stübben, *Der Städteban* (Leipzig: J. R. Gebhardt, 1924).

72 Nuno Portas, "Art déco e suas cidades," *Art Deco na América Latina*, 102.

73 Ibid., 104. For the reference on Potemkin City, see Adolf Loos, *Spoken into the Void (Collected Essays, 1897–1900)* (Cambridge: The MIT Press, 1982).

such as the "picturesque," the "garden" districts and the first version of "zoning," made their way within the grid system. Organized workers' movements in cities like Vienna, Amsterdam, and Berlin, enticed the construction of the modern working class districts by Michel De Klerk (1884–1923), Bruno Taut, Eriel Saarinen, Innocenzo Sabbatini (1891–1987) and "other modern" architects. Through subtle transformations and manipulations of the grid pattern, these improved districts and city expansions demonstrated, in fact, the same awareness of the issues linked to modernity as Le Corbusier's and CIAM's. They addressed topics such as hygienic improvement through better legislation for inner courtyards and patios, water sanitation and distribution, development of parks and systems of parks, working-class blocks or quarters, control of industrial establishments, infrastructure expansion, as well as the public transportation networks scandalously ignored by the Charter of Athens.

It was also along the streets of these "other modern" cities that the twentieth-century modern styles, from neoclassical to Art Nouveau and International Style, succeeded and integrated with each other. Their modernized grids and streets absorbed and incorporated new building types such as parking garages, skyscrapers and civic centers like Rockefeller Center in New York, at times dramatically modifying the city architecture without compromising its urban character. On the one hand, the "other modern" cities — or "Art Deco cities" as coined by Nuno Portas[74] — demonstrated that the maximum individual and artistic expression were able to coexist with an urban morphology that was preconceived and preexisting. On the other hand, they made it clear that this creative potential could only be explored if supported by a firm and comprehensible matrix of public spaces.

Mediterranean Cities

International Style and CIAM partisans saw modern architecture and traditional urbanism of streets, blocks and squares as antithetical, and their interaction unworthy of theoretical consideration. As a consequence they ignored the modern architecture built or designed within the traditional city. The "new city" of Tel Aviv, which has until recently received

View of Avenida Atlántica in the early 1930s with Edificio OK in the foreground. Gusmão, Dourado & Baldassini Ltda, 1928 (Edificio OK). Postcard. Courtesy of the Prefeitura da Cidade do Rio de Janeiro.

scarce attention among urban historians, is perhaps the best case in point. Tel Aviv started as a suburb of Jaffa and had about sixty families in 1908. As immigration increased, its population grew to fifty thousand by 1932, and about three times that number by the middle of the decade. During the 1930s, architects — many of them exiled from Central Europe, including some trained at the Bauhaus — built about three thousand genuine "Bauhaus style" structures on small urban lots, and created an urban environment that, typologically and aesthetically, was very similar to Miami Beach.[75] Most of Tel Aviv was built following the pattern of detached isolated buildings closely aligned along the streets, paseo-like boulevards and inner-block parks originally planned by Patrick Geddes to structure his low-density garden city. In the mid-1930s, *Architectural Forum* dedicated sixteen pages, as part of its monthly international section, to the new urban and architectural work-in-progress in Palestine.[76] It documented schools, apartment houses with projecting balconies and roof terraces that increased the public use of the property, as well as houses of "German origin, counterparts of which could be found in many Berlin suburbs." The editor recalled the Arab tradition of flat or domed roofs, mud or stone walls, and central courtyards, but he noticed another influence, "that of modern architecture in Europe, a type

74 Portas, 105.

75 For Tel Aviv see Neal Payton, "Patrick Geddes and the Plan for Tel Aviv," *The New City: Modern Cities 3*: (New York: Princeton Architectural Press, 1996) 4-25; and Irmel Kamp-Bandau, *Tel Aviv Neues Bauen* (Tübingen: Wasmuth, 1993).

76 *Architectural Forum* was the only publication to dedicate pages to the rapid phenomenon of urban growth in Palestine. It is possible that, given the Jewish constituency of the builders of Miami Beach, this may have had an impact on the architecture of the city. Yet, no indication of such a relationship has been discovered to date.

77 *Architectural Forum* (September 1936), 94.

Plate 143. Tony Garnier, 1917. From Tony Garnier, *Une cité industrielle: étude pour la construction des villes* (1917, reprint, New York: Princeton Architectural Press, 1989).

of building completely foreign to the country, and yet, curiously enough, more in harmony with indigenous architecture than the stilted archeological efforts of the more conservative designers."[77] A few years later Erich Mendelsohn (1889– 1953) wrote: "Tel Aviv's new residential quarters prove that the best constructive and architectural results of the modern movement have already brought about an artistic expression of their own, corresponding to the climatic conditions of the Mediterranean."[78]

Mendelsohn's own works in Palestine embodied the genuine encounter between the spirit of European modernism and the Mediterranean heritage and soil, an encounter that led to true synthesis, to architectural syncretism. He did not abandon any of the modern principles that he had put into use in Germany; he fused them in the language of stone, thus reinventing modernity.[79]

Mendelsohn's commentary on Tel Aviv's new quarters could apply, in fact, to quite a number of new cities or districts that emerged at that time in Mediterranean-like regions. Based upon traditional plans, they were usually built, lot by lot, with Deco or Bauhaus-inspired apartment buildings. The pilotis, white walls, projecting balconies, flat roofs and the horizontal windows that made up the urban landscape of Tel Aviv could, for instance, be found two thousand miles north of Tel Aviv,

along the shores of the Caspian Sea in the former Soviet Union (today Azerbaijan). From 1924 to 1928, planner and architect Alexandre Ivanitski (1881–1947) laid out the new districts of the old town of Baku as a modern gridded town with wide avenues connected to the lakefront.

Like Tel Aviv or Miami Beach, Copacabana was originally planned as a low-rise summer resort for the residents of Rio de Janeiro. In the 1920s, the city experienced a tremendous growth that almost overnight transformed its bayfront single-family neighborhoods into metropolitan quarters. Under the influence of the Agache Plan of 1929–30, special planning laws induced the construction of mid-rise office and apartment buildings along the coastline and in the city center. Copacabana and the Flamengo districts were entirely rebuilt with dense, ten-story high, party-wall apartment buildings, integrating planning advances such as covered commercial passages, interior patios and setback planes in the Manhattan tradition. Avenida Atlántica became the grand urban façade along the beach, harmoniously combining all styles from Art Deco to the International Modern of the 1950s.[79]

On the other side of the ocean, Casablanca evolved, between the two wars, from a walled Arab town into a critical place of experimentation for new building typologies and advanced esthetics. As many Moroccan and French clients were committed to the modernization of the city, outstanding teams of professionals "turned the city into a regulatory, technological, and cultural laboratory," that placed the Moroccan capital ahead of Paris in many ways, and later influenced urban projects in the metropolis.[80] The expansion of Casablanca had been substantially started and subdivided without an overall plan; thus planner Henri Prost had to introduce "corrections," and focused on developing a clear structure of boulevards, squares and parks; he organized the city into a system of functional zones, echoing the German and American practice. Architects built the new "functional" blocks advocated by Prost with elegant, low-rise and mid-rise apartment buildings that contained the first parking garages of any French city. Interestingly, critics also emphasized the Mediterranean roots of the white cubist architecture, and some architects such as Henri Descamps wrote that "it is curious to notice how well a fit the modern international style is to Morocco: it even creates a happier effect than it does in the countries where it was born."[81]

78   Erich Mendelsohn, "Palestine and the World of Tomorrow" (1941). Republished in Ita Heinze-Greenberg, *Eric Mendelsohn, Bauten und Projekte in Palästina (1934–1941)* (München: Scaneg, 1986). On Mendelsohn in Palestine, see Reginald Stephan, ed. *Eric Mendelsohn Architect 1887-1953* (New York: The Monacelli Press, 1999).

79   See *Guia da Arquitectura Art Deco no Rio de Janeiro* (Rio de Janeiro: Prefeitura da Cidade do Rio de Janeiro, 1996), 17-19; and Donat Alfred Agache, *Cidade do Rio de Janeiro, extensão, remodelacao, embellezamento* (Pris: Foyer Brésilien, 1930). The relationship between the two cities remains to be investigated, as Miami Beach developers may have been familiar with the late 1920s boom in the Brazilian capital.

80   Jean-Louis Cohen, "Henri Prost & Casablanca: The Art of Making Successful Cities," *The New City: Modern Cities* 3 (New York: Princeton Architectural Press, 1996): 107.

81   Quoted by Monique Eleb, "Apartments Buildings in Casablanca: Types & Lifestyles 1930–1950," *The New City: Modern Cities*, 96.

In Defense of the Grid

The American ubiquitous grid of streets has been correctly, but excessively, criticized by urban historians and social scientists, as a mere planning expedient to develop land cheaply and quickly. Yet, the history of twentieth-century urbanism has amply demonstrated that, even though it had been generally used in the most elementary fashion, the urban grid was the background of a rational urban system, the "necessary condition" of American urban life. In the early 1900s, Daniel Burnham (1846–1912) and the City Beautiful movement developed urban improvement strategies, inspired by the French planning tradition; they introduced boulevards and civic centers that allowed the grid to "breathe" and acquire more urbanistic character. It is interesting to put into this context the construction of the Grand Concourse area in the Bronx between 1920 and 1940. In an astonishing aesthetic and socio-cultural parallel with Miami Beach, more than four hundred housing structures and important public buildings were built on both sides of the Grand Concourse axis, planned as a grand boulevard at the end of the nineteenth century. They were the works of a small group of architects, many of whom immigrated from Eastern Europe and had limited architectural education. Among them, it is important to mention Horace Ginsbern and his chief designer Marvin Fine (1904–81), a team credited for having designed the Park Hotel (1929–31) and the Noonan Plaza with its large inner garden (1926); the Russian-born Israel Crausman (1899–1991) and the New Yorker Louis Allen Abramson (1887–1985). Many buildings along the boulevards and streets of the attractive neighborhood were intended for the upper middle class and were luxuriously designed with spacious rooms, tiled sun decks, courtyards, interior gardens and often ground-floor shops. Other structures were built by politically active cooperatives. Regardless of the speculative atmosphere of the 1930s "the builders and owners erected apartment houses that they were proud of. Almost without realizing it, they were part of the 1939 World's Fair's spirit of hope for the future."[83]

In most "other modern" cities, the party-wall condition prevailed and the continuity of the street remained intact. By contrast, in Miami Beach and in Los Angeles, but also in Tel Aviv, housing buildings were allowed to become freestanding objects. Yet, these objects fulfilled their

Apartment building, 2121 Grand Concourse, Bronx, New York. Howard Ginsbern, 1936. From *Building a Borough: Architecture and Planning in the Bronx, 1890–1940* (New York: The Bronx Museum of the Arts, 1986).

82 See Mario Gandelsonas, *X-Urbanism: Architecture and the American City* (New York: Princeton Architectural Press, 1999).

83 Richard Plunz, "Reading Bronx Housing, 1890–1940," *Building a Borough: Architecture and Planning in the Bronx, 1890–1940* (New York: The Bronx Museum of the Arts, 1986), 61. Also see Donald G. Sullivan and Brian J. Danforth, *Bronx Art Deco Architecture* (New York: Hunter College, 1976), 10.

84 Steven Holl, *The Alphabetical City* (New York: Pamphlet Architecture, 1980).

urban responsibilities by purposefully defining complex hierarchies of open-air public spaces at different scales, particularly through the use of the Mediterranean-type courtyard. Therein lies the methodological value of the modern "urban assemblages" of Miami Beach, Tel Aviv and Hollywood. Their new and fundamentally modern housing typologies constitute the Mediterranean version of Steven Holl's *Alphabetical City*.[84]

They inevitably bring to mind Tony Garnier's vision of a Mediterranean Utopia, inspired by the rediscovery of the urbanism of Priene and other Greek cities in Asia. Few authors have emphasized the introduction of innovative typologies within the blocks of the *Cité Industrielle*. Eugène Hénard (1849–1923) had advanced new urban types with his *immeubles à redents* (1903–06), but Garnier pioneered the systematic use of detached and formally defined buildings in a mid-density urban fabric in *Une Cité Industrielle* and his project for the "Quartier des Etats-Unis" designed for Lyons in 1920 and partially built between 1929 and 1935. Courtyards, open staircases, flat roofs with terraces created a fine grain of interstitial open spaces that liberated the ground without destroying the very principles of urbanity. The residential zone functioned as "a great park, without any wall or enclosure limiting the terrain," allowing for a free pedestrian movement across the blocks.[85]

Thus, surprisingly and in a highly speculative parallelism, the intellectual progeny of the French planner might be found in Miami Beach, Los Angeles or Tel Aviv where, within the convention of the grid and the lot, architects and developers invented a new and modern type of "traditional city."[86] This new urban typology became a new vernacular in many cities after World War II particularly in Rome (Parioli) and throughout Italy where it became known as the *palazzina*.

Whether or not they knew of Garnier, the builders and architects of Miami Beach never aimed at reaching the intensity of civic grandeur and public space openness that he envisioned for his industrial city; yet, they built — as they did in Copacabana and Tel Aviv — the ultimate public square for the hedonistic society of the twentieth century. The urban beaches became the new, radically modern "public spaces" that Le Corbusier and the CIAM members desperately kept looking for, as they were blind to the emerging new urban realities.

The Grand Concourse boulevard in the Bronx, with Manhattan in the distance. 1930s. Photograph by Culver Pictures.

85 Tony Garnier, *Une Cité Industrielle* (1917; reprint, New York: Princeton Architectural Press, 1989), 14. The regular plot in Garnier's project is 50 feet by 50 feet. In South Beach it is 50 feet by 100 feet to 140 feet. The mention of *Une Cité Industrielle* in relation to Miami Beach was made by Terry Kilian in an interview with Denise Scott-Brown, in *Everyday Masterpieces*, 209.

86 The palazzina invented in the garden city of La Garbatella (south of Rome) and developed in the 1950s by architects such as Luigi Moretti and Marco Ridolfi has not received the attention it deserved as the first new urban type to follow the Renaissance palazzo. Among the few publications about the type, see *Metamorfosi: Quaderni di Architettura* 15 [La palazzina romana degli anni '50] (Roma, 1992).

Miami Beach: The Modern Repository

PHEDRA: *Dis-moi (puisque tu es si sensible aux effets de l'architecture), n'as tu pas observé, en te promenant dans cette ville, que d'entres les édifices dont elle est peuplée, les uns sont muets; les autres parlent; et d'autres enfin, qui sont les plus rares, chantent? Ce n'est pas leur destination, ni même leur figure générale, qui les animent à ce point, ou qui les réduisent au silence. Cela tient au talent de leur constructeur, ou bien à la faveur des Muses.*[87]

Making the case for a relationship between the vernacular, the Mediterranean, Rudofsky's theses and the streets and buildings of Miami Beach can be construed as audacious. It is not certain that the Austrian would have been ready to appreciate the vernacular quality of Miami Beach architecture as did Venturi and Scott Brown when they "stumbled" upon it in the 1970s, and were later invited to develop their masterplan for the renovation of the Washington / Collins corridors.[88] Yet, it is incontrovertible that Miami Beach is a city of "everyday masterpieces." Even to well-educated eyes, it is difficult to distinguish the architects' signatures, as they all worked during the period 1933–1942 in quite a symbiotic spirit. Theirs was "an architecture without architects," in the modern sense. They used a similar vocabulary and urban module, based upon similar lots and achieved a rare consistency of urban fabric. The southern districts of Miami Beach were built on an egalitarian speculative grid, one building at a time, without grand plan or any grand expectation of the future. Private builders and speculators, of relatively minimal resources, followed simple rules and urban regulations. Building types were quickly accepted not only as a means of organizing space and form but also as a means of construction; they entered into the realm of the builder-contractor, and thus became the vernacular-modern of the city.

Miami Beach in the 1930s was a genuine place of encounter between modernity and tradition, between the traditional urban grid and the mass-flowing modernist buildings, between machine-oriented edifices and traditional typologies, between the Temple and the Aeroplane, between the Machine and the Mediterranean. Its architecture integrated "the classical and the traditional, the antiquarian and the mass production, the style and the non-style, the individual and the standard, the use of color and the absolute white, machine symbolism and regional character, monumentality and horizontality."[89] For critics Thomas and Charlotte Benson, it is in this everyday architecture that the "small masters" achieved the true synthesis between classicism and modernism, thus inventing the vernacular modern that the International Style architects did not want to recognize.[90] This style, "modernist classicism," shared with the stripped classicism the rules of symmetry, proportion, grandeur and "correctness." But it absorbed from the modern movement a new sense of space, a treatment of walls as surfaces rather than as load-bearing masses and a completely "modern" approach to materials. In an interview, Denise Scott Brown used the analogy of the "American immigrants" to explain Miami Beach and the Deco-Moderne movement: "The first generation [of immigrants] came over because they were in revolt. They were looking for a New World. The first ethnic immigrants, the first Italian or Irish who came here, came because they were rebels; the next came because they had a brother here. The Deco architects are the people who had a brother. They internalized some of that revolution and then they made it able to be accepted by the market."[91]

In conclusion, the built reality of the "other modern" cities forces us to acknowledge the incalculable and invaluable contribution of the anonymous or forgotten "masters" who built the cities and neighborhoods of the twentieth century, often in the modern style and for the middle class. Moreover, their architecture unequivocally rebuts the anti-democratic equation made in the 1920s and 1930s — and even more so after the war by the orthodox voices of history — between the socio-architectural goals of modernism and the destructive, libertarian agenda of the "open city" and the "end of the street." The urbanists and architects that designed and built them demonstrated — particularly in the "Mediterranean" cities where the cultural heritage of urban life remained alive against all odds — that the idea of universality implicit in the modern project was not incompatible with an architecture established in its context, and that the "traditional" city of streets, squares and blocks was and remains the truest and richest repository of modern architecture.[92]

---

opposite:
Aerial photograph of Tel Aviv, 1990s. © Ofek Aerial Photography.

87 Paul Valéry, *Eupalinos ou l'architecte* (Paris: Gallimard, 1922; new edition by Mario Pani, Monterrey, Mexico: Ediciones Sierra Madre, 1957), 20.

88 Denise Scott Brown, *City of Miami Beach (Florida) Washington Avenue Revitalization Plan* (Miami Beach: City of Miami Beach, 1979).

89 Scott Brown, *Everyday Masterpieces*, 16.

90 See Thomas and Charlotte Benton, "Towards Modernist Classicism," *werk archithese* 23-24 (Nov.-Dec. 1978): 23-27. Quoted in Scott Brown, *Everyday Masterpieces*, 224.

91 See interview of Denise Scott Brown, *Everyday Masterpieces*, 209.

92 This convergence between Tel Aviv and Miami Beach was academically recognized when the City of Tel Aviv organized the International Style Architecture Conference (May 22-28, 1994) and made the City of Miami Beach a co-sponsor of the meeting. The authors attended the conference and are indebted to the organizers for the influence that the wide-ranging papers had on the intellectual framework of this book.

SAMUEL H. GOTTSCHO
AND THE PHOTOGRAPHY OF MIAMI BEACH

Jean-François Lejeune & Allan T. Shulman

The "phenomenon" of early Miami Beach was recorded in folios and features, such as *National Geographic*'s "A Little Journey to Altonia." Here the city was portrayed as a realm of golf courses, polo fields, mansions and harbors, which were the backdrop for athletes and yachtsmen. However, Miami Beach was best documented in the work of three successive commercial photographers: Claude Carson Matlack (1878-1944), Gleason Waite Romer (1887-1971) and Samuel Herman Gottscho (1875-1971).

Claude Matlack was the first to document Miami Beach, arriving in Florida in 1916. He produced thousands of photos of the first generation of the city, particularly its homes and estates. These photos provided a record of architectural glamour as the context for a life of luxury. In contrast, Gleason Romer photographed Miami Beach—and the whole Miami area—for almost forty years, contributing a comprehensive, almost journalistic account of the city's rapid transformation. He pictured the city from every angle, introducing the buildings in the context of the people who occupied them. As Gary Munroe has documented, "Romer's idea was to perpetuate a visual record of Miami's sensational lifestyle."[1] His photographs were often scenes of Miami Beach life, although Romer was primarily a commercial photographer. His photography was the template for countless postcards.

Samuel H. Gottscho was responsible for providing the clearest and most architecturally dramatic images of Miami Beach in the 1930s, extensively photographing the work of Lawrence Murray Dixon, Robert Law Weed and Igor Polevitzky, among others. Samuel Gottscho acquired his first camera in 1896. Until 1920 he photographed part-time, specializing in houses and gardens as he particularly enjoyed nature, country scenes and landscapes. After attending several architectural photography exhibitions, Gottscho decided to improve his work and make the acquaintance of several architects and landscape architects in the New York area. After twenty-three years as a traveling salesman, Gottscho became a professional full-time photographer at the age of fifty. William H. Schleisner (1912–1962), also a photographer, joined the business in 1935. As a commercial photographer, Gottscho photographed many of the most important architectural and urban developments of the Machine Age, documenting the growth of New York City and the 1939 World's Fair in particular. In the tradition of Alfred Stieglitz he portrayed the drama of the modern metropolis. He was much appreciated by architects, working extensively for Raymond Hood and George Howe.

Gottscho photographed the realm of the city, extensively illustrating New York City's skyline. He skillfully portrayed skyscrapers, like Rockefeller Center and Radio City Music Hall. His urban photographs were often framed by open space, as in the example of his famous shots of downtown New York City from across the East River or the Plaza group seen from Central Park. Another theme was the nightlife of cities. His photos often included and even celebrated the elements urban life, like traffic and cars. Taken from a low vantage point, they emphasized the dynamism of the city.

Gottscho's presence in Miami Beach was a sign of the resort's economic and visual importance in the 1930s. His photography was fundamentally classical, always rigorously framed, avoiding the surprising viewpoints and distorted angles then in favor to express architectural modernity. His compositions emphasized balance and geometry — the classical roots of Miami Beach modern architecture — while ignoring the modernist details like pilotis, projecting concrete balconies, and other cubist asymmetries. Yet, street views were rare, unlike his work in New York. Photographs focused on the individual building as subject, and, perhaps at the clients' request, rarely encompassed the emerging urban context. [2]

In 1940 Gottscho initiated a vast project of botanical documentation for the New York Botanical Garden in the Bronx. He illustrated most of this institution's publications and quickly became a leading photographer in the fields of gardens and flower art. His works appeared regularly in the specialized press as well as in many popular magazines such as *Collier's* and *House & Garden*. In the 1950s, Miami Beach became once again a glamorous place and Gottscho was the photographer of the new generation of modern hotels, in particular of Morris Lapidus' landmarks, the Eden Roc and the Fontainebleau.

The firm's archives can be found at the Museum of the City of New York, at Columbia University Avery Library, at the Canadian Center of Architecture in Montréal (CCA) and at the Bass Museum of Art in Miami Beach. The Gottscho-Schleisner Collection at the Library of Congress is comprised of over 29,000 images and negatives, primarily of architectural subjects, including interiors and exteriors of homes, stores, offices, factories, historic buildings and other structures. Subjects are concentrated chiefly in the northeastern United States, especially the New York City area, and Florida. Included are the homes of notable Americans, such as Raymond Loewy, and of several U.S. presidents, as well as color photographs of the 1939 World's Fair.[3]

1   Gleason Waite Romer, *Romer's Miami: Windows to the Past*, ed. Gary Munroe (Miami: Miami-Dade Public Library System, 1985). The authors found no information on Moser & Son, a local firm that extensively documented Lawrence Murray Dixon's works. Their photographs are conserved at the Bass Museum of Art.

2   See for instance Margaret Bourke-White in the United States, and Lucia and László Moholy-Nagy in Europe.

3   Electronic access to the Gottscho-Schleisner Collection at the Library of Congress is: http://memory.loc.gov/ammem/gschtml/gotthome.html.

BIBLIOGRAPHY

Interior of Lawrence Murray Dixon's office, Euclid Avenue, Miami Beach. Lawrence Murray Dixon, 1937. Photograph Samuel Gottscho. Collection Bass Museum of Art, Gift of Lawrence Murray Dixon, Jr.

I. General Works

Architecture in Exile. CD-ROM. Vienna: Science Wonder Productions, Organa, 1995.

Armbruster, Ann. *The Life and Times of Miami Beach*. New York: Alfred A. Knopf, 1995.

Barr, Alfred. *Present Status and Future Direction of the Museum of Modern Art*. MoMA Archives, 1933.

Bass Museum of Art. *The Normandie: Floating Art Deco Palace*. Miami Beach: Bass Museum of Art, 1993.

Bauer, Catherine. "The House That Works." *Fortune*, no. 12 (October 1935): 59-65, 94.

Bayer, Patricia. *Art Deco Architecture — Design, Decoration and Detail from the Twenties and the Thirties*. New York: Harry Abrams, 1992.

Bel Geddes, Norman. *Horizons*. Boston: Little, Brown and Co, 1932.

Benson, Robert. "Douglas Haskell and the Criticism of International Modernism." *Modern Architecture in America: Visions and Revisions*. Eds. Richard Guy Wilson and Sidney K. Robinson. Ames, Iowa: Iowa State University Press, 1991:

Benton, Tom and Charlotte Benton. "Towards Modernist Classicism." *werk archithèse* 23-24 (November 1978): 23-27.

Bollack, Françoise and Tom Killian. *Ely Jacques Kahn, New York Architect*. New York: Acanthus Press, 1995.

Borsi, Franco. *The Monumental Era*. New York: Rizzoli, 1985.

Bossaglia, Rossana. *L'Art Déco*. Bari: Editori Laterza, 1984.

Bossom, Alfred C. "America's National Architecture." *American Architect* 128 (29 July 1925): 77-83.

Bouillon, Jean-Paul. *Art Deco: 1903–1940*. New York: Rizzoli, 1989.

Bozdogan, Sibel. "Against Style: Bruno Taut's Pedagogical Program in Turkey, 1936-1938." *The Education of an Architect: Historiography, Urbanism, and the Growth of Architectural Knowledge — Essays Presented to Stanford Anderson*. Cambridge: The MIT Press, 1997: 163-192.

Brown, Phil. *Catskill Culture: A Mountain Rat's Memories of the Great Jewish Resort Area*. Philadelphia: Temple University Press, 1999.

Cantone, Gaetana and Italo Prozzillo. "La casa di Capri e il Movimento Moderno." *Case di Capri: Ville, palazzi, grandi dimore*. Napoli: Electa Napoli/Edizioni La Conchiglia, 1994: 147-173.

Capitman, Barbara Baer. *Deco Delights: Preserving the Beauty and Joy of Miami Beach Architecture*. New York: E.P. Dutton, 1988.

Capitman, Barbara, Michael D. Kinerk, and Dennis W. Wilhelm. *Rediscovering Art Deco U.S.A.* New York: Viking Studio Books, 1994.

Carter, Randolph, and Reed Cole. *Joseph Urban: Architecture-Theatre-Opera-Film*. New York: Abbeville Press, 1992.

Castillo, Greg. "Modernity, Modernism, and the Quest for Hegemony." *The Other Modern: 1900–2000*. Ed. Gabriele Tagliaventi. Savona: Dogma, 2000.

"A Century of Progress Exposition." *Architectural Forum* 55 (October 1931).

Cerwinske, Laura. *Tropical Deco: The Architecture and Design of Old Miami Beach*. New York: Rizzoli, 1981.

Cheney, Sheldon and Martha Chandler Cheney. *Art and the Machine*. New York: McGraw-Hill, 1936.

Ciucci, Giorgio, Francesco Dal Co, Manieri-Elia Antonio and Manfredo Tafuri. *The American City: From the Civil War to the New Deal*. Cambridge-London: The MIT Press, 1979.

Cohen, Jean-Louis. *Scenes of the World to Come: European Architecture and the American Challenge 1893–1960*. Paris: Flammarion, 1995.

____. "Mouvement moderne." *Dictionnaire de l'architecture du XXè siècle*. Paris: Hazan/Institut français d'architecture, 1996: 630.

Colquhoun, Alan. "Vernacular Classicism," *Modernity and the Classical Tradition (Architectural Essays 1980-1987)*. Cambridge-London: The MIT Press, 1989: 21-31.

"Come to the Fair." *Pencil Points* 19 (September 1938): 536-550

Conant, Paul. "Never-Never Land in San Francisco: First Showing of Designs for the 1939 Fair." *Pencil Points* 18 (June 1937): 377-390.

Cornell, Elias. "The Sky as a Vault: Gunnar Asplund and the articulation of space." *Asplund: A Book*. Eds. Claes Caldenby and Olof Hultin. New York: Rizzoli, 1986: 23-33.

Cret, Paul Philippe. "The Festive Stage Setting." *Architectural Forum* 58-59 (July 1933): 4-5.

___. "Ten Years of Modernism." *Architectural Forum* 58-59 (August 1933): 91-95.

——. "The Hall of Science, A Century of Progess Exhibition." *Architectural Forum* 57 (October 1932): 285-292.

Culot, Maurice, et. al. *Bruxelles Art Déco 1920–1930*. Paris: Norma Editions, 1996.

Curtis, William J. R. *Modern Architecture Since 1900*. London: Phaidon, 1997.

De Long, D. G., Helen Searing and Robert A. M. Stern, eds. *American Architecture: Innovation and Tradition*. New York: Rizzoli, 1986.

De Michelis, Marco. *Heinrich Tessenow, 1876–1950*. Milano: Electa, 1991.

"Design Decade." *Architectural Forum* 73 (October 1940): 217-320.

Diez, Fernando. "Abstração e urbanismo: sobre a relação entre urbanismo e decoração." *Art Déco Na América Latina*. Rio de Janeiro: Prefeitura da Cidade do Rio de Janeiro, 1997: 108-113.

Dos Passos, John. *USA: The Big Money*. Boston: Houghton Mifflin Co., 1937.

Duany, Andres, and Elizabeth Plater-Zyberk. "The Three Traditions of Miami." *Miami Architecture of the Tropics*, 79-89. Eds. Jean-François Lejeune and Maurice Culot. New York: Princeton Architectural Press, 1991.

Dunlop, Beth. "Inventing Antiquity: The Art and Craft of the Mediterranean Revival Architecture." *Journal of Decorative and Propaganda Arts* 23 (1998): 190-207.

Eisenman, Peter. "The Houses of Memory: The Texts of Analogy." *The Architecture of the City*. Cambridge: MIT Press, 1982: 3-11.

Eleb, Monique. "Apartment Buildings in Casablanca: Types and Lifestyles (1930–1950)." *The New City: Modern Cities*. Ed. Jean-François Lejeune. New York: Princeton Architectural Press, 1996: 94-105.

Etlin, Richard A. *Modernism in Italian Architecture, 1890–194*0. Cambridge-London: The MIT Press, 1991.

"Fairs, Their Lusty Ancestry, Their Vigorous Maturity, Their Present Indecisiveness; And What of New York 1939." *Architectural Forum* 64-65 (1936): 171-190

Feather, Maurice. "Some Observations on Building in Florida." *Pencil Points* 18 (July 1937): 615-620.

Federal Writers' Project of the WPA of Florida. The WPA Guide to Florida: *The Federal Writers' Project Guide to 1930s Florida*. New York: Oxford University Press, 1939.

Ferriss, Hugh. *The Metropolis of Tomorrow*. New York: I. Washburn, 1929; reprint by Princeton Architectural Press, 1986.

Fisher, Jane. *Fabulous Hoosier*. New York: Robert M. McBride, 1947.

The Intellectual Migration: Europe and America, 1930–1960. Eds. Donald Fleming and Bernard Bailyn. Cambridge: The MIT Press, 1970.

Florida Editors Association. *An Illustrated Description of the Advantages and Opportunities of the State of Florida and the Progress that has been Achieved with a Biographical Record of those Citizens Whose Endeavor has Produced the Superb Structures — Commercial, Industrial, Agricultural and Political — which Comprise the Strength of this Charming Section*. Florida Editors Association: James O. Jones Company, 1925.

The Florida Tropical Home at A Century of Progress 1933. New York: Kuhne Galleries, 1933.

Ford, Katherine Morrow. "Modern Is Regional." *House & Garden* 80 (March 1941): 35-37, 79.

Frampton, Kenneth. *Modern Architecture: A Critical History*. New York: Oxford University Press, 1980.

Frankl, Paul Theodore. *Form and Re-Form: Handbook of Modern Interiors*. New York: Harper and Brothers, 1930.

___. *New Dimensions: The Decorative Arts of Today in Words & Pictures*. New York: Da Capo Press, 1928.

Frehling, Jennifer. *Henry Hohauser: Miami Beach Moderne 1935–1948*. University of Virginia: Master's Thesis, 1994.

Garnier, Tony. *Une Cité Industrielle: étude pour la construction des villes*. New York: Princeton Architectural Press, 1989 (first published 1917).

Gebhard, David. *The Elusive Image: Regionalism in Twentieth Century Architecture*. Christchurch, New Zealand: School of Fine Arts University of Canterbury, 1993.

___. *George Washington Smith, 1876–1930*. Santa Barbara: The Art Galleries, University of California, 1964.

___. *Kem Weber, the Moderne in Southern California*. Santa Barbara: The Arts Galleries, University of California, 1969.

___. "The Moderne in the United States, 1920–1941." *Architectural Association Quarterly* 2 (July 1970): 4-20.

___. *The National Trust Guide To Art Deco in America*. New York: John Wiley and Sons, 1996.

___. "The Spanish Colonial Revival in Southern California (1895–1930)." *Journal of The Society of Architectural Historians* 37 (May 1967): 131-147.

Gelertner, David. *1939: The Lost World of the Fair*. New York: The Free Press, 1995.

Giedion, Siegfried. "The Dangers and Advantages of Luxury." *Architectural Forum* 70 (May 1939): 348.

Goodhue, Bertram. "Preface." *The Minor Ecclesiastical, Domestic, and Garden Architecture of Southern Spain, V-VIII*. Ed. Austin Whittlesey. New York: Architectural Book Publishing, 1923.

Goodwin, Philip. *Brazil Builds: Architecture New and Old, 1652–1942*. New York: The Museum of Modern Art, 1943.

Gournay, Isabelle. "Leonard Schultze and S. Fullerton Weaver." *Dictionnaire de l'architecture du XXè siècle*. Paris: Hazan/Institut français d'architecture, 1996.

Gravagnuolo, Benedetto. *Adolf Loos, Theory and Works*. New York: Rizzoli, 1982.

___. *Il mito mediterraneo nell'architettura contemporanea*. Napoli: Electa Napoli, 1994.

Green, Henry Allan. *MOSAIC: Jewish Life in Florida: A Documentary Exhibit from 1763 to the Present*. Coral Gables: MOSAIC, 1991.

Hamlin, Talbot F. "A Contemporary American Style: Some Notes on its Qualities and Dangers." *Pencil Points* (February 1938): 99-106.

___. "The Frustrated Monument Complex." *Pencil Points* 22 (October 1941): 78.

Harris, Steven & Deborah Berke. *Architecture of the Everyday*. New York/New Haven: Princeton Architectural Press/Yale Publications on Architecture, 1997.

Haskell, Barbara. *The American Century: Art & Culture 1900–1950*. New York: Whitney Museum of American Art/W. W. Norton & Company, 1999.

Hegemann, Werner and Elbert Peets. *The American Vitruvius: An Architect's Handbook of Civic Art*. New York: Architectural Books Publishing, 1922; reprint by Princeton Architectural Press, 1988.

Hillier, Bevis. *Art Deco of the 20's and 30's*. London: Studio Vista/Dutton Pictureback, 1968.

___. *The World of Art Deco*. New York: E. P. Dutton and Co., 1971.

Hitchcock, Henry Russell and Philip Johnson. *The International Style: Architecture Since 1922*. New York: W.W. Norton, 1932.

Hitchcock, Henry-Russell and Arthur Drexler, eds. *Post-war architecture*. New York, Museum of Modern Art/Arno Press, 1968.

Hochstim, Jan. *The Paintings and Sketches of Louis I. Kahn*. New York: Rizzoli, 1991.

Hoffmann, Josef. "Architektonisches von der Insel Capri." *Der Architekt* 3 (1897): 13.

Hohauser, Henry. *Architecture: Selections from the Works of Henry Hohauser*. Miami: 1939.

Holl, Steven. *The Alphabetical City*. New York: Pamphlet Architecture, 1980.

The Housing Division of the Public Works Administration. "Unit Types of Plans for Low-Rent Housing Projects." *Architectural Record* 77 (March 1935): 153-184.

Howe, George. "What is this Modern Architecture Trying to Express?" *American Architect* 137-138 (May 1930): 22.

Il convegno del paesaggio (1923). Capri: Edizioni La Conchiglia, 1993.

Irmel, Kamp-Bandeau. *Tel Aviv Neues Bauen*. Tübingen: Wasmuth, 1993.

Jacobs, Jane. *The Death and Life of Great American Cities* (New York: Random House, 1961).

Jackson, J. B. "Vernacular." *American Architecture: Innovation and Tradition*. New York: Rizzoli, 1986: 141-152.

Jordy, William H. *American Buildings and Their Architects: The Impact of European Modernism in the Mid-Twentieth Century* (Vols. 3 and 4). Garden City, NY: Doubleday, 1970.

Kiehnel & Elliott. *A Monograph of the Florida Work of Kiehnel & Elliott, Architects*. Miami: 1938.

Kinerk, Michael D. and Dennis W. Wilhelm. "Dream Palaces: The Motion Picture Playhouses in the Sunshine State." *Journal of Decorative and Propaganda Arts* 23 (1998): 208-237.

Kleinberg, Howard. *Miami Beach: A History*. Miami: Centennial Press, 1994.

Kofoed, John Christian. *Moon Over Miami*. New York: Random House, 1955.

Kornwolff, T. (editor). *Modernism in America, 1937–1941*. Williamsburg, Va: Joseph and Margaret Muscarelle Museum of Art, 1985.

La fortuna di Paestum e la memoria moderna del dorico 1750–1830. Firenze: Centro Di, 1986.

Henri Lefebvre, "The Everyday and Everydayness," in Harris, Steven & Deborah Berke. *Architecture of the Everyday* (New York/New Haven: Princeton Architectural Press/Yale Publications on Architecture, 1997), 35.

Lejeune, Jean-François. "Construindo a cidade do lazer ne Era da Máquina: L. Murray Dixon, H. Hohauser, I. Polevitzky e o Moderno Vernacular de Miami Beach." *Art Déco na América Latina* (1 Seminario Internacional, Centro de Arquitectura e Urbanismo do Rio de Janeiro, April 14-16, 1996). Rio de Janeiro: Prefeitura da Cidade do Rio de Janeiro, 1997: 18-27.

___. "Fin-de-siècle." *The New City: Modern Cities*. New York: Princeton Architectural Press, 1996: 125-128.

___. "From Hellerau to the Bauhaus: Memory and Modernity of the German Garden City." *The New City: Modern Cities*. New York: Princeton Architectural Press, 1996: 51-69.

Lescaze, William. "The Functional Approach to School Planning." *Architectural Record* 79 (June 1936): 481-2.

Libby Owens Ford Glass Company. "Glass." *Architectural Forum* 60-61 (1934).

Lichtenstein, Claude, and Franz Engler. *Streamlined: A Metaphor for Progress.* Baden: Lars Müller, 1995.

Loos, Adolf. *Spoken into the Void (Collected Essays, 1897–1900).* Cambridge: MIT Press, 1982.

Loyer, François. "Art Déco." *Dictionnaire de l'architecture moderne.* Paris: Hazan, 1997: 53-55.

Lummus, John Newton. *The Miracle of Miami Beach.* Miami: The Teacher Publishing Co., 1940.

Marchi, Virgilio. *Architettura Futurista.* Foligno: Campitelli, 1924.

Mattie, Erik. *World's Fairs.* New York: Princeton Architectural Press, 1998.

McCoy, Esther. *Five California Architects.* New York: Reinhold Pub. Corp., 1960.

Mehling, Howard. *The Most of Everything: The Story of Miami Beach.* New York: Harcourt, Brace and Company, 1960.

Meikle, Jeffrey. *Twentieth Century Limited Industrial Design in America 1925–1939.* Philadelphia: Temple University Press, 1979.

Mendelsohn, Erich. *The Complete Works.* New York: Princeton Architectural Press, 1992.

___. "Palestine and the World of Tomorrow (1941)." *Erich Mendelsohn, Bauten und Projekte in Palästina (1934–1941).* Ed., Ita Heinze-Greenberg. München: Scaneg, 1986.

Miami Beach Art Deco Guide. Miami Beach: Miami Design Preservation League, 1987.

Millas, Aristides J. and Michael H. Raley. "Old Miami Beach": *A Case Study in Historic Preservation, July 1976–July 1980.* Miami Beach: Miami Design Preservation League, 1994.

Mock, Elizabeth, ed. *Built in the U.S.A.: A Survey of Contemporary American Architecture Since 1932.* New York: Museum of Modern Art/Arno Press, 1944.

Mujica, Francisco. *History of the Skyscraper.* Paris: Archeology and Architecture Press, 1929.

Mumford, Lewis. "Monumentalism, Symbolism and Style." *Architectural Review* (April 1949): 170-180.

___. "Status Quo." *New Yorker* (11 October 1947): 104-10.

Murchinson, Kenneth. "The Drawings for the New Waldorf-Astoria." *Pencil Points* (January 1931): 28-35.

Naylor, Gillian. "Swedish Grace or the Acceptable Face of Modernism." *Modernism in Design.* Ed. Paul Greenhalgh. London: Reaktion Books, 1990: 163-172.

Newcomb, Rexford. *Spanish Colonial Architecture in the United States.* New York: J.J. Augustin, 1937.

"Norman Bel Geddes (1893–1958)." *Rassegna* 60 (1994).

Norton, David. "Miami Beach." *Progressive Architecture* (August 1980): 64-65.

Oldenburg, Claes and Oluf Hultin, eds. *Asplund: A Book.* New York: Rizzoli, 1986.

Olson, Arlene R. "Building to Weather the Depression Decade: Miami Beach 1933–1941." *Southeastern College Art Conference Review* (1977): 169-176.

___. *A Guide to the Architecture of Miami Beach.* Miami: Dade Heritage Trust, 1978.

O'Neill, Eugene. *Dynamo.* New York: H. Liveright, 1929.

Olson, Arlene Rita. *A Guide to the Architecture of Miami Beach.* Miami: Dade Heritage Trust, 1978.

Ormond, Mark. *The Biltmore Revisited: A Photo-Documentary Exhibition of the Miami Biltmore Hotel & Country Club, Coral Gables.* Coral Gables: Metropolitan Museum & Art Center, 1981.

Ortelli, Luca. "Heading South: Asplund's Impressions." *Lotus International*, no. 68 (1991): 23-33.

Pancoast, Russell T. *A Guide to the Architecture of Miami.* Miami: Florida South Chapter AIA, 1963.

"The Pattern Palls... And Is Reexamined." *Architectural Forum* 65 (September 1936): 179-186.

Payton, Neal. "Patrick Geddes and the Plan for Tel Aviv." *The New City: Modern Cities.* New York: Princeton Architectural Press, 1996: 4-25.

Perry, Clarence Arthur. *Housing for the Machine Age.* New York: Russell Sage Foundation, 1939.

Pevsner, Nikolaus. *A History of Building Types.* Princeton, N. J.: Princeton University Press, 1976.

Pinchon, Jean-François. *Robert Mallet-Stevens: Architecture, Furniture, Interior Design.* Cambridge: The MIT Press, 1990.

Pizza, Antonio, ed. J. LL. *Sert and Mediterranean Culture.* Barcelona: Collegi d' Arquitectes de Catalunya, 1997.

"Pleasure Dome." *Time* (19 April 1940): 18.

Plunz, Richard. *A History of Housing in New York City.* New York: Columbia University Press, 1990.

___. "Reading Bronx Housing, 1890–1940." *Building A Borough: Architecture And Planning in the Bronx, 1890–1940.* New York: The Bronx Museum of the Arts, 1986: 30-76.

Pokinski, Deborah Frances. *The Development of the American Modern Style.* Ann Arbor: University of Michigan Press, 1984.

Polyzoides, Stefanos, Roger Sherwood and James Tice. *Courtyard Housing of Los Angeles: A Typological Analysis.* Berkeley: University of California Press, 1982.

Portas, Nuno. "Art Déco e suas Cidades." *Art Déco Na América Latina.* (1 Seminario Internacional, Centro de Arquitectura e Urbanismo do Rio de Janeiro, April 14-16, 1996). Rio de Janeiro: Prefeitura da Cidade do Rio de Janeiro, 1997: 100-107.

Posener, Julius. *From Schinkel to the Bauhaus.* New York: George Wittenborn, Inc., 1972.

Putnam, James. *The New Millenium of Modern Art Museums.* On line. http://www.repubblicarts.kataweb.it/repubblicarts/museum/testo.html. Roma: La Repubblica of the Arts, 1999.

Rainbolt, Victor. *The Town that Climate Built: The Story of the Rise of a City in the American Tropics.* Miami: Parker Art Printing Association, 1924.

Redford, Polly. *Billion Dollar Sandbar.* New York: E. P. Dutton, 1970.

Riley, Terence. *The International Style: Exhibition 15 and the Museum of Modern Art.* New York: Rizzoli/Columbia Books of Architecture, 1992.

Robinson, Cervin and Joel Herschman. *Architecture Transformed: A History of the Photography of Buildings from 1839 to the Present.* New York-Cambridge: The Architectural League of New York & MIT Press, 1987.

Rodriguez, Ivan A., Margot Ammidown, Emily Perry Dieterich, and Bogue Wallin. *From Wilderness to Metropolis: The History and Architecture of Dade County, Florida, 1825–1940.* Miami: Metropolitan Dade County Office of Community Development, Historic Preservation Division, 1982.

Rossi, Aldo. *The Architecture of the City.* Cambridge: MIT Press, 1982.

Rothchild, John. *Up for Grabs.* New York: Viking Books, 1985.

Rowe, Colin. *As I Was Saying: Recollections and Miscellaneous Essays.* Cambridge: MIT Press, 1996.

Rowe, Colin and Fred Koetter. *Collage City.* Cambridge: MIT Press, 1978.

Rudofsky, Bernard. *Architecture Without Architects.* Garden City, NY: Doubleday & Company, 1964.

___. *The Prodigious Builders.* New York-London: Harcourt, Brace & Jovanovitch, 1977.

___. *Streets For People: A Primer for Americans.* Garden City, NY: Doubleday, 1969.

Rydell, Robert W. *All the World's a Fair: Visions of Empire at the American International Expositions, 1876–1916*. Chicago: University of Chicago Press, 1984.

Schinkel, Karl Friedrich. *Reisen nach Italien*. Tagebücher, Briefe, Zeichnungen, Aquarelle. Berlin: Rütten & Loenig, 1979.

Schultze, Leonard. "The Waldorf-Astoria Hotel." *Architecture* 64 (November 1931): 251-305.

Schumacher, Fritz. "Trends in Architectural Thought." *Architectural Forum* 54 (April 1931): 399.

Schwarzer, Mitchell. "Modern Architectural Ideology in Cold War America." *The Education of the Architect: Historiography, Urbanism, and the Growth of Architectural Knowledge* (Essays Presented to Stanford Anderson). Cambridge: The MIT Press, 1997: 87-109.

Scott Brown, Denise. "Revitalizing Miami." *Urban Design International* (Jan-Feb. 1980): 20-25.

Scully, Vincent. "American Architecture: The Real and the Ideal." *American Architecture. Innovation and Tradition*. New York: Rizzoli, 1986: 5-23.

Sembach, Klaus-Jurgen. *Style 1930*. New York: Universe Books, 1986.

Serra, Joselita Raspi, Françoise Astorg Bollack and Tom Killian, eds. *Everyday Masterpieces: Memory and Modernity. A Study of an International Vernacular Architecture Between the Two World Wars*. Modena: Edizioni Panini, 1988.

Sert, Josep Lluis. "Arquitectura sense 'estil' i sense 'arquitecte'." *D'Aci i d'Allà*, no. 179 (December 1934). Reprinted in Pizza, 210.

___. "Raices mediterráneas de la arquitectura moderna." *A. C.*, no. 18 (1935). Reprinted in Pizza, 217-8.

Seventy Years of Miami Architecture: Commercial and Institutional Architecture in Dade County. Miami Beach: Bass Museum of Art, 1991.

Sexton, Randolph Williams. *Spanish Influence on American Architecture and Decoration*. New York: 1926.

Shulman, Allan T. "Igor Polevitzky's Architectural Vision for a Modern Miami." *Journal of Decorative and Propaganda Arts* 23 (1998): 335-359.

___. "Miami Beach as Urban Assemblage: A Unique Culture of Housing." *The New City: Modern Cities*. New York: Princeton Architectural Press, 1996: 25-49.

Singer, Isaac Bashevis. "Introduction." *My Love Affair with Miami Beach*. Richard Nagler. New York: Simon & Schuster, 1991.

Smith, Terry. *Making the Modern: Industry, Art, and Design in America*. Chicago & London: The University of Chicago Press, 1993.

Sobin, Harris J. "Miami Deco Roots and Meanings." *Time Present, Time Past: The Art Deco District*. Eds. Barbara Capitman and Diane Camber. Miami Beach: Miami Design Preservation League, 1980: 11-12.

Stein, Clarence S. "A Triumph of the Spanish Colonial Style." *The Architecture and the Gardens of the San Diego Exposition; A Pictorial Survey Of The Aesthetic Features of the Panama California International Exposition*. San Francisco: P. Elder and Company, 1916: 12-18.

Stephan, Reginald, ed. *Eric Mendelsohn Architect 1887-1953*. New York: The Monacelli Press, 1999.

Stern, Jewel. *Jewel Stern/Project Skyline: Modern/Moderne/Modernistic Miami Beach Hotel Architecture/Circa 1949*. Akron: Akron Art Institute, 1979.

Stern, Robert A. M., Gregory Gilmartin, and Thomas Mellins. *New York 1930: Architecture and Urbanism Between The Two World Wars*. New York: Rizzoli, 1987.

Stuart, John A. "Pragmatism Meets Exoticism: Interview with Paul Silverthorne." *Journal of Decorative and Propaganda Arts* 23 (1998): 360-381.

"Style of Buildings." *Official Guide Book of the Fair*. Chicago: A Century of Progress, 1933.

Sullivan, Donald G. and Brian J. Danforth. *Bronx Art Deco Architecture*. New York: Hunter College, 1976.

Sussman, Warren, ed. *Culture and Commitment*. New York: George Braziller, 1973.

Taut, Bruno. *Architekturlehre*. Hamburg: Verlag für der Studium der Arbeiterbewegung, 1977.

Treib, Marc. *An Everyday Modernism: The Houses of William Wurster*. San Francisco: San Francisco Museum of Modern Art, 1995.

Urban, Joseph. *Theaters*. New York: Theatre Arts, Inc., 1929.

Valéry, Paul. *Eupalinos ou l'architecte*. Paris: Gallimard, 1922.

Venturi, Robert. *Complexity and Contradiction in Architecture*. New York: The Museum of Modern Art, 1966.

Venturi, Robert, Denise Scott Brown and Steven Izenour. *Learning from Las Vegas*. Cambridge: MIT Press, 1972.

Vidler, Anthony. "History of Follies," in B.J. Archer, *Follies: Architecture for the Late-Twentieth-Century Landscape*. New York: Rizzoli, 1983: 8-9.

Vigato, Jean-Claude. *Le jeu des modèles — Les modèles en jeu*. Villers-les-Nancy: CEMPA, 1980.

von Goethe, Wolfgang. *Italienische Reise (Italian Journey)*. Princeton: Princeton University Press, 1989.

Walker, Ralph Thomas. "The Relation of Skyscrapers to our Life." *Architectural Forum* 52 (May 1930): 689-695.

Weed, Robert Law. *Robert Law Weed, Architect*. New York: Architectural Catalog Co., 1937.

Weisgal, Meyer W., ed. *Palestine Book: Official Publication of the Jewish Palestine Pavilion at the New York World's Fair 1939*. New York: New York American Committee for Jewish Palestine Participation at the New York World's Fair for the Benefit of the Jewish Palestine Building Fund, 1939.

Whitworth, Henry P. "The Outdoor Living Room." *Florida Architecture and Allied Arts* (1935): unpaginated.

Wilson, Richard Guy. "Modernized Classicism and Washington, D.C." *American Public Architecture: European Roots and Native Expressions, Papers on Art History from the Pennsylvania State University*. Eds. Craig Zabel and Susan Scott Munshower. University Park, PA: Pennsylvania State University, 1989: 272-286.

Wilson, Richard Guy, Dianne H. Pilgrim, and Dickran Tashjian. *The Machine Age in America, 1918–1941*. New York: Harry N. Abrams, 1986.

Winslow, Carleton M. *The Architecture and the Gardens of the San Diego Exposition; A Pictorial Survey Of the Aesthetic Features of the Panama California International Exposition*. San Francisco: P. Elder and Company, 1916.

Wirth, Louis. "Urbanism As A Way of Life." *American Journal of Sociology*, no. 44 (July 1938): 1-24.

Wodum, Howard and Harry Estill Moore. *American Regionalism: A Cultural-Historical Approach to National Integration*. New York: 1938.

Wojtowicz, Robert. *Lewis Mumford & American Modernism: Utopian Theories for Architecture and Urban Planning*. Cambridge: Cambridge University Press, 1996.

___. *Sidewalk Critic: Lewis Mumford's Writings on New York*. New York: Princeton Architectural Press, 1998.

Wright, Henry. "The Modern Apartment House." *Architectural Record* 65 (March 1929).

Zevi, Bruno. *Eric Mendelsohn*. New York: Rizzoli, 1985.

Zieman, Irving. *Miami Beach in Rhyme*. Boston: Meador Publishing Company, 1954.

II. Lawrence Murray Dixon:
Periodicals and Other Publications

"The Adams Hotel." *Album of Florida and West Indies Hotel.* Miami Beach: Davis & Campbell, 1938: 56.

"The Atlantis Hotel, Miami Beach." *Architectural Record* 80 (July 1936): 52-54.

"Beach Plaza Hotel, Miami Beach." *Album of Florida and West Indies Hotels.* Miami Beach: Davis & Campbell, 1938: 40.

"Boom Over Miami Beach." *Architectural Forum* 73 (December 1940): 10.

"Building Types: Markowitz & Resnick Store." *Architectural Record* 82 (October 1937): 132-133.

"Coburn Country Day School, Miami Beach, Florida." *Architectural Record* 79 (June 1936): 469-470.

Dixon, Lawrence Murray. "Form for Senior Classification (Experience and Record in Professional Practice)." 4 June 1947.

Dixon, Lawrence Murray, Jr. "Lawrence Murray Dixon's Tropical Architecture." Typewritten manuscript. Collection Bass Museum of Art.

"Florida Architecture: An Outstanding U. S. Resort Center Turns to Modern for its New Residences and Commercial Buildings." *Architectural Forum* 69 (December 1938): 449-464.

"Fourteen Examples of the Better House of Concrete: L. Murray Dixon Residence, Miami Beach." *American Architect and Architecture* 149 (August 1936): 45.

"The Goldwasser Shop, Miami Beach." *Architectural Forum* 69 (December 1938): 456.

"House for Mrs. Ruth Norton Natelson, Miami Beach." *Architectural Forum* 68 (March 1938): 252-253.

"Lake Drive Apartments on Flamingo Drive, Miami Beach — Building Types." *Architectural Record* 82 (October 1937): 132-134.

"The President Hotel, Miami Beach." *Album of Florida and West Indies Hotels.* Miami Beach: Davis & Campbell, 1938: 44.

Solera, Maria Lourdes. *Miami Beach During the Streamline Decade and L. Murray Dixon.* University of Virginia: Master's Thesis, 1991.

"The Tides Hotel, Miami Beach; Lawrence Murray Dixon, Architect." *Architectural Forum* 69 (December 1938): 452-453.

"Two Apartments, Miami Beach, Florida." *American Architect and Architecture* 149 (November 1936): 359-361.

III. Lawrence Murray Dixon:
Newspapers: Hotels, Apartment hotels, and Commercial Structures

Advertisement, "Florence Villa Apartments." *Miami Herald,* 9 December 1934.

"New Akers Apartments Open At Beach." *Miami Daily News,* 13 January 1935.

"New Apartment Is Open Today At Miami Beach: Modern Construction and Beautiful Furniture Feature Akers Homes." *Miami Daily News,* 13 January 1935.

"Akers Apartments Open For Inspection Today." *Miami Daily News,* 13 January 1935.

"New Apartment is Completed on Oceanfront: 15-Unit Park View Now Ready for Occupancy At Miami Beach." *Miami Daily News,* 20 January 1935.

"New Pine Tree Drive Residence." *Miami Herald,* 17 February 1935.

"Coburn School Building Which Will Be Constructed In Bay Drive." *Miami Herald,* 12 May 1935.

"Ground Is Broken For New Building: Coburn School Will Erect Structure in Bay Drive, Normandy Isle." *Miami Herald,* 12 May 1935.

"Fireproof Structure To Contain 150 Rooms, Penthouses And Tower." *Miami Herald,* 19 May 1935.

"Construction Starts on Nine-Story Atlantis Hotel on Ocean Front Plot in Miami Beach." *Miami Herald,* 19 May 1935.

"Apartment Building Of 24 Units Being Erected." *Miami Herald,* 9 June 1935.

"Apartment Building Under Construction: Structure Being Erected In Miami Beach At Cost of $40,000." *Miami Daily News,* 9 June 1935.

"Store And Apartment Building For Miami Beach." *Miami Herald,* 14 July 1935.

"Apartment Planned In Store Structure: Erection Will Start This Week of Building For Arthur J. Sporberg." *Miami Herald,* 14 July 1935.

"Hotel Under Construction In Miami Beach." *Miami Herald,* 21 July 1935.

"Building Under Construction At Miami Beach." *Miami Herald,* 8 September 1935.

"...Throughout the Metropolitan Miami Area." *Miami Herald,* 6 October 1935.

"Apartment Building Under Construction: Plans Provide For Mechanical Ventilation Designed For Tropic Areas." *Miami Herald,* 15 December 1935.

"New Miami Beach Hostelry Will Open." *Miami Herald,* 29 December 1935.

"Grand Plaza, Overlooking Indian Creek and Ocean Beach, is Modern Structure." *Miami Herald,* 29 December 1935.

"Miami Beach Hotel's Formal Opening Set: New Ocean Front Hostelry Now Is Receiving Guests And Advance Reservations." *Miami Herald,* 12 January 1936.

"New Two-Story Structure is in Pine Tree Drive, Miami Beach." *Miami Herald* , 19 January 1936.

"The Atlantis, Distinctive Miami Beach Hostelry, Opens Doors Today." *Miami Herald,* 19 January 1936.

Advertisement, "The Atlantis." *Miami Herald,* 19 January 1936.

"52-Room President Hotel Being Constructed." *Miami Herald,* 15 March 1936.

"Home In Miami Beach Bought By Capitalist: Extensive Alterations Planned For Collins Avenue Residence Before Being Occupied." *Miami Herald,* 26 April 1936.

"Construction Begun On Apartment." *Miami Herald,* 17 May 1936.

"Apartment Building Of Eight Units Being Constructed At Miami Beach." *Miami Herald,* 24 May 1936.

"70-Room Hotel On Normandy Isles." *Miami Herald,* 14 June 1936.

"Hotel To Be Built In Miami Beach." *Miami Herald,* 6 September 1936.

"Apartment Group Under Construction In Bay Drive, Normandy Isle."*iami Herald,* 6 December 1936.

"Glass Brick Used In Front Facade Of Apartment." *Miami Herald,* 17 January 1937.

"Architectural Skill Shown In Apartment: Glass Brick Are, [sic] Used In all Areas of Front Façade of Building." *Miami Herald*, 17 January 1937.

"Construction Of Miami Beach Hotel At Cost Of $80,000 Begins On March 15." *Miami Herald*, 7 March 1937.

"Three-Unit Miami Beach Store Building To Cost $15,000." *Miami Herald*, 28 March 1937.

"Seymour Building Plans Are Finished." *Miami Herald*, 4 April 1937.

"Two Twelve-Unit Miami Beach Apartments To Represent $80,000 Investment." *Miami Herald*, 18 April 1937.

"Store Building Contract Awarded." *Miami Herald*, 30 May 1937.

"Eighteen-Unit Apartment Building Will Be Built." *Miami Herald*, 11 July 1937.

"New Hotel For Miami Beach." *Miami Herald*, 1 August 1937.

"New Ocean Front Hotel Is Opened." Miami Daily News, 2 January 1938.

"Hotels Number One for Each 75 Beach Residents?" *Miami Daily News*, 23 January 1938.

"Advanced Type Apartment Under Construction At Beach." *Miami Daily News*, 28 May 1938.

"Construction on the 60-Unit Adams Apartment Hotel." *Miami Herald*, 12 June 1938.

"Construction Starts On Swanky Apartment Building At Beach." *Miami Daily News*, 12 June 1938.

"Modern Design Throughout." *Miami Herald*, 10 July 1938.

"Featuring A Novel Arrangement... ." *Miami Herald*, 10 July 1938.

"New Hotel Is Planned At Miami Beach." *Miami Daily News*, 24 July 1938.

"Outstanding Apartment Under Construction At Miami Beach." *Miami Daily News*, 7 August 1938.

"Store Building... ." *Miami Herald*, 14 August 1938.

"20-Unit Apartment Building." *Miami Herald*, 4 September 1938.

"First Unit Of $500,000 Project Starts At Miami Beach." *Miami Daily News*, 11 September 1938.

"Pink Stone Used To Rebuild Beach Store." *Miami Daily News*, 25 September 1938.

"Frederick Hotel Under Way At Miami Beach To Cost $70,000." *Miami Daily News*, 2 October 1938.

"Twelve-Unit." *Miami Herald*, 13 November 1938.

"Nearing Completion." *Miami Herald*, 20 November 1938.

"Twelve-Unit Apartment." *Miami Herald*, 27 November 1938.

"Snyder Builds Own Home On San Marco." *Miami Daily News*, 4 December 1938.

"Unit In Beach Building Plans." *Miami Daily News* , 18 December 1938.

"Every Apartment Has Access." *Miami Herald*, 11 June 1939.

"New Kent Hotel To Have Advanced Construction." *Miami Daily News*, 9 July 1939.

"Work Starts On New Hotel: 3-Story, 52-Room Kent Building Rising On Collins Avenue." *Miami Herald*, 9 July 1939.

"Another Modern Structure." *Miami Herald*, 9 July 1939.

"$63,000 Hotel Begun." *Miami Herald*, 23 July 1939.

"Another Modern Type Hotel." *Miami Herald*, 30 July 1939.

"Hotel Imperial Gets Under Way On Ocean Drive Location." *Miami Daily News*, 30 July 1939.

"Lobby And Recreation Room." *Miami Herald*, 6 August 1939.

"Streamlined Marlin Hotel." *Miami Herald*, 13 August 1939.

"Beach Shop Going Up On 71st St." *Miami Daily News*, 17 August 1939.

"Miami Beach Apartment To Cost $38,000." *Miami Daily News*, 20 August 1939.

"Palmer House Under Construction." *Miami Herald*, 3 September 1939.

"New York Interests Buy Beach Hotel." *Miami Daily News*, 3 September 1939.

"Rounded Facade." *Miami Herald*, 22 October 1939.

"New Block Planned For Lincoln Road." *Miami Daily News*, 26 November 1939.

"Dr. Manuel De La Cruz is Building...." *Miami Herald*, 7 January 1940.

"A quadrangle 32-Unit Apartment Building...." *Miami Herald*, 21 April 1940.

"$40,000 Building Planned For Lincoln Road." *Miami Herald*, 5 May 1940.

"$180,000 Paid For $200-Foot Oceanfront Block: Construction of 3 Beach Hotels Costs $538,000." *Miami Herald*, 9 June 1940.

"Two Miami Beach Hotels To Cost $379,500." *Miami Herald*, 28 July 1940.

"A Generous Allotment of Windows...." *Miami Herald*, 8 September 1940.

"Richard Store Company...." *Miami Herald*, 8 September 1940.

"$68,000 Hotel Being Erected: Bernard Cohen Pays $28,500 For Site On Ocean Drive." *Miami Herald*, 15 September 1940.

"$160,000 Hotel Is Planned: Structure To Replace Lear School On Collins Avenue." *Miami Herald*, 9 February 1941.

"Contract Awarded For $145,000 Hotel On Ocean Drive." *Miami Herald*, 27 April 1941.

"Contracts Let For 2 Hotels Costing $421,000: Sovereign and Caribbean To Be Erected At Beach." *Miami Herald*, 15 June 1941.

"Panama Corporation...." *Miami Herald*, 15 June 1941.

"Under Construction is this 76-room Hotel...." *Miami Herald*, 28 September 1941.

IV. Miami Beach Architects:

Periodicals and Other Material

"Apartment Hotel, Miami Beach, Florida; Martin L. Hampton, Architect." *Architectural Forum* 65 (September 1936): 217-218.

"Boom Over Miami Beach." *Architectural Forum* 73 (December 1940): 10.

Brochure. "The Call of Miami Beach." 25 August 1925. Collection Historical Museum of Southern Florida.

Brochure. "Florida at the NY World's Fair." 1939. The Mitchell Wolfson Jr. Collection, The Wolfsonian-Florida International University.

Brochure. "Homes Miami Beach Florida." A consortium of The Miami Beach Ocean View Company, United Companies Realty Corporation, Miami Beach Improvement Company and Alton Beach Realty Company, Collection Historical Museum of South Florida.

Brochure. "The Lure of Miami Beach, Florida." Collection Historical Museum of Southern Florida.

Brochure. "Paradise Under the Sun." Archives and Special Collections, Otto G. Richter Library University of Miami.

Brochure. "Winter Homes for Southern Florida: A Book of Design." Collection Historical Museum of Southern Florida.

Cheney, Howard Lovewell. "Post Office for Miami Beach." *Architectural Concrete* 5 (March 1939): 3-4.

Collection of Henry Hohauser newspaper clippings, architectural renderings, photocopied blueprints, etc. The Mitchell Wolfson Jr. Collection, The Wolfsonian-Florida International University.

"Designed for an Ocean View, The Shelborne Hotel; Igor B. Polevitzky and T. Trip Russell, Architects." *Interior Design and Decoration* 17 (August 1941): 22-25.

"Florida Architecture: An Outstanding U. S. Resort Center Turns to Modern for its New Residences and Commercial Buildings." *Architectural Forum* 69 (December 1938): 449-464.

Florida Architecture and Allied Arts. Collection 1935-1941.

"Florida House for Alvin Grief, Rivo Alto Island. Igor B. Polevitzky, T. Trip Russell, Architects." *Architectural Forum* 69 (December 1938): 462-464.

"Florida House Planned to Suit Climate and Location, Igor B. Polevitzky, T. Trip Russell, Architects." *Architectural Record* 86 (July 1939): 49-50.

Frehling, Jennifer. *Henry Hohauser: Miami Beach Moderne 1935–1948*. University of Virginia: Master's Thesis, 1994.

Hohauser, Henry. *Architecture: Selections from the Works of Henry Hohauser*. Miami: 1939.

"House for Jay Greenwald Miami Beach; Igor B. Polevitzky and Thomas Trip Russell, Architects." *The Architectural Forum* 71 (October 1939): 294-295.

"Houses for Occasional Occupancy." *Architectural Forum* 87 (March 1940): 61-80.

Kiehnel & Elliott. *A Monograph of the Florida Work of Kiehnel & Elliott, Architects*. Miami: 1938.

Kiehnel, Richard. "Past, Present & Future Building Conditions of Metropolitan Miami." *Florida Architecture and Allied Arts* (1935): unpaginated.

LaGorce, John Oliver. *A Little Journey to Altonia: The Lure of a Clockless Land Where Summer Basks in the Lap of Winter*. Indianapolis, Indiana: Carl G. Fisher, 1918.

"Lincoln Center Building, Miami Beach; Igor B. Polevitzky and T. Trip Russell." *Architectural Forum* 69 (December 1938): 450-451.

"Miami Beach is Calling You." *Miami Beach Hotel & Apartment Book, Season 1940–41*. Miami Beach: Miami Beach Chamber of Commerce, 1940.

"Miami Beach: The Albion Hotel and Office Building, by the Architects Igor B. Polevitzky and T. Trip Russell." *Architectural Record* 87 (March 1940): 44-48.

"Miami Beach Today..." *American Architect* 147 (March 1935): 15-42.

A Modernistic Florida Home at Miami Beach. Miami: Dade County Newsdealers Supply Co., 1940.

Works of Igor Polevitzky and Thomas Triplett Russell. The Collection of Thomas Triplett Russell, compilation date unknown.

Schultze and Weaver, Lloyd Morgan Architects Collection. The Mitchell Wolfson Jr. Collection, Florida International University.

Scott Brown, Denise. *City of Miami Beach (Florida) Washington Avenue Revitalization Plan*. Miami Beach: City of Miami Beach, 1979.

"The Shelborne Hotel, Miami Beach; Igor B. Polevitzky and T. Trip Russell, Architects." *Florida Architecture and Allied Arts* (1941): 32.

"The Shelborne Hotel, Miami Beach; Igor B. Polevitzky and T. Trip Russell, Architects." *Architectural Record* 90 (July 1941): 41-46.

Silverthorne, Paul. Art Deco Interior Designer, An Oral History by Paul Silverthorne, January 1997. The Mitchell Wolfson Jr. Collection, Florida International University.

A Store on Miami Beach (Saks Fifth Avenue), Polevitzky and Russell Architects." *Architect and Building News* 164 (8 November 1940): 86-87.

Washington Storage Company. *Commercial Building for Messrs*. Mathews, Miami Beach/L.L. Robertson & L.R. Patterson, Architects. Miami Beach: Robertson & Patterson, 1927.

Whitworth, Henry P. "The Outdoor Living Room." *Florida Architecture and Allied Arts* (1935): unpaginated.

"The Work of Polevitzky and Russell 1936-1941." *The Architectural Record* 90 (July 1941): 42-46.

VI. Miami Beach Architects:

Selected Local Newspapers Articles

"Kiehnel, Richard." *Miami Herald*, 2 June 1935.

"Plans are Completed by Nunally Company for $200,000 Store Building: Construction Work Will Start At Once." *Miami Herald*, 2 June 1935.

"Robert Law Weed Architect." *Miami Herald*, 16 June 1935.

"New Apartment In Española Way, Miami Beach." *Miami Herald*, (9 June 1935.

"Work Is Started On Hotel Building: Barclay-Plaza In Miami Beach Is Owned By George E. Willis." *Miami Herald*, 30 June 1935.

"Four-Unit Apartment Completed." *Miami Herald*, 5 July 1936.

"Art Gallery Is Completed at Miami Beach." *Miami Daily News*, 26 December 1937.

"Architects Predict Sky Cities: Beach Visitors Say Towering Buildings will be Communicated with by Airplane Taxis." *Miami Daily News*, March 17, 1938.

"Hotel in Miami Beach Reveals World's Fair Influence: Essex House Project Will Cost $145,000." *Miami Daily News*, 18 September 1938.

"Miami Inspires Architectural Magazine Plash: 'Better Types' of Work Cited by Forum 25 Indicating Trend," *Miami Daily News*, 18 December 1938.

"Yes, Sir, It Is A Fire Station." *Miami Herald*, 25 December 1938.

Ludlow, William Orr. "Florida Architecture Praised." *Miami Herald*, 5 March 1939.

"Albion is Completed on Beach Site: Modern Trend is Featured in New Resort on Lincoln Road." *Miami Daily News*, 10 December 1939.

"$250,000 Hotel to Open Today on Miami Beach: Royal Palm at 1545 Collins Avenue, Contains 73 Rooms." *Miami Daily News*, 17 December 1939.

"Seven Questions That the Prospective Homeowner Must Ask." *Miami Herald*, 27 May 1940.

"Henry Hohauser Architecture." *Miami Beach Building Journal*, April 1947.

VII. Samuel H. Gottscho:

Databases and articles

Architecture and interior design for 20th century America Photographs by Samuel Gottscho and William Schleisner 1935- 1955. Washington, D.C.: Prints and Photographs Division, Library of Congress, 1997.
Electronic access: http://memory.loc.gov/ammem/gschtml/gotthome.html

Costantini, Paolo. "Brooklyn Public Library (photography by Samuel H. Gottscho)." *Casabella* v. 61 (July/Aug. 1997): 80-81.

Deschin, Jacob. "Gottscho/Always in Love with his Medium." *Popular Photography* (April 1965): 28-30.

Gottscho, Samuel H. *Early years, with images of family, self- portraits, landscapes and architectural interiors (1910-12)*. Album in Gottscho-Schleisner Collection (Library of Congress).

___. *Reference prints, 1919-1920, numbers 2133-2377*. Album (1919-1920) in Gottscho-Schleisner Collection (Library of Congress).

___. *Miami Beach: Architecture and Gardens (1930-1947)*. Album in Gottscho-Schleisner Collection (Library of Congress).

___. *Seventy-One Years of My Life with Photography*. Unpublished manuscript. Gottscho-Schleisner Collection (Library of Congress).

"Reviews: Architecture and Interior Design for 20th Century America: Photographs by Samuel Gottscho and William Schleisner, 1935-1955." *Microform & Imaging Review*, vol. 28, no. 2 (1999): 68.

Romer, Gleason Waite; Gary Munroe, ed. *Romer's Miami : Windows to the Past*. Miami: Miami-Dade Public Library System, 1985.

Exterior of Lawrence Murray Dixon's office, Euclid Avenue, Miami Beach. Lawrence Murray Dixon, 1937. Photograph Samuel Gottscho. Collection Bass Museum of Art, Gift of Lawrence Murray Dixon, Jr.

Bold numbers in the index refer to illustrations.